Second Language Learning Theories

Second Edition

ROSAMOND MITCHELL
Modern Languages, University of Southampton

FLORENCE MYLES
Modern Languages, University of Southampton

Hodder Arnold

A MEMBER OF THE HODDER HEADLINE GROUP

First published in Great Britain in 1998
Second edition published in Great Britain in 2004 by
Hodder Arnold, a member of the Hodder Headline Group,
338 Euston Road, London NW1 3BH

http://www.hoddereducation.com

Distributed in the United States of America by
Oxford University Press Inc.,
198 Madison Avenue, New York, NY10016

The advice and information in this book are believed to be true and
accurate at the date of going to press, but neither the author nor the publisher
can accept any legal responsibility or liability for any errors or omissions.

British Library Cataloguing in Publication Data
A catalogue record for this book is available from the British Library

Library of Congress Cataloging-in-Publication Data
A catalog record for this book is available from the Library of Congress

ISBN-10: 0 340 80766 0
ISBN-13: 978 0 340 80766 8

5 6 7 8 9 10

Typeset in 10/13pt Plantin by Phoenix Photosetting, Chatham, Kent
Printed and bound in India by Replika Press Pvt. Ltd.

What do you think about this book? Or any other Hodder Arnold title?
Please sent your comments to www.hoddereducation.com

To Paul, Francis and David

Contents

Acknowledgements

The authors and publishers wish to thank the following for permission to use copyright material:

Ablex Publishing Corporation/ Greenwood Publishing: extract from 'Collective scaffolding in second language learning', by R. Donato, in *Vygotskian approaches to second language research*, edited by J.P. Lantolf and G. Appel, 1994.

Academic Press/ Elsevier: figure from 'From discourse to syntax: grammar as a processing strategy', by T Givón, in *Syntax and Semantics* 12, 1979. Academic Press and the authors: table from 'Information-processing approaches to research on second language and use', by B. McLaughlin and R. Heredia, in *Handbook of second language acquisition*, edited by W.C. Ritchie and T.K. Bhatia, 1996.

Addison Wesley Longman/ Pearson Education: extracts from *Achieving understanding: discourse in intercultural encounters,* by K. Bremer, C. Roberts, M.T. Vasseur, M. Simonot and P. Broeder, 1996. Extract from *Linguistic minorities and modernity* by M. Heller, 1999. Material adapted from 'You can't learn without goofing: an analysis of children's second language errors' by H. Dulay and M. Burt, in *Error analysis*, edited by J. Richards, 1974.

Blackwell Publishing: excerpt from 'Negative feedback as regulation and second language learning in the Zone of Proximal Development', by A. Aljaafreh and J.P. Lantolf, *Modern Language Journal* 78, 1994. Excerpt from 'A sociocultural perspective on language learning strategies: the role of mediation', by R. Donato and D. McCormick, *Modern Language Journal* 78, 1994. Excerpt from 'Adult second language learners' use of private speech: a review of studies', by S.G. McCafferty, *Modern Language Journal* 78, 1994. Material adapted from 'Is there a "natural sequence" in adult second language learning?', by N. Bailey, C. Madden and S.Krashen, *Language Learning* 24, 1974.

Cambridge University Press: figure and extract from 'Input, interaction and second language production', by S. Gass and E. M. Varonis, *Studies in Second Language Acquisition* 16, 1994. Table and extract from 'Negative feedback in child NS-NNS conversation', by R. Oliver, *Studies in Second Language Acquisition* 17, 1995. Table from *Learning strategies in second language acquisition*, by J. O'Malley and A. Chamot, 1990. Table from *Second Language Acquisition and Universal Grammar* by L. White, 2003.

Gunter Narr Verlag: extracts from *The syntax of conversation in interlanguage development*, by C. Sato, 1990.

John Benjamins B V: extracts from *Utterance structure: developing grammars again*, by W. Klein and C. Perdue, 1992. Table from 'Competing constraints on variation in the speech of adult Chinese learners of English' by R.J. Bayley, in *Second language acquisition and linguistic variation*, edited by R. Bayley and D. R. Preston, 1996. Tables from 'Variationist perspectives on second language acquisition' by D. R. Preston, in *Second language acquisition and linguistic variation*, edited by R. Bayley and D. R. Preston, 1996. Extract from 'External appropriations as a strategy for participating in intercultural multi-party conversations' by G. Pallotti, in *Culture in communication*, edited by A. Di Luzio, S. Gunthner and F. Orletti, 2001.

Lawrence Erlbaum: extracts from *Second language acquisition processes in the classroom* by A. S. Ohta, 2001.

MIT Press: figure adapted from *Rethinking innateness: a connectionist perspective on development*, by J. Elman, E. Bates, M. Johnson, A. Karmiloff-Smith, D. Parisi and K. Plunkett, 1996.

Multilingual Matters Ltd: extract from 'Language and the guided construction of knowledge', by N. Mercer, in *Language and Education*, edited by G. Blue and R. F. Mitchell, 1996. Figure from *Approaches to second language acquisition*, by R. Towell and R. Hawkins, 1994.

Oxford University Press: figures from *Language two* by H. Dulay, M. Burt and S. Krashen, reproduced by permission of Oxford University Press. Copyright © 1982 Oxford University Press, Inc. Figure from *The study of second language acquisition*, by R. Ellis, reproduced by permission of Oxford University Press. Copyright © Rod Ellis 1994. Figure from *Conditions for second language learning*, by B. Spolsky, reproduced by permission of Oxford University Press. Copyright © B. Spolsky 1989. Extract from 'The role of consciousness in language learning' by R. Schmidt, *Applied Linguistics* 11, 1990, reproduced by permission of Oxford University Press and the author. Teachers of English to Speakers of Other Languages Inc. (TESOL: permission conveyed through Copyright Clearance Center, Inc.): table from 'The impact of interaction on comprehension', by T. Pica, R. Young and C. Doughty, *TESOL Quarterly* 21, 1987. Extracts from 'L2 literacy and the design of the self: a case study of a teenager writing on the internet' by W. S. E. Lam, *TESOL Quarterly* 34, 2000. Extracts from 'Disputes in child L2 learning' by K. Toohey, *TESOL Quarterly* 35, 2001.

Every effort has been made to trace all copyright holders of material. Any rights not acknowledged here will be acknowledged in subsequent printings if sufficient notice is given to the publishers.

Introduction

Aims of this book

This book is the result of collaboration between a linguist with research interests in second language acquisition (Myles) and an educationist with research interests in second language teaching and learning in the classroom (Mitchell). Our general aim is to provide an up-to-date, introductory overview of the current state of second language learning (SLL) studies. Our intended audience is wide: undergraduates following first degrees in language or linguistics; graduate students embarking on courses in foreign language education/EFL/applied linguistics; and a broader audience of teachers and other professionals concerned with second-language education and development. SLL is a field of research with potential to make its own distinctive contribution to fundamental understandings, for example of the workings of the human mind or the nature of language. It also has the potential to inform the improvement of social practice in many fields, most obviously in language education. We are interested in SLL from both perspectives, and are concerned to make it intelligible to the widest possible audience.

Our first (1998) edition was strongly influenced by the 1987 volume by McLaughlin, *Theories of Second Language Learning*, which provided a selective and authoritative introduction to key second-language learning theories of the day. In this second edition, our primary aim remains the same: to introduce the reader to those theoretical orientations on language learning that seem currently most productive and interesting for our intended audience. We have revised our text throughout to reflect the substantial developments that have taken place in the field in the last few years, so that the work aims to be fully up to date for a 21st century readership. New studies have been incorporated as examples, and theoretical advances are presented and explained. The evaluation sections in each chapter have been expanded and generally the book is rebalanced in favour of newer material.

All commentators recognize that although the field of second language learning research has been extremely active and productive in recent decades, we have not yet arrived at a unified or comprehensive view as to how second languages are learnt. We have therefore organized this book as a presentation and critical review of a number of different theories of SLL, which can broadly be viewed as linguistic, psycholinguistic and socio-linguistic. Indeed, the 'map' of the field we proposed in the first edition largely survives today, reflecting the fact that strands of research already active 20 years ago have continued to flourish. The most obvious example is the ongoing linguistic research inspired by the Universal Grammar theory of Noam Chomsky. However, while this vein of theorizing and empirical investigation remains active and productive, it has not succeeded in capturing the whole field, nor indeed has it attempted to do so. No single theoretical position has achieved dominance, and new theoretical orientations continue to appear. Whether or not this is a desirable state of affairs has been an issue of some controversy for SLL researchers (Beretta, 1993; van Lier, 1994; Lantolf, 1996; Gregg, 2003). On the whole, though we accept fully the arguments for the need for cumulative programmes of research within the framework of a particular theory, we incline towards a pluralist view of SLL theorizing. In any case, it is obvious that students entering the field today need a broad introduction to a range of theoretical positions, with the tools to evaluate their goals, strengths and limitations, and this is what we aim to offer.

Distinctive features of this book

As one sign of the vigour and dynamism of SLL research, a good number of surveys and reviews are already on the market. Reflecting the variety of the field, these books vary in their focus and aims. Some are written to argue the case for a single theoretical position (Sharwood Smith, 1994; Carroll, 2000; Hawkins, 2001; White, 2003); some are encyclopaedic in scope and ambition (R. Ellis, 1994; Ritchie and Bhatia, 1996; Doughty and Long, 2003); and some pay detailed attention to research methods and data analysis (Larsen-Freeman and Long, 1991).

This book is intended as an introduction to the field, for students without a substantial prior background in linguistics. We have adopted a 'pluralist' approach, and made a selection from across the range of SLL studies, of a range of theoretical positions that we believe are most active and significant. Some of the theories we review are well-established in SLL research, but evolving in the light of new evidence (e.g. Universal Grammar theory; reviewed in Chapter 3); others are relative newcomers to SLL studies, but offer a productive challenge to established thinking (e.g. connectionism discussed in Chapter 4, or socio-cultural theory discussed in Chapter 7).

From its early days, SLL research has been a varied field, involving a variety of disciplinary perspectives. However, it is fair to say that the dominant theoretical influences have been linguistic and psycholinguistic, and this continues to be reflected in many contemporary reviews of the subject (Gass and Selinker, 1994; Ritchie and Bhatia, 1996; Hawkins, 2001; Long and Doughty, 2003). This has been the case despite widespread acceptance of the sociolinguistic construct of communicative competence as the goal of second language learning and teaching (Brumfit and Johnson, 1979).

A distinctive feature of our first edition was its extended treatment of some theoretical positions that view the language learning process as essentially social, and which also view the learner as essentially a social being, whose identity is continually reconstructed through the processes of engagement with the second language and its speech community. In the second edition these treatments have been extended and updated. To illustrate the first of these positions we focus on Vygotskian socio-cultural theory, now well established in the SLL field as part of its growing influence on educational thinking and learning theory more generally (discussed in Chapter 7). To illustrate the second, we look at recent work in the ethnography of second-language communication, and in second language socialization; *see* discussion in Chapter 8.

Just as we have been selective in choosing the theories we wish to discuss, we have also been selective in reviewing the empirical evidence that underpins these theories. Our overall approach has been to illustrate a particular theoretical position by discussion of a small number of key studies that have been inspired by that approach. We use these studies to illustrate: the methodologies that are characteristic of the different traditions in SLL research (from controlled laboratory-based studies of people learning artificial languages to naturalistic observation of informal learning in the community); the scope and nature of the language 'facts' that are felt to be important; and the kinds of generalizations which are drawn. Where appropriate, we refer our readers to more comprehensive treatments of the research evidence relevant to different theoretical positions.

Lastly, the field of SLL research and theorizing has historically depended heavily on theories of first language learning, as well as on theoretical and descriptive linguistics. We think that students entering the field need to understand something about these origins, and have therefore included brief overviews of relevant thinking in first-language acquisition research, at several points in the book.

Ways of comparing SLL perspectives

We want to encourage our readers to compare and contrast the various theoretical perspectives we discuss in the book, so that they can get a better sense of the kinds of issues that different theories are trying to explain, and the extent to which they are supported to date with empirical evidence.

In reviewing our chosen perspectives, therefore, we evaluate each individual theory systematically, paying attention to the following factors:

- the claims and scope of the theory
- the view of language involved in the theory
- the view of the language learning process
- the view of the learner
- the nature and extent of empirical support.

In Chapter 1 we discuss each of these factors briefly, introducing key terminology and critical issues that have proved important in distinguishing one theory from another.

I

Second language learning: key concepts and issues

1.1 Introduction

This preparatory chapter provides an overview of key concepts and issues that will recur throughout the book in our discussions of individual perspectives on second language learning (SLL). We offer introductory definitions of a range of key terms, and try to equip the reader with the means to compare the goals and claims of particular theories with one another. We summarize key issues, and indicate where they will be explored in more detail later in the book.

The main themes to be dealt with in the following sections are:

1.2 What makes for a 'good' explanation or theory
1.3 Views on the nature of language
1.4 Views of the language learning process
1.5 Views of the language learner
1.6 Links between language learning theory and social practice.

First, however, we must offer a preliminary definition of our most basic concept, 'second language learning'. We define this broadly, to include the learning of any language, to any level, provided only that the learning of the 'second' language takes place some time later than the acquisition of the first language. (Simultaneous infant bilingualism is a specialist topic, with its own literature, which we do not try to address in this book; *see* relevant sections in Hamers and Blanc, 1989; Romaine, 1995; Dopke, 2000; Tokuhama-Espinosa, 2000.)

For us, therefore, 'second languages' are any languages other than the learner's 'native language' or 'mother tongue'. They include both languages of wider communication encountered within the local region or community (e.g. at the workplace or in the media) and truly foreign languages, which have no immediately local uses or speakers. They may indeed be a second language learners are working with, in a literal sense, or they may be their third, fourth, or even fifth language. It is sensible to include 'foreign' languages under our more general term of 'second' languages, because we believe that the underlying learning processes are essentially the same for more local and for more remote target languages, despite differing learning purposes and circumstances.

We are also interested in all kinds of learning, whether formal, planned and systematic (as in classroom-based learning) or informal and unstructured (as when a new language is 'picked up' in the community). Some second language researchers have proposed a principled distinction between formal, conscious **learning** and informal, unconscious **acquisition**. This distinction attracted much criticism when argued in a strong form by Stephen Krashen; it still has both its active supporters and its critics (Zobl, 1995; Robinson, 1997). It is difficult to sustain systematically when surveying SLL research in the broad way proposed here, and unless specially indicated, we will be using both terms interchangeably.

1.2   What makes for a good theory?

Second language learning is an immensely complex phenomenon. Millions of human beings have experience of SLL, and may have a good practical understanding of the activities that helped them to learn (or perhaps blocked them from learning). But this practical experience, and the commonsense knowledge which it leads to, are clearly not enough to help us understand fully how the process happens. We know, for a start, that people cannot reliably describe the language rules that they have somehow internalized, nor the inner mechanisms which process, store and retrieve many aspects of that new language.

We need to understand SLL better than we do, for two basic reasons:

1.   Because improved knowledge in this particular domain is interesting in itself, and can also contribute to more general understanding about the nature of language, of human learning and of intercultural communication, and thus about the human mind itself, as well as how all these are interrelated and affect each other.

2.   Because the knowledge will be useful. If we become better at explaining the learning process, and are better able to account for both success and failure in SLL, there will be a payoff for millions of teachers, and tens of millions of students and other learners, who are struggling with the task.

We can only pursue a better understanding of SLL in an organized and productive way if our efforts are guided by some form of theory. For our purposes, a **theory** is a more or less abstract set of claims about the units that are significant within the phenomenon under study, the relationships that exist between them and the processes that bring about change. Thus, a theory aims not just at description but also at explanation. Theories may be embryonic and restricted in scope, or more elaborate, explicit and comprehensive. They may deal with different areas of interest to us; thus, a **property theory** will be primarily concerned with modelling the nature of the language system that is to be acquired, whereas a **transition theory** will be primarily concerned with modelling the change or developmental processes of language acquisition. (A particular transition theory for SLL may deal only with a particular stage or phase of learning, or with the learning of some particular sub-aspect of language; or it may propose learning mechanisms which are much more general in scope.) Worthwhile theories are produced collaboratively, and evolve through a process of **systematic enquiry** in which the claims of the theory are assessed against some kind of evidence or data. This may take place through a process of **hypothesis testing** through formal experiment, or through more ecological procedures, where naturally occurring data are analysed and interpreted (*see* Brumfit and Mitchell, 1990, for fuller discussion and exemplification of methods). Lastly, the process of theory building is a reflexive one; new developments in the theory lead to the need to collect new information and explore different phenomena and different patterns in the potentially infinite world of 'facts' and data. Puzzling 'facts', and patterns which fail to fit in with expectations, lead to new theoretical insights.

To make these ideas more concrete, an example of a particular theory or 'model' of SLL is shown in Figure 1.1, taken from Spolsky, 1989, p. 28.

This model represents a 'general theory of second language learning' (Spolsky, 1989, p. 14). The model encapsulates this researcher's theoretical views on the overall relationship between contextual factors, individual learner differences, learning opportunities and learning outcomes. It is thus an ambitious model in the breadth of phenomena it is trying to explain. The rectangular boxes show the factors (or **variables**) that the researcher believes are most significant for learning, that is, where variation can lead to differences in success or failure. The arrows connecting the various boxes show directions of influence. The contents of the various boxes are defined at great length, as consisting of clusters of interacting 'Conditions' (74 in all; Spolsky, 1989, pp. 16–25), which make language learning success more or less likely. These 'conditions' summarize the results of a great variety of empirical language learning research, as Spolsky interprets it.

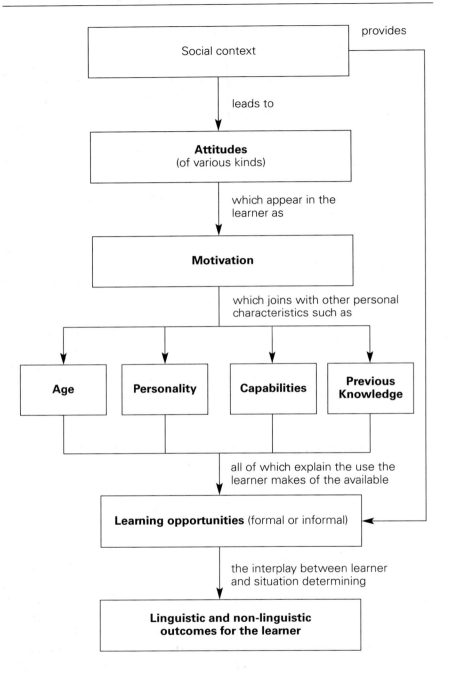

Fig. 1.1 Spolsky's general model of second language learning (*Source*: Spolsky, 1989, p. 28)

How would we begin to 'evaluate' this or any other model, or even more modestly, to decide that this was a view of the language learning process with which we felt comfortable and within which we wanted to work? This would depend partly on broader philosophical positions; for example, are we satisfied with an account of human learning that sees individual differences as both relatively fixed, and also highly influential for learning? It would also depend on the particular focus of our own interests, within SLL; this particular model seems well-adapted for the study of individual learners, but has relatively little to say about the social relationships in which they engage, for example.

But whatever the particular focus of a given theory, we would expect to find the following:

- Clear and explicit statements of the ground the theory is supposed to cover, and the claims it is making.
- Systematic procedures for confirming or disconfirming the theory, through data gathering and interpretation: a good theory must be testable or falsifiable in some way.
- Not only descriptions of second-language phenomena, but attempts to explain why they are so, and to propose mechanisms for change.
- Last but not least, engagement with other theories in the field, and serious attempts to account for at least some of the phenomena that are 'common ground' in ongoing public discussion (Long, 1990a). The remaining sections of this chapter offer a preliminary overview of numbers of these.

(For fuller discussion of evaluation criteria, *see* McLaughlin 1987, pp. 12–18; Long, 1993; Gregg, 2003.)

1.3   Views on the nature of language

1.3.1   Levels of language

Linguists have traditionally viewed language as a complex communication system, which must be analysed on a number of levels: **phonology**, **syntax**, **morphology**, **semantics** and **lexis**, **pragmatics**, and **discourse**. (Readers unsure about this basic descriptive terminology will find help from a range of introductory linguistics texts, such as Graddol *et al.*, 1994; Fromkin and Rodman, 1997). They have differed about the degree of separateness or integration of these levels; for example, while Chomsky (1957, p. 17) argued at one time that 'grammar is autonomous and independent of meaning', another tradition initiated by the British linguist, Firth, claims that 'there is no boundary between lexis and grammar: lexis and grammar are interdependent' (Stubbs, 1996, p. 36). When examining different perspectives on SLL, we will first of all be looking at the levels of language that these linguists attempt to take into account, and the relative degree of priority they attribute to the different levels. (Does language-learning start with words, or with discourse?) We will also examine the degree of integration or separation that they assume, across the various levels. We will find that the control of syntax and morphology is commonly seen as somehow 'central' to language learning, and that most general SLL theories try to account for development in this area. Other levels of language receive much more variable attention, and some areas are commonly treated in a semi-autonomous way, as specialist fields; this is often true for SLL-oriented studies of pragmatics and of lexical development, for example (*see* Kasper and Rose, 2003, on pragmatics; Singleton, 1999, or Nation, 2001, on vocabulary).

1.3.2   Competence and performance

Throughout the 20th century, linguists also disagreed in other ways over their main focus of interest and of study. Should this be the collection and analysis of actual attested samples of language in use; for example, by recording and analysing people's speech? Or, should it be to theorize underlying principles and rules that govern language behaviour, in its potentially infinite variety? The linguist, Noam Chomsky, famously argued that it is the business of theoretical linguistics to study and model underlying language **competence**, rather than the **performance** data of actual utterances that people have produced (Chomsky, 1965). By competence, Chomsky is referring to the abstract and hidden representation of language knowledge held inside our minds, with its potential to create and understand original utterances in a given language. As we shall see, this view has been influential in much SLL research.

However, for linguists committed to this dualist position, there are difficulties in studying competence. Language performance data are believed to be imperfect reflections of competence, partly because of the processing complications that are involved in speaking or other forms of language production, and which lead to errors and slips. More importantly, it is believed that, in principle, the infinite creativity of the underlying system can never adequately be reflected in a finite data sample (*see* Chomsky, 1965, p. 18). Strictly speaking, many researchers of language competence believe it can be accessed only indirectly, and under controlled conditions, through different types of tests such as **grammati-**

cality judgement tests (roughly, when people are offered sample sentences, which are in (dis)agreement with the rules proposed for the underlying competence, and are invited to say whether they think they are grammatical or not; Sorace, 1996).

This split between competence and performance has *never* been accepted by all linguists, however, with linguists in the British tradition of Firth and Halliday (for example) arguing for radically different models in which this distinction between competence and performance does not appear. In a recent review of this tradition, Stubbs quotes Firth as describing such dualisms as 'a quite unnecessary nuisance' (Firth, 1957, p. 2n, quoted in Stubbs, 1996, p. 44). In the Firthian view, the only option for linguists is to study language in use, and there is no opposition between language as system and observed instances of language behaviour; the only difference is one of perspective.

Of course, the abstract language system cannot be 'read' directly off small samples of actual text, any more than the underlying climate of some geographical regions of the world can be modelled from today's weather (a metaphor of Michael Halliday, quoted in Stubbs, 1996, pp 44–5). The arrival of **corpus linguistics**, in which very large corpora comprising millions of words of running text can be stored electronically and analysed with a growing range of software tools, has revitalized the writing of 'observation-based grammars' (Aarts, 1991), of the integrated kind favoured by Firthian linguistics. 'Work with corpora provides new ways of considering the relation between data and theory, by showing how theory can be grounded in publicly accessible corpus data' (Stubbs, 1996, p. 46). For example, the English corpus-based work of the COBUILD team, directed by John Sinclair, has claimed to reveal 'quite unsuspected patterns of language' (Sinclair, 1991, p. xvii), offering new insights into the interconnectedness of lexis and grammar. Within the field of second language acquisition, recent advances in software development are also making it possible to analyse large databases of learner language, both from a 'bottom-up' perspective (to find patterns in the data) and from a 'top-down' perspective (to test specific hypotheses) (Granger, 1998; MacWhinney, 2000a, 2000b; Rutherford and Thomas, 2001; Granger *et al.*, 2002; Marsden *et al.,* 2002).

In making sense of contemporary perspectives on SLL, then, we need to take account of the extent to which a competence or performance distinction is assumed. This will have significant consequences for the research methodologies associated with various positions; for example, the extent to which these pay attention to naturalistic corpora of learner language, spoken and written, or rely on more controlled and focused – but more indirect – testing of learners' underlying knowledge. For obvious reasons, theorists' views on the relationship between competence and performance are also closely linked to their view of the language learning process itself, and in particular, to their view of the ways in which **language use** (i.e. speaking or writing a language) can contribute to **language learning** (i.e. developing grammatical or lexical competence in the language).

1.4   The language learning process

1.4.1   Nature and nurture

Discussions about processes of SLL have always been coloured by debates on fundamental issues in human learning more generally. One of these is the **nature–nurture** debate. How much of human learning derives from innate predispositions, that is, some form of genetic pre-programming, and how much of it derives from social and cultural experiences that influence us as we grow up? In the 20th century, the best-known controversy on this issue as far as first language learning was concerned involved the behaviourist psychologist, B. F. Skinner, and the linguist, Noam Chomsky. Skinner attempted to argue that language in all its essentials could be and was taught to the young child, by the same mechanisms that he believed accounted for other types of learning. (In Skinner's case, the mechanisms were those envisaged by general behaviourist learning theory – essentially, copying and memorizing behaviours encountered in the surrounding environment. From this point of view, children could learn language primarily by imitating the speech of their caretakers. The details of the argument are discussed further in Chapter 2.)

Chomsky, on the other hand, has argued consistently for the view that human language is too complex to be learnt in its entirety, from the performance data actually available to the child; we must therefore have some innate predisposition to expect natural languages to be organized in particular ways and not others. For example, all natural languages have word classes, such as Noun and Verb, and grammar rules that apply to these word classes. It is this type of information which Chomsky doubts children could discover from scratch, in the speech they hear around them. Instead, he argues that there must be some innate core of abstract knowledge about language form, which pre-specifies a framework for all natural human languages. This core of knowledge is currently known as **Universal Grammar** (*see* Chapter 3 for detailed discussion).

For our purposes, it is enough to note that child language specialists now generally accept the basic notion of an innate predisposition to language, though this cannot account for all aspects of language development, which results from an interaction between innate and environmental factors. That is, complementary mechanisms, including active involvement in language use, are equally essential for the development of communicative competence (*see* Foster-Cohen, 1999).

How does the nature–nurture debate affect SLL theories? If humans are endowed with an innate predisposition for language then perhaps they should be able to learn as many languages as they need or want to, provided (important provisos!) that the time, circumstances and motivation are available. On the other hand, the environmental circumstances for SLL differ systematically from first-language learning, except where infants are reared in multilingual surroundings. Should we be aiming to reproduce the 'natural' circumstances of first-language learning as far as possible for the SLL student? This was a fashionable view in the 1970s, but one which downplayed some very real social and psychological obstacles. In the last 30 years there has been a closer and more critical examination of 'environmental' factors which seem to influence SLL; some of these are detailed briefly below, in Section 1.4.8, and will be elaborated on in a number of following chapters (especially Chapters 6, 7 and 8).

1.4.2   Modularity

A further issue of controversy for students of the human brain and mind has been the extent to which the mind should be viewed as **modular** or unitary. That is, should we see the mind as a single, flexible organism, with one general set of procedures for learning and storing different kinds of knowledge and skills? Or, is it more helpfully understood as a bundle of **modules**, with distinctive mechanisms relevant to different types of knowledge (Fodor, 1983; Smith and Tsimpli, 1995; Lorenzo and Longa, 2003)?

The modular view has consistently found support from within linguistics, most famously in the further debate between Chomsky and the child development psychologist, Jean Piaget. This debate is reported in Piatelli-Palmarini (1980), and has been re-examined many times: Johnson (1996, pp. 6–30) offers a helpful summary. Briefly, Piaget argued that language was simply one manifestation of the more general skill of symbolic representation, acquired as a stage in general cognitive development; no special mechanism was therefore required to account for first language acquisition. Chomsky's general view is that not only is language too complex to be learnt from environmental exposure (his criticism of Skinner), it is also too distinctive in its structure to be 'learnable' by general cognitive means. Universal Grammar is thus endowed with its own distinctive mechanisms for learning (so-called **parameter-setting**; *see* Chapter 3 below).

There are many linguists today who support the concept of a distinctive language module in the mind, the more so as there seems to be a dissociation between the development of cognition and of language in some cases (Bishop and Mogford, 1993; Smith and Tsimpli, 1995; Bishop, 2001; Lorenzo and Longa 2003). As we shall see later in the book, there are also those who argue that language competence itself is modular, with different aspects of language knowledge being stored and accessed in distinctive ways. However, there is still no general agreement on the number and nature of such modules, or how they relate to other aspects of cognition.

1.4.3   Modularity and second language learning

The possible role of an innate, specialist language module in SLL has been much discussed in recent years. If such innate mechanisms indeed exist, there are four logical possibilities:

1.   They continue to operate during SLL, and make key aspects of SLL possible, in the same way that they make first-language learning possible.
2.   After the acquisition of the first language in early childhood, these mechanisms cease to be operable, and second languages must be learnt by other means.
3.   The mechanisms themselves are no longer operable, but the first language provides a model of a natural language and how it works, which can be 'copied' in some way when learning a second language.
4.   Distinctive learning mechanisms for language remain available, but only in part, and must be supplemented by other means. (From a Universal Grammar point of view, this would mean that Universal Grammar was itself modular, with some modules still available and others not.)

The first position was popularized in the SLL field by Stephen Krashen in the 1970s, in a basic form (*see* Chapter 2). Although Krashen's theoretical views have been criticized, this has by no means led to the disappearance of modular proposals to account for SLL. Instead, this particular perspective has been revitalized by the continuing development of Chomsky's Universal Grammar proposals (Chomsky, 1995, 2000; Cook and Newson, 1996; Herschensohn, 2000; Hawkins, 2001; White, 2003). An example is Sharwood Smith (1994), who argues not only for the continuing contribution of a Universal Grammar 'module' to SLL, but for a view of SLL that is itself modular, so that a range of distinct learning mechanisms contribute to the learning of different aspects of language. (Thus vocabulary and pragmatics, for example, would be learnt by mechanisms quite different from those which account for grammar learning; Sharwood Smith, 1994, p. 171.) Such Universal Grammar-based views are discussed more fully below in Chapter 3.

On the other hand, thinking about the general learning mechanisms that may be operating at least for adult learners of second languages has also developed considerably further since the original proposals of McLaughlin (1987, pp. 133–53) for example. The work of the cognitive psychologist J. R. Anderson, on human learning from an information-processing perspective, has been applied to various aspects of SLL by different researchers (O'Malley and Chamot, 1990; Towell and Hawkins, 1994; Johnson, 1996). This work is reviewed in detail in Chapter 4 below; here, it is worth pointing out the attempt of Towell and Hawkins in particular to integrate information-processing with Universal Grammar, as two complementary mechanisms that together develop second-language fluency as well as second-language knowledge. There has also been a significant recent revival of interest in behaviourist (associative) theories of learning with reference to language, especially in the work termed 'connectionism', which models SLL processes in computer simulations (N.C. Ellis, 2003). These revitalized generalist theories are discussed further in Chapter 4 below.

1.4.4 'Systematicity' and variability in SLL

When the utterances produced by second-language learners are examined and compared with traditionally accepted target language norms, they are often condemned as full of errors or mistakes. Traditionally, language teachers have often viewed these errors as the result of carelessness or lack of concentration on the part of learners. If only learners would try harder, surely their productions could accurately reflect the target language rules that they had been taught! In the mid-20th century, under the influence of behaviourist learning theory, errors were often viewed as the result of 'bad habits', which could be eradicated if only learners did enough rote learning and pattern drilling using target language models.

As will be shown in more detail in Chapter 2, one of the big lessons that has been learnt from the research of recent decades is that though learners' second-language utterances may be deviant by comparison with target language norms, they are by no means lacking in **system**. Errors and mistakes are patterned, and although some regular errors are caused by the influence of the first language, this is by no means true of all of them. Instead, there is a good deal of evidence that learners work their way through a number of **developmental stages,** from apparently primitive and deviant versions of the second language, to progressively more elaborate and target-like versions. Just like fully proficient users of a language, their language productions can be described by a set of underlying rules; these interim rules have their own integrity and are not just inadequately applied versions of the target language rules.

One clear example, which has been studied for a range of target languages, concerns the formation of negative sentences. It has commonly been found that learners start off by tacking a negative particle of some kind on to the beginning or the end of an utterance (*no you are playing here*). Next, they learn to insert a negative particle of some kind into the verb phrase (*Mariana not coming today*) and, finally, they learn to manipulate modifications to auxiliaries and other details of negation morphology, in line with the full target language rules for negation (*I can't play that one*) (English examples from R. Ellis, 1994, p. 100). This kind of data has commonly been interpreted to show that, at least as far as key parts of the second language grammar are concerned, learners' development follows a common **route,** even if the speed (or **rate**) at which learners actually travel along this common route may be very different.

This **systematicity** in the language produced by second-language learners is of course paralleled in the early stages through which first language learners also pass in a highly regular manner, described more fully in Chapter 2. Towell and Hawkins (1994, p. 5) identify it as one of the key features that SLL theories are required to explain, and throughout the book we will be examining how current explanations handle this feature.

However, learner language (or **interlanguage**, as it is commonly called) is not only characterized by systematicity. Learner language systems are presumably – indeed, hopefully – unstable and in course of change; certainly, they are also characterized by high degrees of **variability** (Towell and Hawkins, 1994, p. 5). Most obviously, learners' utterances seem to vary from moment to moment, in the types of 'errors' that are made, and learners seem liable to switch between a range of correct and incorrect forms over lengthy periods of time. A well-known example offered by R. Ellis (1985a) involves a child learner of English as a second language who seemed to produce the utterances *no look my card, don't look my card* interchangeably over an extended period. Myles *et al.* (1998) produced similar data from a classroom learner of French as a second language, who variably produced forms such as *non animal, je n'ai pas de animal* within the same 20 minutes or so (to say that he did not have a pet; the correct French form should be *je n'ai pas d'animal*). Here, in contrast to the underlying systematicity earlier claimed for the development of rules of negation, we see performance varying quite substantially from moment to moment.

Like systematicity, variability is also found in child language development. However, the variability found among second-language learners is undoubtedly more 'extreme' than that found for children; again, variability is described by Towell *et al.* (1996) as a central feature of learner interlanguage that SLL theories have to explain, and we will see various attempts to do this in later chapters (especially Chapters 4 and 8).

1.4.5   Creativity and routines in SLL

In the last section, we referred to evidence which shows that learners' interlanguage productions can be described as systematic, at least in part. This systematicity is linked to another key concept, that of originality or **creativity**. Learners' surface utterances can be linked to underlying rule systems, even if these seem primitive and deviant compared with the target language system. It logically follows that learners can produce original utterances, that is, that their rule system can **generate** utterances appropriate to a given context, which the learner has never heard before.

There is, of course, plenty of commonsense evidence that learners can put their second language knowledge to creative use, even at the very earliest stages of SLL. It becomes most obvious that this is happening when learners produce utterances like the highly deviant *non animal* (no animal = 'I haven't got any pet'), which we cited before. This is not an utterance that any native speaker of French would produce (other than, perhaps, a very young child); much the most likely way that the learner has produced it is through applying a very early interlanguage rule for negation, in combination with some basic vocabulary.

But how did this same learner manage to produce the near-target *je n'ai pas de animal*, with its negative particles correctly inserted within the verb phrase, within a few minutes of the earlier form? For us, the most likely explanation is that at this point he was reproducing an utterance that he has indeed heard before (and probably rehearsed), which has been memorized as an unanalysed whole, that is, a formula or a **prefabricated chunk**.

Work in corpus linguistics has led to the increasing recognition that formulas and routines play an important part in everyday language use by native speakers; when we talk, our everyday first-language utterances are a complex mix of creativity and prefabrication (Sinclair, 1991). In first-language acquisition research also, the use of unanalysed chunks by young children has commonly been observed (Wray, 2002; Tomasello, 2003). For first language learners, the contribution of chunks seems limited by processing constraints; for older second-language learners, however, memorization of lengthy, unanalysed language routines is much more possible. (Think of those opera singers who successfully memorize and deliver entire arias, in languages they do not otherwise control!)

Analysis of second language data produced by classroom learners, in particular, shows extensive and systematic use of chunks to fulfil communicative needs in the early stages (Myles *et al.*, 1998, 1999). Studies of informal learners also provide some evidence of chunk use. This phenomenon has attracted relatively little attention in recent times, compared with that given to learner creativity and systematicity. However, we believe it is common enough in second language spontaneous production (and not only in the opera house) to receive more sustained attention from SLL theory, and this is now happening to some extent (Weinert, 1995; Wray, 2002).

1.4.6   Incomplete success and fossilization

Young children learning their first language embark on the enterprise in widely varying situations around the world, sometimes in conditions of extreme poverty and deprivation, whether physical or social. Yet with remarkable uniformity, at the end of five years or so, they have achieved a very substantial measure of success. Teachers and students know to their cost that this is by no means the case with second languages, embarked on after these critical early years. Few, if any, adult learners ever come to blend indistinguishably with the community of target language 'native speakers'; most remain noticeably different in their pronunciation, and many continue to make grammar mistakes and to search for words, even when well-motivated to learn, after years of study, residence or work in contact with the target language.

If the eventual aim of the SLL process is to become indistinguishable from native speaker usage, therefore, it is typified by **incomplete success**. Indeed, while some learners go on learning, and arrive very close to the target language norm, others seem to cease to make any visible progress, no matter how many language classes they attend, or how actively they continue to use their second language for communicative purposes. The term **fossilization** is commonly used to describe this phenomenon, when a learner's second language system seems to 'freeze', or become stuck, at some more or less deviant stage.

These phenomena of incomplete success and fossilization are also significant 'facts' about the process of SLL, which any serious theory must eventually explain. As we will see, explanations of two basic types have been offered. The first group of explanations are **psycholinguistic**: the language-specific learning mechanisms available to the young child simply cease to work for older learners, at least partly, and no amount of study and effort can recreate them. The second group of explanations are **socio-linguistic**: older second language learners do not have the social opportunities, or the motivation, to identify completely with the native speaker community, but may instead value their distinctive identity as learners or as members of an identifiable minority group. These ideas are discussed in more detail in the relevant chapters that follow.

1.4.7   Cross-linguistic influences in SLL

Everyday observation tells us that learners' performance in a second language is influenced by the language, or languages, that they already know. This is routinely obvious from learners' 'foreign accent'; that is, pronunciation that bears traces of the phonology of their first language. It is also obvious when learners make certain characteristic mistakes, such as when a native speaker of English says something in French like *je suis douze*, an utterance parallel to the English 'I am twelve'. (The correct French expression would be *j'ai douze ans* = I have twelve years.)

This kind of phenomenon in learner productions is often called **language transfer**. But how important is it, and what exactly is being transferred? Second language researchers have been through several 'swings of the pendulum' on this question, as Gass (1996) puts it, and as we shall see in a little more detail in Chapter 2. Behaviourist theorists viewed language transfer as an important source of error and interference in SLL, because first-language 'habits' were so tenacious and deeply rooted. The interlanguage theorists who followed downplayed the influence of the first language in SLL however, because of their preoccupation with identifying creative processes at work in second language development. They pointed out that many second language errors could not be traced to first language influence, and they were primarily concerned with discovering patterns and developmental sequences on this creative front.

Theorists today, as we shall see, generally accept once more that cross-linguistic influences play an important role in SLL. However, we will still find widely differing views on the extent and nature of these influences. In Chapter 5 below we discuss multilingual research on the acquisition of a range of second languages by adult migrants in Europe, conducted by a team sponsored by the European Science Foundation (ESF). These ESF researchers argue that the early grammars produced by learners in their multilingual study show little trace of first language influence, though they do not discount the likelihood of increasing variation due to first-language influence as second-language grammars become more complex. Other researchers have claimed that learners with different first languages progress at somewhat different rates, and even follow different acquisitional routes, at least in some areas of the target grammar (Keller-Cohen, 1979; Zobl, 1982, both quoted in Gass, 1996, pp. 322–3).

From a Universal Grammar perspective, the language transfer problem is looked at somewhat differently. If second language learners have continuing **direct** access to their underlying Universal Grammar, first language influence will affect only the more peripheral areas of second language development. If, on the other hand, learners' only access to Universal Grammar is **indirect**, via the working example of a natural language that the first language provides, then first language influence lies at the heart of SLL. In Chapter 3 we will review some of the evidence for these different views current among different Universal Grammar-inspired researchers, and we will see that the dichotomy between direct or indirect access is being replaced by more complex hypotheses about the role of the first language in second language acquisition.

1.4.8   The relationship between second language use and SLL

In Section 1.3.2 above, we considered the distinction between language **competence** and **performance**, which many linguists have found useful. Here, we look more closely at the concept of performance, and in particular, look at the possible relationship between using (i.e. performing in) a second language, and learning (i.e. developing one's competence in) that same language.

We should note first of all, of course, that 'performing' in a language not only involves speaking it. Making sense of the language data that we hear around us is an equally essential aspect of performance. Indeed, it is basic common ground among all theorists of language learning, of whatever description, that it is necessary to interpret and to process incoming language data in some form, for normal language development to take place.

There is thus a consensus that language **input** of some kind is essential for normal language learning. In fact, during the late 1970s and early 1980s, the view was argued by Stephen Krashen and others that input (at the right level of difficulty) was all that was necessary for second language acquisition to take place (Krashen, 1982, 1985; *see* fuller discussion of the **comprehensible input hypothesis** in Chapter 2). More recent theorists have viewed Krashen's early formulation as inadequate. However, it has inspired a range of theory-building and associated empirical research about the role of input in SLL, which we review in Chapter 6 (Long, 1996; Carroll, 2000; VanPatten, 2002).

Krashen was unusual in not seeing any central role for language production in his theory of second language acquisition. Most other theoretical viewpoints support in some form the commonsense view that speaking a language is helpful for learning it, though they offer a wide variety of explanations as to why this should be the case. For example, behaviourist learning theory saw regular (oral) practice as helpful in forming correct language 'habits'. This view became less popular, as part of linguists' general loss of interest in behaviourist thinking, although it is enjoying something of a revival because of developing interest in **connectionism**; *see* Chapter 4.

Other contemporary theorists continue to lay stress on the 'practice' function of language production, especially in building up **fluency** and **control** of an emergent second language system. For example, information-processing theorists commonly argue that language competence consists of both a **knowledge** component ('knowing that') and a **skill** component ('knowing how'). While they may accept a variety of possible sources for the first component, ranging from parameter-setting in a Universal Grammar framework (Towell and Hawkins, 1994) to systematic classroom instruction (Johnson, 1996), researchers in this perspective agree in seeing a vital role for second language use or second language performance in developing the second, skill component (*see* Chapter 4 for fuller discussion).

An even more strongly contrasting view to that of Krashen is the so-called **comprehensible output** hypothesis, argued by Swain and colleagues (Swain, 1985; Swain and Lapkin, 1995). Swain points out that much incoming second language input is comprehensible, without any need for a full grammatical analysis. If we do not need to pay attention to the grammar, in order to understand the message, why should we be compelled to learn it? On the other hand, when we try to say something in our chosen second language, we are forced to make grammatical choices and hypotheses in order to put our utterances together. The act of speaking forces us to try out our ideas about how the target grammar actually works, and of course gives us the chance of getting some feedback from interlocutors who may fail to understand our efforts.

So far in this section, we have seen that theorists can hold different views on the contribution both of language **input** and language **output** to language learning. However, another way of distinguishing among current theories of SLL from a 'performance' perspective concerns their view of second-language **interaction** – when the speaking and listening in which the learner engages is viewed as an integral and mutually influential whole, such as in everyday conversation. Two major perspectives on interaction are apparent: one psycholinguistic, one sociolinguistic.

From a psycholinguistic point of view, second language interaction is mainly interesting because of the opportunities it seems to offer to individual second language learners, to fine-tune the language input they are receiving. This ensures that the input is well adapted to their internal needs (i.e. to the present state of development of their second language knowledge). What this means is that learners need the chance to talk with native speakers in a fairly open-ended way, to ask questions and to clarify meanings when they do not immediately understand. Under these conditions, it is believed that the utterances that result will be at the right level of difficulty to promote learning: in Krashen's terms, they will provide true 'comprehensible input'. Conversational episodes involving the regular **negotiation of meaning** have been intensively studied by many researchers influenced by Krashen (e.g. Long, 1996), whose work is discussed in Chapter 6.

Interaction is also interesting to linguistic theorists, because of recent controversies over whether the provision of **negative evidence** is necessary or helpful for second language development. By 'negative evidence' is meant some kind of input that lets the learner know that a particular form is *not* acceptable according to target language norms. In second language interaction this might take different forms, ranging from a formal correction offered by a teacher, to a more informal rephrasing of a learner's second language utterance, offered by a native-speaking conversational partner.

Why is there a controversy about negative evidence in SLL? The problem is that correction often seems ineffective – and not only because second language learners are lazy. It seems that learners often cannot benefit from correction, but continue to make the same mistakes however much feedback is offered. For some current theorists, any natural language must therefore be learnable from **positive** evidence alone, and corrective feedback is largely irrelevant. Others continue to see value in corrections and negative evidence, though it is generally accepted that these will be useful only when they relate to 'hot spots' currently being restructured in the learner's emerging second language system, or to its more peripheral aspects.

These different (psycho)linguistic views have one thing in common, however; they view the learner as operating and developing a relatively autonomous second language system, and they see interaction as a way of feeding that system with more or less fine-tuned input data, whether positive or negative. **Sociolinguistic** views of interaction are very different.

Here, the language learning process is viewed as essentially social; both the identity of the learner, and his or her language knowledge, are collaboratively constructed and reconstructed in the course of interaction. The details of how this is supposed to work vary from one theory to another, as we shall see. Some theorists stress a broad view of the SLL process as an apprenticeship into a range of new discourse practices (Hall, 1995); others are more concerned with analysing the detail of interaction between more expert and less expert speakers, to determine how the learner is **scaffolded** into using (and presumably learning) new second-language forms (Ohta, 2001). These more social interpretations of second language interaction and its consequences for SLL are examined in some detail in Chapters 7 and 8.

1.5   Views of the language learner

Who is the second language learner, and how is he or she introduced to us, in current SLL research?

We have already made it clear that the infant bilingual (i.e. a child who is exposed to more than one language from birth and acquires them more or less simultaneously in the first few years of life) is not the subject of this book. Instead, 'second language' research generally deals with learners who embark on the learning of an additional language, at least some years after they have started to acquire their first language. This learning may take place formally and systematically, in a classroom setting; or it may take place through informal social contact, through work, through migration or other social forces that bring speakers of different languages into contact and make communication a necessity.

So, second language learners may be children, or they may be adults; they may be learning the target language formally in school or college, or 'picking it up' in the playground or the workplace. They may be learning a highly localized language, which will help them to become insiders in a local speech community; or the target language may be a language of wider communication relevant to their region, which gives access to economic development and public life.

Indeed, in the first part of the 21st century, the target language is highly likely to be English; a recent estimate suggests that while around 375 million people speak English as their first language, another billion or so are using it as a second language, or learning to do so (Graddol, 1997, p. 10). Certainly it is true that much research on SLL, whether with children or adults, is concerned with the learning of English, or with a small number of other languages (French, German, Japanese, Spanish . . .). There are many multilingual communities today (e.g. townships around fast-growing mega-cities) where SLL involves a much wider range of languages. However, these have been comparatively little studied.

It is possible to distinguish three main points of view, or sets of priorities, among SLL researchers as far as the learner is concerned: the linguistic perspective, which is concerned with modelling language structures and processes within the mind; the social psychological perspective, which is concerned with modelling individual differences among learners, and their implications for eventual learning success; and the socio-cultural perspective, which is concerned with learners as social beings and members of social groups and networks. These different perspectives are briefly introduced in following sections.

1.5.1   The learner as language processor

Linguists and psycholinguists have typically been concerned primarily with analysing and modelling the **inner mental mechanisms** available to the individual learner, for processing, learning and storing new language knowledge. As far as language learning in particular is concerned, their aim is to document and explain the developmental route along which learners travel. (We have already seen that the **route** of development is the sequence of linguistic stages through which learners seem to pass.) Researchers for whom this is the prime goal are less concerned with the speed or **rate** of development, or indeed with the degree of ultimate second language success. Thus they tend to minimize or disregard social and contextual differences among learners; their aim is to document universal mental processes available to all normal human beings.

As we shall see, however, there is some controversy among researchers in this psycholinguistic tradition on the question of **age**. Do child and adult second language learners learn in essentially similar ways? Or, is there a **critical age** that divides younger and older learners, a moment when early learning mechanisms atrophy and are replaced or at least supplemented by other compensatory ways of learning? The balance of evidence has been interpreted by Long (1990b) in favour of the existence of such a cut-off point, and many other researchers agree with some version of a view that 'younger = better in the long run' (Singleton, 1995, p. 3). Other researchers argue that this debate is far from resolved (for an overview, *see* Birdsong, 1999). However, explanations of why this should be are still provisional; *see* Chapter 3 below.

1.5.2   Differences between individual learners

Real-life observation quickly tells us, however, that even if second-language learners can be shown to be following a common developmental route, they differ greatly in the degree of success that they achieve. Social psychologists have argued consistently that these differences in learning outcomes must be due to **individual differences** among learners, and many proposals have been made concerning the characteristics that supposedly cause these differences.

In a two-part review, Gardner and MacIntyre (1992, 1993) divide what they see as the most important learner traits into two groups: the **cognitive** and the **affective** (emotional). Here, we follow their account and summarize very briefly the factors claimed to have the most significant influence on SLL success. For fuller treatment of this social psychological perspective on learner difference, we refer the reader to sources such as R. Ellis, 1994, pp. 467–560; Skehan, 1998; Dörnyei, 2001a, 2001b; Robinson, 2001, 2002; Dörnyei and Skehan, 2002.

1.5.2.1   Cognitive factors

Intelligence: not very surprisingly perhaps, there is clear evidence that second-language students who are above average on formal measures of intelligence or general academic attainment tend to do well in SLL, at least in formal classroom settings.

Language aptitude: is there really such a thing as a 'gift' for language learning, distinct from general intelligence, as folk wisdom often holds? The best known formal test of language aptitude was designed in the 1950s by Carroll and Sapon (1959, in Gardner and MacIntyre, 1992, p. 214). This 'Modern Language Aptitude Test' assesses a number of sub-skills believed to be predictive of SLL success: (a) phonetic coding ability; (b) grammatical sensitivity; (c) memory abilities; and (d) inductive language learning ability. In general, learners' scores on this and other similar tests do indeed 'correlate with . . . achievement in a second language' (Gardner and MacIntyre, 1992, p. 215), and in a range of contexts measures of aptitude have been shown to be one of the strongest available predictors of success (Harley and Hart, 1997).

Language learning strategies: do more successful language learners set about the task in some distinctive way? Do they have at their disposal some special repertoire of ways of learning, or **strategies**? If this were true, could these even be taught to other, hitherto less successful learners? Much research has been done to describe and categorize the strategies used by learners at different levels, and to link strategy use to learning outcomes; it is clear that more proficient learners do indeed employ strategies that are different from those used by the less proficient (Oxford and Crookall, 1989, quoted in Gardner and MacIntyre, 1992, p. 217). Whether the strategies cause the learning, or the learning itself enables different strategies to be used, has not been fully clarified, however. We look more closely at learning strategies and their role in acquisition in Chapter 4.

1.5.2.2   Affective factors

Language attitudes: social psychologists have long been interested in the idea that the attitudes of the learner towards the target language, its speakers and the learning context, may all play some part in explaining success or lack of it. Research on second language attitudes has largely been conducted within the framework of broader research on motivation, of which attitudes form one part.

Motivation: for Gardner and MacIntyre (1993, p. 2), the motivated individual 'is one who wants to achieve a particular goal, devotes considerable effort to achieve this goal, and experiences satisfaction in the activities associated with achieving this goal'. So, motivation is a complex construct, defined by three main components: 'desire to achieve a goal, effort extended in this direction, and satisfaction with the task' (Gardner and MacIntyre, 1993, p. 2). Gardner and his Canadian colleagues have carried out a long programme of work on motivation with English Canadian school students learning French as a second language, and have developed a range of formal instruments to measure motivation. Over the years consistent relationships have been demonstrated between language attitudes, motivation and second-language achievement, with the strongest relationships obtaining between motivation and achievement (Masgoret and Gardner, 2003); these relationships are complex, however, as the factors interact and influence each other. Dornyei and Otto (1998, p. 48, cited in Dörnyei, 2001b, p. 86) recognized the dynamic and changing nature of motivation over time, in their so-called 'process model' of second-language motivation.

Language anxiety and willingness to communicate: the final learner characteristic that Gardner and MacIntyre consider to hold a relationship with learning success is language anxiety (and its obverse, self-confidence). For these authors, language anxiety 'is seen as a stable personality trait referring to the propensity for an individual to react in a nervous manner when speaking . . . in the second language' (Gardner and MacIntyre, 1993, p. 5). It is typified by self-belittling, feelings of apprehension, and even bodily responses such as a faster heartbeat! The anxious learner is also less willing to speak in class, or to engage target language speakers in informal interaction. Gardner and MacIntyre cite many studies that suggest that language anxiety has a negative relationship with learning success, and some others that suggest the opposite, for learner self-confidence. More recently, a broad overarching construct 'willingness to communicate' has been proposed as a mediating factor in second-language use and SLL (MacIntyre et al., 2002). This construct includes anxiety and confidence alongside a range of other variables which together produce 'readiness to enter into discourse at a particular time with a specific person or persons, using a L2' (MacIntyre et al., 1998, p. 547, cited in Dornyei and Skehan, 2002, p. 13).

1.5.3   The learner as social being

The two perspectives on the learner that we have highlighted so far have concentrated (a) on universal characteristics and (b) on individual characteristics. But it is also necessary to view the second language learner as essentially a social being, taking part in structured social networks and social practices, and we will encounter later in this book some of the researchers who do just that. Indeed, after some decades when psycholinguistic and individualist perspectives on second language learners predominated, recent research is redressing the balance, as will be seen in Chapters 7 and 8 below.

Interest in learners as social beings will lead to concern with their relationship with the social context in which their language learning is taking place, and the structuring of the learning opportunities that this makes available. The learning process itself may also be viewed as essentially social, and inextricably entangled in second language use and second language interaction. Two major characteristics distinguish this social view of the learner from the 'individual differences' view that we have just dipped into.

First, interest in the learner as a social being leads to concern with a range of socially constructed elements in learners' identities, and their relationship with learning – so **social class, power, ethnicity** and **gender** make their appearance as potentially significant for SLL research. Second, the relationship between the individual learner and the social context of learning is viewed as **dynamic**, reflexive and constantly changing. The 'individual differences' tradition saw that relationship as being governed by a bundle of learner traits or characteristics (such as aptitude, anxiety, etc.), which were relatively fixed and slow to change. More socially oriented researchers view motivation, learner anxiety, etc., as being constantly reconstructed through ongoing second-language experience and second-language interaction.

1.6   Links with social practice

Is SLL theory 'useful'? Does it have any immediate practical applications in the real world, most obviously in the second language classroom? In our field, theorists have been and remain divided on this point. Beretta and colleagues (1993) argued for 'pure' theory in SLL, uncluttered by requirements for practical application. Van Lier (1994), Rampton (1995b) and others have argued for a socially engaged perspective, where theoretical development is rooted in, and responsive to, social practice and language education, in particular. Yet others have argued that second language teaching in particular should be guided systematically by SLL research findings (Krashen, 1985).

This tension has partly been addressed by the emergence of 'instructed language learning' as a distinct sub-area of research (*see* recent surveys by Spada, 1997; Cook, 2001; Robinson, 2001, 2002; Doughty, 2003). However, much of the theorizing and empirical evidence reviewed in this book cannot be captured within this particular sub-field. We think that language teachers, who will form an important segment of our readership, will themselves want to take stock of the relations between the theories we survey, and their own beliefs and experiences in the classroom. They will, in other words, want to make some judgement on the 'usefulness' of theorizing in making sense of their own experience and their practice, while not necessarily changing it. In our general conclusions to this book, therefore, we end by some brief consideration of the connections we ourselves perceive between learning theory and classroom practice.

1.7   Conclusion

This chapter has aimed to introduce a range of recurrent concepts and issues that most theorists agree will have to be taken into account, if we are to arrive eventually at any complete account of SLL. In Chapter 2 we provide a brief narrative account of the recent history of SLL research, plus summary descriptions of some of the more specific language learning phenomena that any theory must explain. We then move in remaining chapters of the book to a closer examination of a number of broad perspectives, or families of theories, with their distinctive views of the key questions that must be answered and the key phenomena that need to be explained.

2

The recent history of second language learning research

2.1 Introduction

In order to understand current developments in second language learning (SLL) research, it is helpful to retrace its recent history. We will see throughout this chapter that the kind of questions researchers are asking today are for the most part firmly rooted in earlier developments in linguistics, psychology, sociology and pedagogy.

The aim of this chapter is not to provide the reader with an exhaustive description of early approaches, but rather to explore the theoretical foundations of today's thinking. More detailed reviews can be found in other sources (Dulay *et al.*, 1982; Selinker, 1992). We will limit ourselves to the post-war period, which has seen the development of theorizing about SLL from an adjunct to language pedagogy, to an autonomous field of research. The period since the 1950s can be divided into three main phases.

We will start with the 1950s and 1960s, and a short description of how it was believed that second languages were learnt at the time. We will then describe the impact of the 'Chomskyan revolution' in linguistics on the field of language acquisition: initially on the study of first language acquisition and subsequently on that of second language acquisition. This had a huge impact on psycholinguistics in the 1970s, and we will see that its influence is still very much felt today.

We will then briefly consider the period from the 1980s onwards, which has witnessed the development of second language acquisition theorizing as a relatively autonomous field of inquiry (a 'coming of age', as Sharwood Smith (1994, p. ix) put it). During this period, the impact of Chomskyan linguistics has continued to be profound, but ideas coming from a range of other fields have also become increasingly significant. Research strands initiated in the 1980s will then systematically be reviewed and evaluated in the rest of the book, as well as some newer trends that made their appearance in the 1990s, such as connectionism or socio-cultural theory.

2.2   The 1950s and 1960s

In the 1950s and early 1960s, theorizing about SLL was still very much an adjunct to the practical business of language teaching. However, the idea that language teaching methods had to be justified in terms of an underlying learning theory was well-established, since the pedagogic reform movements of the late-19th century at least (*see* Howatt, 1984, pp. 169–208 for an account of these). The writings of language teaching experts in the 1950s and 1960s include serious considerations of learning theory, as preliminaries to their practical recommendations (Lado, 1964; Rivers, 1964, 1968).

As far as its linguistic content was concerned, 'progressive' 1950s language pedagogy drew on a version of structuralism developed by the British linguist, Palmer, in the 1920s, and subsequently by Fries and his Michigan colleagues in the 1940s. Howatt sums up this approach as follows:

1. The conviction that language systems consisted of a finite set of 'patterns' or 'structures' which acted as models . . . for the production of an infinite number of similarly constructed sentences;
2. The belief that repetition and practice resulted in the formation of accurate and fluent foreign language habits;
3. A methodology which set out to teach 'the basics' before encouraging learners to communicate their own thoughts and ideas.

(Howatt, 1988, pp. 14–15)

Howatt's summary makes it clear that the learning theory to which language teaching experts and reformers were appealing at this time was the general learning theory then dominant in mainstream psychology, **behaviourism**, which we explain more fully in the next section.

2.2.1   Behaviourism

In the behaviourist view (Watson, 1924; Thorndike, 1932; Bloomfield, 1933; Skinner 1957), language learning is seen like any other kind of learning, as the formation of **habits**. It stems from work in psychology that saw the learning of any kind of behaviour as being based on the notions of **stimulus** and **response**. This view sees human beings as being exposed to numerous **stimuli** in their environment. The response they give to such stimuli will be reinforced if successful, that is, if some desired outcome is obtained. Through repeated **reinforcement**, a certain stimulus will elicit the same response time and again, which will then become a habit. The learning of any skill is seen as the formation of habits, that is, the creation of stimulus–response pairings, which become stronger with reinforcement. Applied to language learning, a certain situation will call for a certain response; for example, meeting someone will call for some kind of greeting, and the response will be reinforced if the desired outcome is obtained, that is, if the greeting is understood. In the case of communication breakdown the particular response will not be reinforced, and the learner will abandon it in favour of a response that it is hoped will be successful and therefore reinforced.

When learning a first language, the process is relatively simple: all we have to do is learn a set of new habits as we learn to respond to stimuli in our environment. When learning a second language, however, we run into problems: we already have a set of well-established responses in our mother tongue. The SLL process therefore involves replacing those habits by a set of new ones. The complication is that the old first-language habits interfere with this process, either helping or inhibiting it. If structures in the second language are similar to those of the first, then learning will take place easily. If, however, structures are realized differently in the first and the second language, then learning will be difficult. As Lado put it at the time:

> We know from the observation of many cases that the grammatical structure of the native language tends to be transferred to the foreign language . . . we have here the major source of difficulty or ease in learning the foreign language . . . Those structures that are different will be difficult.
>
> (Lado, 1957, pp. 58–9, cited in Dulay *et al.*, 1982, p. 99)

Take the example of an English (as a first language) learner learning French as a second language and wanting to say *I am twelve years old*, which in French is realized as *J'ai douze ans* (= I have 12 years), and now consider the same learner learning the same structure in German, which is realized as *Ich bin zwölf Jahre alt* (= I am 12 years old). According to a behaviourist view of learning, the German structure would be much easier and quicker to learn, and the French one more difficult, the English structure acting as a facilitator in one instance, and an inhibitor in the other. Indeed, it may well be the case that English learners have more difficulty with the French structure than the German one, as many French teachers would testify after hearing their pupils repeatedly saying **Je suis douze* (I am 12) (note: asterisks are traditionally used in linguistics in order to indicate ungrammatical sentences), but more about that later.

From a teaching point of view, the implications of this approach were twofold. First, it was strongly believed that practice makes perfect; in other words, learning would take place by imitating and repeating the same structures time after time.

Second, teachers needed to focus their teaching on structures which were believed to be difficult, and as we saw above, difficult structures would be those that were different in the first and second languages, as was the case for the English–French pair cited above. The teacher of French, in our example, would need to engage his or her pupils in many drilling exercises in order for them to produce the French structure correctly.

The logical outcome of such beliefs about the learning process was that effective teaching would concentrate on areas of difference, and that the best pedagogical tool for foreign language teachers was therefore a sound knowledge of those areas. Researchers embarked on the huge task of comparing pairs of languages in order to pinpoint areas of difference, therefore of difficulty. This was termed **Contrastive Analysis** (or CA for short) and can be traced back to Fries, who wrote in the introduction to his book *Teaching and Learning English as a Foreign Language*: 'The most effective materials are those that are based upon a scientific description of the language to be learned, carefully compared with a parallel description of the native language of the learner' (Fries, 1945, p. 9, cited in Dulay *et al.*, 1982, p. 98). Work in this tradition has some continuing influence on second or foreign language pedagogy (Howatt, 1988, p. 25) despite the many criticisms it has suffered, which we will now discuss.

2.2.2   Behaviourism under attack

Starting in the 1950s and continuing in the 1960s, both linguistics and psychology witnessed major developments. Linguistics saw a shift from structural linguistics, which was based on the description of the surface structure of a large corpus of language, to generative linguistics that emphasized the rule-governed and creative nature of human language. This shift had been initiated by the publication in 1957 of *Syntactic Structures*, the first of many influential books by Noam Chomsky.

In the field of psychology, the pre-eminent role for the environment – which was argued by Skinner – in shaping the child's learning and behaviour was losing ground in favour of more developmentalist views of learning, such as Piaget's cognitive developmental theory, in which inner forces drive the child, in interaction with the environment (Piaget and Inhelder, 1966; Piaget, 1970; Piatelli-Palmarini, 1980).

The clash of views about the way in which we learn language came to a head at the end of the 1950s with two publications. These were Skinner's *Verbal Behavior* in 1957, which outlined in detail his behaviourist view of learning as applied to language, and Chomsky's review of Skinner's book, published in 1959, which was a fierce critique of Skinner's views.

Chomsky's criticisms centred on a number of issues:

- The creativity of language: children do not learn and reproduce a large set of sentences, but they routinely create new sentences that they have never learnt before. This is only possible because they internalize rules rather than strings of words; extremely common examples of utterances such as *it breaked* or *Mummy goed* show clearly that children are not copying the language around them but applying rules. Chomsky was incensed by the idea that you could compare the behaviour of rats in a laboratory, learning to perform simple tasks, to the behaviour of children learning language without direct teaching, a fundamentally different task because of its sheer complexity and abstractness.

- Given the complexity and abstractness of linguistic rules (e.g. the rules underlying the formation of questions in many languages, or the rules underlying the use of reflexive pronouns in English discussed in Chapter 3), it is amazing that children are able to master them so quickly and efficiently, especially given the limited input they receive. This has been termed 'Plato's problem' (Chomsky, 1987), and refers specifically to the fact that some of the structural properties of language, given their complexity, could not possibly be expected to be learnt on the basis of the samples of language to which children are exposed. Furthermore, children have been shown not to be usually corrected on the form of their utterances but rather on their truth values. When correction does take place, it seems to have very little effect on the development of language structure.

For the above reasons, Chomsky claimed that children have an innate faculty that guides them in their learning of language. Given a body of speech, children are programmed to discover its rules, and are guided in doing that by an innate knowledge of what the rules should look like. We will leave fuller discussion of Chomsky's ideas until Chapter 3. Suffice to say for now that this revolutionary approach to the study of language gave a great stimulus to the field of psycholinguistics, and especially to the study of language acquisition.

The next section reviews work that took place in the 1970s, which was heavily influenced by these new ideas.

2.3   The 1970s

2.3.1   First language acquisition

The work outlined above was a great stimulus to investigations of the acquisition of language in young children, by researchers such as Klima and

Bellugi (1966), Slobin (1970) or Brown (1973). These investigators found striking similarities in the language learning behaviour of young children, whatever the language they were learning. It seems that children all over the world go through similar **stages**, use similar constructions in order to express similar meanings, and make the same kinds of errors. The stages can be summarized as follows (Aitchison, 1989, p. 75):

Language stage	*Beginning age**
Crying	Birth
Cooing	6 weeks
Babbling	6 months
Intonation patterns	8 months
One-word utterances	1 year
Two-word utterances	18 months
Word inflections	2 years
Questions, negatives	2 years 3 months
Rare or complex constructions	5 years
Mature speech	10 years

These stages are not language-specific, although their actual realization obviously is.

Similarly, when studying the emergence of a number of structures in English, a consistent **order of acquisition** was found. Brown's (1973) so-called 'morpheme study' is probably the best-known first language study of that time, and was to be very influential for second language acquisition research. In an in-depth study of three children of different backgrounds, he compared the development of 14 grammatical morphemes in English. Brown found that although the rate at which children learnt these morphemes varied, the order in which they acquired them remained the same for all children, as listed below in a simplified form:

Present progressive	*boy sing**ing***
Prepositions	*dolly **in** car*
Plural	*sweeti**es***
Past Irregular	***broke***
Possessive	*baby**'s** biscuit*
Articles	***a** car*
Past regular	*want**ed***
Third person singular	*eat**s***
Auxiliary *be*	*he **is** running*

---

*The ages are given as a very rough guideline only; children vary considerably both in the age of onset of a given phase, and in how fast they proceed from one phase to another. All children normally go through the stages in the order indicated, however.

What is striking is that, not only do children acquire a number of grammatical morphemes in a fixed order, but they also follow fairly rigid stages during the acquisition of a given area of grammar. For example, children all over the world not only acquire negatives around the same age, but they also mark the negative in similar ways in all languages, by initially attaching some negative marker to the outside of the sentence: *no go to bed, pas faut boire* (= not need drinking), etc., and gradually moving the negative marker inside the sentence, following the stages exemplified below for English (R. Ellis 1994, p. 78, based on Klima and Bellugi, 1966, and Cazden, 1972):

Stage 1: Negative utterances consist of a 'nucleus' (i.e. the positive proposition) either preceded or followed by a negator.
wear mitten no
not a teddy bear

Stage 2: Negators are now incorporated into affirmative clauses. Negators at this stage include *don't* and *can't*, used as unitary items. Negative commands appear.
there no squirrels
you can't dance
don't bite me yet

Stage 3: Negators are now always incorporated into affirmative clauses. The 'Auxiliary + not' rule has been acquired, as *don't, can't,* etc., are now analysed. But some mistakes still occur (e.g. copula *be* is omitted from negative utterances and double negatives occur).
I don't have a book
Paul can't have one
I not crying
no one didn't come

These stages are not unlike the stages followed by second language learners, which were outlined in Chapter 1 (1.4.4). Similar phenomena can be observed for the acquisition of interrogatives and other structures.

Another important characteristic of child language that started to receive attention is that it is rule-governed, even if initially the rules children create do not correspond to adult ones. As early as the two-word stage, children express relationships between elements in a sentence, such as possession, negation or location, in a consistent way. Also, it has been demonstrated convincingly that when children produce an adult-like form which is the result of the application of a rule, such as for example adding *-s* to *dog* in order to produce the plural form *dogs*, they are not merely imitating and repeating parrot-fashion the adult language around them. Two kinds of evidence prove that very clearly. First, children commonly produce forms such as *sheeps* or *breads*, which they have never heard before and are therefore not imitating. Second, some ingenious and now famous experiments were carried out with very young children back in the 1950s (Berko, 1958) in which children were shown a picture of a strange bird-like creature and told, for example, *this is a wug*; they were then shown a picture of two of those creatures and told, *Now there's another one. There are two of them. There are two . . . ?* The children almost invariably replied *wugs* (91% of them), showing that they do not merely learn plurals by remembering each plural form they hear, but that they extract a plural rule from the language they hear, and then apply that rule to their own productions. This experiment did not only contain a series of nonsense nouns, but also nonsense verbs; for example, children were shown a picture of a person doing some strange action and told, *This person knows how to gling. He is glinging. Yesterday, he did the same thing. Yesterday, he . . . ?* Children consistently answered *glinged* (77% of them), again showing that they had created a rule for forming the past tense. In fact, children go through a stage, initially, of correctly supplying irregular past-tense forms, such as *took* or *went*, on the basis of having learnt these forms individually,* before having created the past-tense rule. When they do so, they start producing forms such as *taked* and *goed*, which can persist for a very long time despite attempts at correction by worried parents who might think their child is regressing. It is only much later that children will be able to take on board exceptions to rules.

The fact that children do not seem to correct their 'errors' on the basis of adult overt or implied correction of children's utterances is well-documented in the first language acquisition literature. The following dialogue is typical of the uselessness of such attempts (quoted in Pinker, 1994, p. 281). The psycholinguist Martin Braine once tried for several weeks to stamp out one of his daughter's grammatical errors. Here is the result:

Child:	Want other one spoon, Daddy
Father:	You mean, you want THE OTHER SPOON
Child:	Yes, I want other one spoon, please, Daddy
Father:	Can you say 'the other spoon'?
Child:	Other . . . one . . . spoon
Father:	Say . . . 'other'

---

*It is important to note that a large proportion of the verbs which are commonplace in the linguistic environment of the child have irregular past tense forms. For example, verbs such as *give, run, do, come, sit, sleep, fall, find, eat, hit, break*, will form part of both the early vocabulary used by the child, and of the typical verbs used by adults when addressing children.

Child:	Other
Father:	'Spoon'
Child:	Spoon
Father:	'Other . . . spoon'
Child:	Other . . . spoon. Now give me other one spoon?

This famous example is typical of such attempts, and this child is neither slow in her development, nor particularly stubborn; it is as if she cannot make the alternative proposed by her father fit into her current grammar.

From this necessarily brief and oversimplified account of 1970s first language acquisition research, the following characteristics emerge:

- children go through stages
- these stages are very similar across children for a given language, although the rate at which individual children progress through them is highly variable
- these stages are similar across languages
- child language is rule-governed and systematic, and the rules created by the child do not necessarily correspond to adult ones
- children are resistant to correction
- children's processing capacity limits the number of rules they can apply at any one time, and they will revert to earlier hypotheses when two or more rules compete.

These findings seemed to support Chomsky's claims that children follow some kind of pre-programmed, internal route in acquiring language.

2.3.2   Second language learning: the birth of Error Analysis

The findings reported above soon came to the attention of researchers and teachers interested in second language acquisition. This was the case, not only because of their intrinsic interest, but also because the predictions made by Contrastive Analysis did not seem to be borne out in practice. Teachers were finding out in the classroom that constructions that were different in pairs of languages were not necessarily difficult, and that constructions that were similar in two languages were not necessarily easy either. Moreover, difficulty sometimes occurred in one direction but not the other. For example, the placement of unstressed object pronouns in English and French differs: whereas English says *I like them*, French says *Je les aime* (*I them like*). Contrastive Analysis would therefore predict that object pronoun placement would be difficult for both English learners of French and French learners of English. This is not the case, however; whereas English learners of French do have problems with this construction and produce errors such as ***J'aime **les** in initial stages, French learners of English do not produce errors of the type I **them** like, as would be predicted by Contrastive Analysis. The task of comparing pairs of languages in order to design efficient language teaching programmes now seemed to be disproportionately huge in relation to its predictive powers: if it could not adequately predict areas of difficulty, then the whole enterprise seemed to be pointless.

These two factors combined – developments in first language acquisition and disillusionment with Contrastive Analysis – meant that researchers and teachers became increasingly interested in the language produced by learners, rather than the target language or the mother tongue. This was the origin of **Error Analysis**, the systematic investigation of second language learners' errors. The language produced by learners began to be seen as a linguistic system in its own right, worthy of description. Corder (1967) was the first to focus attention on the importance of studying learners' errors, as it became evident that they did not all originate in the first language by any means. The predictions of Contrastive Analysis, that all errors would be caused by interference from the first language, were shown to be unfounded, as many studies showed convincingly that the majority of errors could not be traced to the first language, and also that areas where the first language should have prevented errors were not always error-free. For example, Hernández-Chávez (1972) showed that although the plural is realized in almost exactly the same way in Spanish and in English, Spanish children learning English still went through a phase of omitting plural marking. Such studies became commonplace, and a book-length treatment of the topic appeared in 1974 (Richards' Error Analysis: Perspectives on Second Language Learning).

In a review of studies looking at the proportion of errors that can be traced back to the first language, R. Ellis (1985a) found that there was considerable variation in the findings, with results ranging from three per cent of errors attributed to the first language (Dulay and Burt, 1973) to 51% (Tran-Chi-Chau, 1975), with a majority of studies finding around a third of all errors traceable to the first language. Error Analysis thus showed clearly that the majority of the errors made by second language learners do not come from their first language.

The next question therefore was: where do such errors come from? They are not target-like, and they are not first language-like; they must be learner-internal in origin. Researchers started trying to classify these errors in order to understand them, and to compare them with errors made by children learning their mother tongue. This was happening at the same time as the developments in first language acquisition, which we mentioned above, whereby child language was now seen as an object of study in its own right, rather than as an approximation of adult language. In SLL research, coupled with the interest in understanding learner-internal errors, interest in the overall character of the second language system was also growing.

The term **interlanguage** was coined in 1972, by Selinker, to refer to the language produced by learners, both as a system which can be described at any one point in time as resulting from systematic rules, and as the series of interlocking systems that characterize learner progression. In other words, the interlanguage concept relies on two fundamental notions: the language produced by the learner is a **system** in its own right, obeying its own rules; and it is a **dynamic** system, evolving over time. Interlanguage studies thus moved one step beyond Error Analysis, by focusing on the learner system as a whole, rather than only on its non-target-like features.

2.3.3 Morpheme studies and second language learning

As far as second language acquisition research is concerned, the most important empirical findings of this period were probably the results of the so-called **morpheme studies**, and at a conceptual level, Krashen's **Monitor Model**, which was a logical theoretical development arising from such studies.

The second language morpheme studies were inspired by the work of Roger Brown (1973) in first language acquisition, which we mentioned briefly above. Brown had found a consistent order of emergence of 14 grammatical morphemes in English in his longitudinal study. The same order was confirmed by other researchers, for example by De Villiers and De Villiers (1973) in their cross-sectional study* of 20 children acquiring English as a first language.

Researchers in second language acquisition set about investigating the acquisition of the same grammatical morphemes in second-language learners. Dulay and Burt (1973, 1974, 1975) were the first to undertake such studies, reporting first of all on the accuracy of production of eight of

---

*A longitudinal study is where a (usually small) group of subjects is studied over a period of time. A cross-sectional study, on the other hand, investigates a (usually large) group of subjects at one point in time. In the case of developmental studies, cross-sectional studies take representative samples of subjects at different stages of development and compare their behaviour, inferring development when behaviour changes between two stages. Both types of studies have their advantages and disadvantages, and have been used extensively in language acquisition research.

Brown's morphemes in Spanish-speaking children acquiring English as a second language (Dulay and Burt, 1973). Their study was cross-sectional and was based on the speech of three groups of Spanish-speaking children of different abilities (in terms of their length of exposure to English as immigrants in the USA).

There were 151 children in the study, and the method used for eliciting speech was the Bilingual Syntax Measure, a structured conversation elicitation technique based on cartoons and designed to elicit certain grammatical constructions. It was found that 'the acquisition sequences obtained from the three groups of children were strikingly similar. This was so even though each group on the whole was at a different level of English proficiency' (Dulay et al., 1982, p. 204). Dulay and Burt (1974) also carried out a similar study, but this time using children from different first languages, namely Chinese and Spanish. They found very similar acquisition orders for these structures for both Spanish and Chinese children for 11 of Brown's grammatical morphemes. Encouraged by these results, Dulay and Burt (1975) extended their study to include 536 Spanish- and Chinese-speaking children of varying levels of proficiency in English as a second language, and they investigated 13 of Brown's original morphemes. They found a clear hierarchy for the acquisition of these morphemes, with four different groups of morphemes being acquired in a set order, no matter what the first language, as shown in Figure 2.1 (from Dulay et al., 1982, p. 208).

Dulay and Burt (1982, pp. 207–9) conclude: 'It is highly probable that *children of different language backgrounds learning English in a variety of host country environments acquire eleven grammatical morphemes in a similar order*'.

If the results seem clear as far as child second-language learners are concerned, it does not necessarily follow that adults would also exhibit the same order of acquisition. After all, children might approach the task of SLL more like the learning of a first language than adults do.

Bailey et al. (1974) conducted a similar study with adults. They used the same elicitation method (Bilingual Syntax Measure) in order to investigate the accuracy of production of the eight morphemes studied by Dulay and Burt (1973), in 73 adult learners of English from 12 different first-language backgrounds. The results were very similar to those reported in the case of children by Dulay and Burt (1973, 1974), as shown in Figure 2.2 (taken from Dulay et al., 1982, p. 210).

These morpheme acquisition studies attracted criticism, both at the time and subsequently; this critique is reviewed (by Gass and Selinker (1994), pp. 84–7). (The criticisms are mainly about the elicitation technique used in the early studies, which it was thought biased the results, and also about

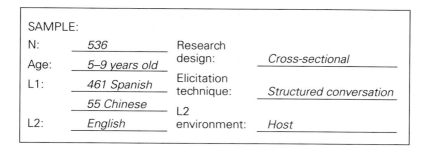

SAMPLE:

N: 536   Research design: Cross-sectional

Age: 5–9 years old

L1:   461 Spanish   Elicitation technique: Structured conversation

            55 Chinese   L2

L2:   English   environment: Host

Acquisition hierarchy observed

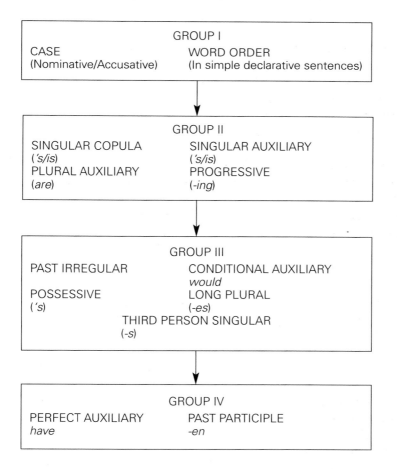

GROUP I

CASE
(Nominative/Accusative)

WORD ORDER
(In simple declarative sentences)

GROUP II

SINGULAR COPULA
(*'s/is*)
PLURAL AUXILIARY
(*are*)

SINGULAR AUXILIARY
(*'s/is*)
PROGRESSIVE
(*-ing*)

GROUP III

PAST IRREGULAR

POSSESSIVE
(*'s*)

CONDITIONAL AUXILIARY
would
LONG PLURAL
(*-es*)
THIRD PERSON SINGULAR
(*-s*)

GROUP IV

PERFECT AUXILIARY
have

PAST PARTICIPLE
-en

Fig. 2.1 Acquisition hierarchy for 13 English grammatical morphemes for Spanish-speaking and Cantonese-speaking children (*Source*: Dulay *et al.*, 1982, p. 208)

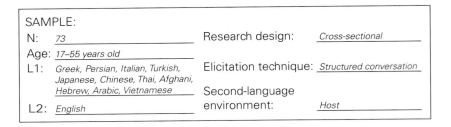

SAMPLE:

N: _73_   Research design: _Cross-sectional_

Age: _17–55 years old_

L1: _Greek, Persian, Italian, Turkish,_   Elicitation technique: _Structured conversation_
     Japanese, Chinese, Thai, Afghani,
     Hebrew, Arabic, Vietnamese   Second-language

L2: _English_   environment: _Host_

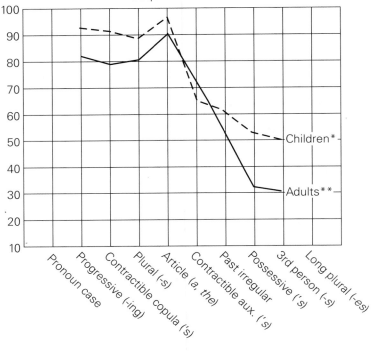

Fig. 2.2 Comparison of adult and child acquisition sequences for eight grammatical morphemes (*Source*: Dulay *et al.*, 1982, p. 210)

the assumption that relative accuracy of production reflects acquisition sequences.)* However, the basic argument that both child and adult learners of English as a second language developed accuracy in a number of grammatical morphemes in a set order, no matter what the context of learning (classroom, naturalistic, mixed), survived the critique. The fact that this set order did not match the order found by Brown or De Villiers and De Villiers for first language acquisition is neither here nor there. The existence of such an order suggested that second-language learners are guided by internal principles that are largely independent of their first language; this was a serious blow for any proponents of Contrastive Analysis.

Moreover, soon after, a number of studies were reported which strongly suggested that systematic staged development could be found in a number of syntactic domains as well. For example, the acquisition of negative structures in English as a second language was shown to occur in well-defined stages, by several early studies (Ravem, 1968; Milon, 1974; Cazden et al., 1975; Wode, 1978, 1981; Adams 1978; Butterworth and Hatch 1978; R. Ellis, 1994, p. 99). Similar stages were also noted in the acquisition of negatives in German as a second language (Felix, 1978; Lange, 1979; Pienemann, 1981; Clahsen, 1982). In summary: 'Despite the differences in the final states towards which learners of English and German are targeted, marked similarities in the sequence of acquisition of negatives in the two languages can be seen' (R. Ellis, 1994, p. 101). Moreover, the acquisition of negatives in English by second language learners is not dissimilar to that of children acquiring English as their first language (*see* Section 2.3.1 above).

The acquisition of other syntactic structures, such as interrogatives and relative clauses in English, word order in German, etc., are also well-documented as exhibiting uniform patterns of acquisition, whatever the first language of the learner (R. Ellis, 1994, pp. 99–105, provides a comprehensive review of early studies). Moreover, the stages followed by second language learners in the acquisition of these other areas of syntax show corresponding similarities to those followed by children learning their first language.

Thus, the 1970s witnessed a wealth of studies investigating development in second language learners that seemed to show convincingly that it is systematic, that it is largely independent of the first language of the learner, and

---

*The morpheme studies measured the accuracy of production of their subjects on the grammatical morphemes studied. Subjects were deemed to have acquired a morpheme if they supplied it correctly in at least 90% of the obligatory contexts (e.g. if they produced the morpheme -s in at least 90% of the cases when the context required a plural noun). Researchers then equated accuracy of production with acquisition, and have been criticized for doing that.

that it presents many similarities with first language acquisition, even though there are differences. These were major empirical findings that undermined contemporary beliefs about how second languages are acquired.

Before moving to examine the theoretical proposals advanced to explain such findings, let us pause for an instant on the last point, namely the finding that acquisitional patterns in first and second language learning were both similar and different, as it is still today an issue that is fiercely debated and highly controversial. Remember that the discovery of acquisition sequences in first language acquisition was linked to the theory that children are endowed with a language faculty that guides them in the hypotheses they make about the language around them. Brown's order of acquisition of grammatical morphemes was seen as evidence to support this view. So, what can we make of the finding that second language learners also follow an order of acquisition, but that this order is different? The fact that they do follow such an order suggests that they are indeed guided by some set of internal principles, as children are. On the other hand, the fact that this order varies from that found for first languages, suggests that these internal principles are different, in some respects at least.

A somewhat confused picture therefore emerges from the empirical work characteristic of the 1970s, and the 1980s research agenda has tried to address some of these issues. But before we turn to the 1980s, we need to consider a highly influential attempt to conceptualize these issues in the first comprehensive model of second language acquisition, Krashen's Monitor Model.

2.3.4   Krashen's Monitor Model

Krashen's theory evolved in the late 1970s in a series of articles (Krashen, 1977a, 1977b, 1978), as a result of the findings outlined above. Krashen thereafter refined and expanded his ideas in the early 1980s in a series of books (Krashen, 1981, 1982, 1985).*

Krashen based his general theory around a set of five basic hypotheses:

1.   the Acquisition-Learning hypothesis
2.   the Monitor hypothesis
3.   the Natural Order hypothesis
4.   the Input hypothesis
5.   the Affective Filter hypothesis.

We shall briefly outline each of these in turn.

*For a useful and comprehensive critique of Krashen's work, *see* McLaughlin (1987, pp. 19–58).

2.3.4.1   The Acquisition-Learning hypothesis

This hypothesis has been highly influential, and, albeit in a different form, still remains the source of much debate today. The basic premise is that language **acquisition**, on the one hand, and **learning**, on the other, are separate processes. Acquisition refers to the 'subconscious process identical in all important ways to the process children utilize in acquiring their first language' (Krashen, 1985, p. 1) and learning refers to the 'conscious process that results in "knowing about" language' (Krashen, 1985, p. 1). In other words, acquisition is the result of natural interaction with the language via meaningful communication, which sets in motion developmental processes akin to those outlined in first language acquisition, and learning is the result of classroom experience, in which the learner is made to focus on form and to learn about the linguistic rules of the target language.

The contrast between the naturalistic environment and the classroom environment is not the crucial issue, however. What is claimed to be important is the difference between meaningful communication, on the one hand, which can very well take place in the language classroom, and which will trigger subconscious processes, and conscious attention to form, on the other, which can also take place in naturalistic settings, especially with older learners who might explicitly request grammatical information from people around them. Krashen has been criticized for his vague definition of what constitutes conscious versus subconscious processes, as they are very difficult to test in practice: how can we tell when a learner's production is the result of a conscious process and when it is not? Nonetheless, this contrast between acquisition and learning has been very influential, especially among foreign language teachers who saw it as an explanation of the lack of correspondence between error correction and direct teaching, on the one hand, and their students' accuracy of performance, on the other. If there was some kind of internal mechanism constraining learners' development, then it could account for the fact that some structures, even simple ones like the third-person singular -s in English (*he likes*), can be so frustrating to teach, with learners knowing the rule consciously, but often being unable to apply it in spontaneous conversation. In Krashen's terminology, learners would have learnt the rule, but not acquired it.

What is also very problematic in this distinction is Krashen's claim that learning cannot turn into acquisition, that is, that language knowledge acquired or learnt by these different routes cannot eventually become integrated into a unified whole (Krashen and Scarcella, 1978). Other 1980s researchers disagreed (Gregg, 1984; McLaughlin, 1987) and the debate about whether different kinds of knowledge interact or remain separate is still alive today, even though the terms used might differ (Schwartz, 1993; Towell and Hawkins, 1994; Zobl, 1995; Myles *et al.*, 1999).

2.3.4.2   The Monitor hypothesis

> According to Krashen, 'learning' and 'acquisition' are used in very specific ways in second-language performance. The Monitor Hypothesis states that 'learning has only one function, and that is as a Monitor or editor' and that learning comes into play only to 'make changes in the form of our utterance, after it has been "produced" by the acquired system' (1982, 15). Acquisition 'initiates' the speaker's utterances and is responsible for fluency. Thus the Monitor is thought to alter the output of the acquired system before or after the utterance is actually written or spoken, but the utterance is initiated entirely by the acquired system.
>
> (McLaughlin, 1987, p. 24)

It is quite clear from the above that the Monitor does not operate all the time. Given enough time, when a focus on form is important for learners, and when learners know the grammatical rule needed, they might make use of the Monitor in order to consciously modify the output produced by the acquired system. Needless to say, the pressures and demands of conversing in the second language in real time do not often allow for such monitoring to take place. Krashen's Monitor hypothesis has been criticized for that reason, and also for the fact that attempts to test its predictions have been unsuccessful, for example in studies comparing learners' performance when given more time (Hulstijn and Hulstijn, 1984) or being made to focus on form (Houck *et al.*, 1978; Krashen and Scarcella, 1978), or checking whether learners who are able to explain the rules perform better than learners who do not (Hulstijn and Hulstijn, 1984).

Krashen used the concept of the Monitor in order to explain individual differences in learners. He suggests that it is possible to find Monitor 'over-users' who do not like making mistakes and are therefore constantly checking what they produce against the conscious stock of rules they possess. Their speech is consequently very halting and non-fluent. On the other hand, Monitor 'under-users' do not seem to care very much about the errors they make, and for them, speed and fluency are more important. Such learners rely exclusively on the acquired system and do not seem able or willing to consciously apply anything they have learnt to their output. In between the two are the supposed 'optimal' Monitor users, who use the Monitor hypothesis when it is appropriate, that is, when it does not interfere with communication.

The problem with such claims, even though they might have some intuitive appeal, is that they are at present impossible to test empirically: how do we know when a learner is consciously applying a rule or not, or, in other words, whether the source of the rule that has been applied is the acquired system or the learnt system?

2.3.4.3   The Natural Order hypothesis

We acquire the rules of language in a predictable order, some rules tending to come early and others late. The order does not appear to be determined solely by formal simplicity and there is evidence that it is independent of the order in which rules are taught in language classes.

(Krashen, 1985, p. 1)

Although there is evidently some truth in such a statement, it has been criticized for being too strong. It ignores well-documented cases of language transfer, or of individual variability. Not only are such cases ignored; there is no place for them in Krashen's theory. Krashen's Natural Order hypothesis has also been criticized for being based almost exclusively on the morpheme studies with their known methodological problems, and which, in any case, reflect accuracy of production rather than acquisition sequences.

A weak version of the Natural Order hypothesis is undoubtedly supported by the kind of empirical evidence on SLL that we reviewed in sections 2.3.2 and 2.3.3 above. However, Krashen gives us little help in understanding why this should be the case.

2.3.4.4   The Input hypothesis

The Input hypothesis is linked to the Natural Order hypothesis in that it claims that we move along the developmental continuum by receiving **comprehensible input**. Comprehensible input is defined as second language input just beyond the learner's current second language competence, in terms of its syntactic complexity. If a learner's current competence is i then comprehensible input is $i + 1$, the next step in the developmental sequence. Input which is either too simple (already acquired) or too complex ($i + 2 / 3 / 4 \ldots$) will not be useful for acquisition. Krashen views the Input hypothesis as central to his model of second language acquisition:

(a) Speaking is a result of acquisition and not its cause. Speech cannot be taught directly but 'emerges' on its own as a result of building competence via comprehensible input.

(b) If input is understood, and there is enough of it, the necessary grammar is automatically provided. The language teacher need not attempt deliberately to teach the next structure along the natural order – it will be provided in just the right quantities and automatically reviewed if the student receives a sufficient amount of comprehensible input.

(Krashen, 1985, p. 2)

Krashen's Input hypothesis has been frequently criticized for being vague and imprecise: how do we determine level i, and level $i + 1$? Nowhere is this vital point made clear. Moreover, Krashen's claim is somewhat circular: acquisition takes place if the learner receives comprehensible input, and comprehensible input (it is claimed) has been provided if acquisition takes place. The theory becomes impossible to verify, as no independently testable definitions are given of what comprehensible input actually consists of, and therefore of how it might relate to acquisition. Nor, of course, does the theory specify the internal workings of the 'Language Acquisition Device' where acquisition actually takes place – this remains an opaque black box.

2.3.4.5   The Affective Filter hypothesis

As we have just seen, Krashen believes that learners need to receive comprehensible input for language acquisition to take place. This is not sufficient, however. Learners also need to 'let that input in', as it were. This is the role of the so-called Affective Filter, which supposedly determines how receptive to comprehensible input a learner is going to be.

> The Affective Filter Hypothesis captures the relationship between affective variables and the process of second language acquisition by positing that acquirers vary with respect to the strength or level of their affective filters. Those whose attitudes are not optimal for second language acquisition will not only tend to seek less input, but they will also have a high or strong affective filter – even if they understand the message, the input will not reach that part of the brain responsible for language acquisition, or the Language Acquisition Device. Those with attitudes more conducive to second language acquisition will not only seek and obtain more input, they will also have a lower or weaker filter. They will be more open to the input, and it will strike 'deeper'.
>
> (Krashen, 1982, p. 31)

Although both researchers and teachers would agree that affective variables play an important role in second language acquisition, Krashen's Affective Filter remains vague and atheoretical. For example, many self-conscious adolescents suffer from low self-esteem and therefore presumably have a 'high' filter. Are they therefore all bad language learners? And are all the confident and extrovert adults (with a 'low' filter) good language learners? Clearly, they are not. Moreover, how does the Affective Filter actually work? All these issues remain vague and unexplored.

To conclude, in this brief account we have reflected criticisms of Krashen's five hypotheses and of his overall model, which have been current almost since Krashen first advanced them. It remains true nonetheless that Krashen's ideas have been highly influential in shaping many research agendas and projects, and in so doing, considerably advancing our understanding of second language acquisition. The Input hypothesis, for example, has stimulated a major ongoing tradition of theorizing and empirical research on input and interaction, reviewed below in Chapter 6. Krashen's main overall weakness was the presentation of what were just hypotheses that remained to be tested, as a comprehensive model that had empirical validity. He then used his hypotheses prematurely as a basis for drawing pedagogical implications.

2.3.5   Schumann's pidginization or acculturation model

Other models appeared in the 1970s, which attempted similarly to theorize second language acquisition findings. We will mention very briefly here one other model, as it views second language acquisition from a radically different angle, and also remained influential during subsequent decades.

Schumann first proposed his pidginization or acculturation model in the late 1970s (Schumann, 1978a, 1978b, 1978c). On the basis of naturalistic studies of untutored learners, he noticed that early interlanguage resembled pidgin languages (i.e. simplified trading languages which lack native speakers; Sebba, 1997), with characteristic features such as fixed word order and lack of inflections. Second language acquisition was compared to the complexification of pidgins, and this process was linked to degree of acculturation of the learners. The closer they feel to the target language speech community, the better learners will 'acculturate', and the more successful their SLL will be. The more alienated from that community they perceive themselves to be, the more pidgin-like their second language will remain.

This model was influential in opening up alternative lines of research comparing second language acquisition with pidginization and creolization, and in bringing to the fore social psychological variables and their role in SLL. For a substantial period, Schumann's proposals were the most theoretically ambitious claims about second language acquisition, which drew on sociolinguistic thinking. In Chapter 8 we revisit this model, briefly, alongside other, newer sociolinguistic approaches.

2.4   The 1980s and beyond

We will not review this period in detail here, as the rest of the book is devoted to outlining the different approaches and the empirical work attached to them, which followed from the 1980s to the present day. In this section, we will briefly summarize the ongoing research agenda that arose from the major developments of the 1970s.

By the mid-1980s, SLL research was no longer subordinate to the immediate practical requirements of curriculum planning and language pedagogy. Instead, it had matured into a much more autonomous field of inquiry, encompassing a number of substantial programmes of research, with their distinctive theoretical orientations and methodologies. The links with other related disciplines have by no means disappeared, however, and we will see throughout this book that many new links have developed. Research into the structure of language(s) and its use continues to be extensively drawn upon, and so is research into language variation and change. New links have emerged with cognitive science (e.g. the development of fluency; the role of consciousness), with neuro-psychology (e.g. connectionist models; modularity of the brain) and with socio-cultural frameworks (Vygotskyan learning theory) that have greatly enriched our perception of the many facets of second language acquisition. But the SLL research agenda continues to focus on a number of fundamental issues carried forward from the 1970s, as follows:

1.   The role of internal mechanisms
     (a)   Language-specific: how similar are the first and second language acquisition processes, and how far are the similarities caused by language-specific mechanisms still being activated? If language-specific mechanisms are important, how can they best be modelled? How relevant is the current Chomskyan conception of Universal Grammar?
     (b)   Cognitive: in what respects are second language learning and processing similar to the learning and processing of any other complex skill?
2.   The role of the first language
     It is clear that cross-linguistic influences from the first and other languages are operating in second language acquisition, but it is also clear that such language transfer is selective: some first-language properties transfer and others do not. An important aspect of today's research agenda is still to understand better the phenomenon of transfer.

3. The role of psychological variables

    How do individual characteristics of the learner, such as motivation, personality, language aptitude, etc., affect the learning process?

4. The role of social and environmental factors

    How similar is the learning of a second language to the creation of pidgins and creoles? How does the overall socialization of the second language learner relate to the language learning process?

5. The role of the input

    What is the role of instruction in shaping or speeding up development? What is the relationship between the input and internal mechanisms? Do certain interaction patterns facilitate learning?

We will now turn to examine how these issues have been tackled across the range of current perspectives on SLL, starting in Chapter 3 with linguistics-inspired attempts to model the contents of the 'black box' of the Language Acquisition Device, left largely unexplored in the proposals of Krashen.

3
Linguistics and language learning: the Universal Grammar approach

Evidently each language is the result of the interplay of two factors: the initial state and the course of experience. We can think of the initial state as a 'language acquisition device' that takes experience as 'input' and gives the language as an 'output' – an 'output' that is internally represented in the mind/brain.

(Chomsky, 2000, p. 4)

3.1 Introduction

In this chapter, we start to consider individual theoretical perspectives on second language learning (SLL) in greater detail. Our first topic is the Universal Grammar approach, developed by the American linguist, Noam Chomsky, and numerous followers over the last few decades. We have concentrated on this particular linguistic approach because it has been much the strongest linguistic influence on second language acquisition research in recent years, and has inspired a great wealth of studies, articles and books on second language acquisition, both empirical and theoretical (for full length treatments, *see* Herschensohn, 2000; Hawkins, 2001; White, 2003).

The main aim of linguistic theory is twofold: first, to characterize what human languages are like (descriptive adequacy), and second, to explain why they are that way (explanatory adequacy). In terms of second language acquisition, what a linguistic approach attempts to do is no different; its aims are to describe the language produced by second language learners, and to explain why the language they produce is the way it is. The main emphasis of the research reviewed in this chapter is therefore on the product(s) of the acquisition process, in its various guises over the course of development, from a descriptive as well as an explanatory point of view. Universal Grammar is therefore a property theory (as defined in Chapter 1), that is, it attempts to characterize the underlying linguistic knowledge in second-language learners' minds. In contrast, a detailed examination of the learning process itself (transition theory) will be the main concern of the cognitive approaches that we describe in Chapter 4.

First in this chapter, we will give a broad definition of the aims of the Chomskyan tradition in linguistic research, in order to delimit the aspects of second language acquisition to which this tradition is most relevant. Second, we will examine the concept of Universal Grammar itself in some detail, and lastly, we will move on to consider its application in SLL research.

3.2   Why a Universal Grammar?

3.2.1   Aims of linguistic research

Linguistic theory is not primarily concerned with second language acquisition. Its main goals, as defined for example in Chomsky 1986a,* are to answer three basic questions about human language:

1.   What constitutes knowledge of language?
2.   How is knowledge of language acquired?
3.   How is knowledge of language put to use?

('Knowledge of language' is an ambiguous term. Here, it means the subconscious mental representation of language that underlies all language use.)

All three questions are also of concern to SLA researchers. They can be briefly developed as follows:

3.2.1.1   What constitutes knowledge of language?

Linguistic theory aims to describe the mental representations of language that are stored in the human mind. It aims to define what all human languages have in common, as well as the distinctive characteristics that

---

*Chomsky (1988, p. 3) added another question to this list which is of concern to the brain scientist rather than the linguist: 'What are the physical mechanisms that serve as the material basis for this system of knowledge and for the use of this knowledge?' (cited in Salkie 1990). This question is not directly relevant to the present discussion.

make human language different from other systems of communication. It also needs to specify in what way individual human languages can differ from one another. Although all human languages have a great deal in common, which enables us to translate from one language to another without too many difficulties, it is equally obvious that they are also different from one another, as our struggle to learn foreign languages clearly shows. However, Chomsky (2000) argues that to a Martian landing on Earth, the differences between human languages would seem like variations on a single theme.

The Universal Grammar approach claims that all human beings inherit a universal set of **principles** and **parameters** that control the shape human languages can take, and which are what make human languages similar to one another. In his *Government and Binding* theory, Chomsky (1981, 1986a, 1986b) argues that the core of human language must comprise these two components. His proposed principles are unvarying and apply to all natural languages; in contrast, parameters possess a limited number of open values which characterize differences between languages (parametric variation). Examples of such principles and parameters will be given later on in this chapter. More recently, in his Minimalist Program, Chomsky (1995, 2000) argues that the core of human language is the lexicon (the word store), which can be characterized as follows:

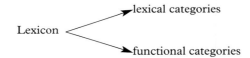

We will define these categories in more detail later; basically, lexical categories include 'content' words such as verbs and nouns, and functional categories include 'grammatical' words such as determiners or auxiliaries, as well as abstract grammatical features such as Tense or Agreement, which may be realized morphologically.

In the Minimalist Program, parametric variation is located within the lexicon, primarily within functional categories, which are characterized by a bundle of functional features that vary from language to language, causing the various surface differences in word order, morphology, etc., which we are familiar with.

One of the main interests of the Universal Grammar approach for second language acquisition research is that it provides a detailed descriptive framework which enables researchers to formulate well-defined hypotheses about the task facing the learner, and to analyse learner language in a more focused manner. For example, first and second languages can be compared in terms of their parameter settings, and implications for learning can be drawn. Moreover, it is a general theory of language, which should therefore encompass any theory dealing specifically with learner language, seen as just another version of human language.

3.2.1.2   How is knowledge of language acquired?

How does the child create the mental construct that is language? Chomsky first resorted to the concept of Universal Grammar because he believes that children could not learn their first language so quickly and effortlessly without the help of an innate language faculty to guide them. The arguments put forward, often referred to as the 'logical problem of language learning', are that on the basis of messy input (spoken language is full of false starts, slips of the tongue, etc.), children create a mental representation of language which not only goes beyond the input they are exposed to, but is also strikingly similar to that of other native speakers of the same language variety. Children achieve this at an age when they have difficulty grasping abstract concepts, yet language is probably the most abstract piece of knowledge they will ever possess. If there is a biologically endowed Universal Grammar, this would make the task facing children much easier, by providing a genetic blueprint which determines in advance the shape which language will take. This would also explain why the different languages of the world are strikingly similar in many respects.

If we now turn to the problem of SLL, learners are faced with the same logical problem of having to construct a grammar of the second language on the basis of more or less fragmentary input, and of having to construct abstract representations on the basis of the limited samples of language they actually encounter. But although the task facing them is the same, this does not mean to say that second language learners necessarily set about tackling it in the same way as children. After all, their needs are very different, if only because they are already successful communicators in one language, and because they already have a mental representation of language, with the parameters set to the values of their native language. Moreover, second language learners are cognitively mature and therefore presumably much more resourceful as far as their ability to solve problems and to deal with abstract concepts is concerned. From a theoretical point of view, therefore, different possible scenarios are open to consideration:

- Second language grammars are constrained by Universal Grammar. The second language is one example of a natural language, and it is constrained by Universal Grammar in the same way as native grammars are. Within this view, there is a range of different possibilities that we will review later. For example, some researchers believe that second language learners start off with the parameter settings of their first language, and reset them on the basis of input. Others believe that second language learners have available to them from the onset the full range of Universal Grammar parameters, like first language childlearners, and do not resort to first language parameter settings in the first instance. Others still believe that second languages gradually draw on Universal Grammar, and that (for example) functional categories are not available to learners at the beginning of the learning process. All these approaches believe that the second language grammar can (but does not necessarily) become native-like.

- Universal Grammar does not constrain second-language grammars or Universal Grammar is impaired. Some researchers believe that second language grammars are fundamentally different from first language grammars because they are not constrained any longer by Universal Grammar, and learners have to resort to general learning mechanisms, giving rise to 'wild' grammars, that is, grammars which do not necessarily conform to the general rules underlying natural human languages. Other researchers believe that only the principles and parameters instantiated (activated) in the learners' first language will be available, and that parameter resetting is impossible. Within this view, the second language grammar is still Universal Grammar constrained in the sense that it does not violate Universal Grammar principles and parameters (it is not 'wild'), but it cannot become the same as that of first language speakers of the same language.

There is considerable controversy around all these issues, and there are many representatives of each of these positions in the literature about second language acquisition. We revisit them below in Section 3.5.

3.2.1.3 How is knowledge of language put to use?

The Universal Grammar approach to language is concerned with knowledge of language, that is, with the abstract mental representation of language and the computational mechanisms associated with it, which all human beings possess, called **competence**. It is not about **performance**, about how language is used in real life. Performance is the domain of a theory of language use, in which linguistic competence is only one aspect, and factors such as the brain's information-processing capacity also come into play. A complete theory of language also has to define how we access our knowledge base, and how it relates to a number of sociolinguistic and psycholinguistic variables. Although Chomsky acknowledges that this is an important area for research, he has been concerned almost exclusively with addressing the first two issues. This is also true for Universal Grammar-inspired research in second language acquisition, although some researchers are increasingly attempting to reconcile the two objectives.

3.2.2   Arguments from first language acquisition

In this section, we will review in some more detail the arguments that support the existence of an innate language faculty in children. We will base our discussion on the brief outline presented in Chapter 2 of what we know about first language acquisition, the main characteristics of which are summarized succinctly below:

- children go through developmental stages
- these stages are very similar across children for a given language, although the rate at which individual children progress through them is variable
- these stages are similar across languages
- child language is rule-governed and systematic, and the rules created by the child do not necessarily correspond to adult ones
- children are resistant to correction
- children's processing capacity limits the number of rules they can apply at any one time, and they will revert to earlier hypotheses when two or more rules compete.

Universalists could not conclude from the evidence presented above alone that there must be a specific language module in the brain. These regularities, although very striking, could be attributed to the more general cognitive make-up of human beings which leads them to process information, whether linguistic or not, in the way they do. After all, children learning maths or learning to play the piano also go through fairly well-defined stages, although not at such a young age, and not necessarily so successfully.

However, another striking feature of child language is that it does not seem to be linked in any clear way to intelligence. In fact, children vary greatly in the age at which they go through each developmental step, and in how fast they go through each stage. By age three or four, though, individual differences have largely disappeared, and the late starter has usually caught up with the precocious child. Moreover, early onset of language is not linked to intelligence; Steinberg (1993) states that 'many very famous people, including Albert Einstein, are reputed to have been slow to talk'.

Not only is language development not directly linked to intelligence, but it is also one of the most complex and abstract pieces of knowledge children have to cope with at such an early age, perhaps even during the entire course of their life. To give an example of the complexities of language which children have to disentangle, just consider the following reflexive sentences, some of them grammatical and others ungrammatical:

   a.   *John* saw *himself*.
   b.   **Himself* saw *John*.
   c.   Looking after *himself* bores *John*.
   d.   John said that *Fred* liked *himself*.
   e.   **John* said that Fred liked *himself*.
   f.   *John* told *Bill* to wash *himself*.
   g.   **John* told *Bill* to wash *himself*.
   h.   *John* promised *Bill* to wash *himself*.
   i.   *John* believes *himself* to be intelligent.
   j.   **John* believes that *himself* is intelligent.
   k.   *John* showed *Bill* a picture of *himself*.

(Examples are taken from White, 1989, cited in Lightbown and Spada, 1993, pp. 9–10. In all these sentences, the noun and the pronoun that refer to the same person are printed in italics.)

Now imagine you are the child trying to work out what the relationship between the reflexive pronoun and its antecedent is; you might conclude from (a) and (b) that the reflexive pronoun must follow the noun it refers to, but (c) disproves this. Sentences (d), (e), (f) and (g) might lead you to believe that the closest noun is the antecedent, but (h) shows that this cannot be right either. It is also evident from (h) that the reflexive and its antecedent do not have to be in the same clause. Furthermore, the reflexive can be in subject position in (i), an untensed clause, but not in (j), a tensed clause. Moreover, the reflexive can sometimes have two possible antecedents, as in (k) where *himself* can refer to either *John* or *Bill*.

These few sentences should be enough to convince you of the magnitude of the task facing children; how can they make sense of this, and invariably arrive at the correct rule?

In support of the view that language is not linked to intelligence, there is also a large body of evidence from children with cognitive deficits who develop language normally (Bishop and Mogford, 1993; Smith, 1999; Bishop 2001). For example, Bellugi *et al.* (1993) studied children suffering from Williams' syndrome, a rare metabolic disorder that causes heart defects, mental retardation and a distinctive facial appearance. These investigators demonstrated that these children show dissociation between language development and the kind of supposed cognitive prerequisites that Piaget and his followers would argue are necessary for language development. Sophisticated use of language with complex syntax and adult-like vocabulary is found in individuals whose overall mental development is otherwise very slow and remains below that of a seven-year-old.

Smith and Tsimpli (1995) studied in detail the extraordinary case of a brain-damaged man, Christopher, who is institutionalized because he is unable to look after himself, but who can read, write and communicate in any of 15–20 languages:

> The most salient feature is a striking mismatch between his verbal and non-verbal abilities, supported by test results over a prolonged period and with recent documentation across a wide range of different tests. The basic generalisation is that he combines a relatively low performance IQ with an average or above average verbal IQ.
>
> (Smith and Tsimpli, 1995, p. 4)

Evidence of the opposite is also found: children who are cognitively 'normal', but whose language is impaired, sometimes severely. This condition, known as 'specific language impairment' (SLI), is characterized by language being deficient in specific ways, such as 'difficulties with productive rules of word-formation, the morphosyntactic prerequisites of feature agreement and construction of complex phonological units' (Lorenzo and Longa, 2003) (see also Van der Lely, 1998; Van der Lely and Ullman, 2001; van der Lely and Battell, 2003). One English-speaking family has been studied recently, in which 16 out of 30 members in the last three generations suffer from specific language impairment, suggesting that it is an inherited disorder, and that some aspects of language at least might be genetically controlled (Gopnik and Crago, 1991; Pinker, 1994; Van der Lely, 1996; Van der Lely and Ullman, 1996; Cook, 1997; Smith, 1999). Recently, the gene FOXP2 has been discovered, whose mutation apparently leads to specific language impairment (Lai et al., 2001).

Not only does language seem to be largely separate from other aspects of cognition – although the two interact of course – but within language itself, different modules also seem to be relatively independent of one another. We find further evidence in brain-damaged adults that language is separate from other kinds of cognitive faculties; people who suffer strokes or other localized injuries to the brain will have very different symptoms depending on the location of their injury. Damage to the left hemisphere of the brain will usually result in language deficit, as in the majority of people (around 90%) it is the left hemisphere that controls language. Moreover, the exact location of the injury within the left hemisphere is often linked to particular kinds of language deficit. Damage to the region in front of and just above the left ear (Broca's area) usually results in effortful, hesitant and very non-fluent speech, with virtually no grammatical structure in evidence, consisting largely of specific nouns with few verbs, and poorly articulated. The comprehension of speech, in contrast, usually remains good. This condition is called Broca's aphasia, and is in many respects the mirror image of Wernicke's aphasia, which usually results from an injury to the region of the brain around and under the left ear (Wernicke's area). In the case of Wernicke's aphasia, patients produce effortless, fluent and rapid speech, which is generally grammatically complex and well-structured, but which is lacking in content words with specific meaning; these patients produce very general nouns and verbs, such as *something, stuff, got, put* or *did*, and their speech is so vague that it is usually totally incomprehensible. In this condition, the comprehension of speech is severely impaired.

The picture we have just outlined of the relationship between brain and language is necessarily very oversimplified. (For more detailed accounts, see for example Harris and Coltheart, 1986; Caplan 1987, 1992; Sabouraud, 1995; Jenkins, 2000; Lorenzo and Longa, 2003). Nonetheless, it shows clearly that specific areas of the brain deal with specific aspects of language, and that suffering from a language deficit does not necessarily mean having lost language completely, but usually means having problems with one or more aspects of language. Recent advances in brain-imaging techniques have also shown that specific areas of the brain are activated when using different aspects of language, although the picture is becoming more complex as techniques become more sophisticated (Carter, 1998).

All this evidence put together has been used by universalists to posit that there must be some kind of innate language faculty that is biologically triggered, in order to explain why language in children just seems to 'grow', in the same way as teeth develop and children start walking. An influential book by Lenneberg (1967), called *The Biological Foundations of Language*, outlined the characteristics that are typical of biologically triggered behaviour and argued that language conforms to the criteria used in order to define such behaviour.

Aitchison (1989, p. 67) presents Lenneberg's criteria as a list of six features:

1. 'The behaviour emerges before it is necessary'. Children start talking long before they need to: they are still being fed and looked after, and therefore do not need language for their survival.

2. 'Its appearance is not the result of a conscious decision'. It is quite obvious that children do not get up one morning and decide to start talking, whereas they might consciously decide to learn to ride a bike or play the piano.
3. 'Its emergence is not triggered by external events (though the surrounding environment must be sufficiently 'rich' for it to develop adequately)'. Although children need language around them in order to learn it, there is no single event that will suddenly trigger language development.
4. 'Direct teaching and intensive practice have relatively little effect'. We have seen in Chapter 2 how oblivious children seem to be to correction.
5. 'There is a regular sequence of 'milestones' as the behaviour develops, and these can usually be correlated with age and other aspects of development'. In the same way as a baby will sit up before standing up before walking before running, we have seen how children go through well-defined stages in their language development, which tend to run parallel to physical development. The onset of the first words usually roughly corresponds to the onset of walking for example.
6. 'There may be a "critical period" for the acquisition of the behaviour'. It is often argued that, in the same way as some species of birds have to be exposed to their species' song in order to learn it before a certain age, human beings have to be exposed to language before puberty in order for language to develop. This is a controversial issue; the evidence from children who have been deprived of language in their early years is difficult to interpret, as it is not usually known whether they were normal at birth or had suffered some kind of brain damage (Curtiss, 1977, 1988; Eubank and Gregg, 1999; Smith, 1999). We will examine later in this chapter the evidence that adult second language learners bring to this ongoing debate (Birdsong, 1999).

After having reviewed the kind of argumentation used by universalists in order to propose the existence of a language-specific module in the brain, which allows the child to learn language so easily and effortlessly, let us now turn to the question of what this so-called language faculty or Universal Grammar might be like.

3.3   What does Universal Grammar consist of?

The aim of this chapter is not to give a full account of Universal Grammar and all its principles and parameters, but to understand how it has been applied to the study of language acquisition. Generative linguistics has changed considerably in the last 50 years or so, from the early phase of phrase structure rules to the recent Minimalist Program. Although these changes have been significant, and have been frustrating at times for applied linguists wanting to know which version of the theory to adopt for their empirical investigations, its primary goal has remained the same: to characterize the innate language faculty. The varying emphases over the years have essentially been the result of the tension between the two contradictory goals of such an endeavour. The search for 'descriptive adequacy' has attempted to account for the details of increasing numbers of typologically unrelated languages, while the search for 'explanatory adequacy' has aimed to make effective cross-language generalizations:

> A theory of language must show how each particular language can be derived from a uniform initial state under the 'boundary conditions' set by experience. . . . The search for descriptive adequacy seems to lead to ever-greater complexity and variety of rule systems, while the search for explanatory adequacy requires that language structure must be invariant, except at the margins.
>
> (Chomsky, 2000, p. 7)

Next, we will examine more concretely some examples of principles and parameters, that is, the content of Universal Grammar.

3.3.1   Principles

We have seen earlier that, according to this view of language learning, the first language learner's initial state is supposed to consist of a set of universal principles. Furthermore, languages vary in limited ways, expressible in terms of parameters that need to be fixed in one of a few possible settings (usually two).

What does this mean in practice? The general idea is that language learning is highly constrained in advance, thus making the task for the child much more manageable. In the following section, we will work our way through one concrete example of a principle and its associated parameters, in order to see how these concepts have been applied to the problem of language learning.

The universal principle we are going to use as our first example is the principle of **structure-dependency**, which states that language is organized in such a way that it crucially depends on the structural relationships between elements in a sentence (such as words, morphemes, etc.). What this means is that words are regrouped into higher-level structures that are the units that form the basis of language. Intuitively, we know that this is the case. In the following sentences:

(a) *She bought a new car yesterday.*
(b) *My friend bought a new car yesterday.*
(c) *The friend that I met in Australia last year bought a new car yesterday.*
(d) *The friend I am closest to and who was so supportive when I lost my job two years ago bought a new car yesterday.*

we know that *she, my friend, the friend that I met in Australia last year* and *the friend I am closest to and who was so supportive when I lost my job two years ago* are the same kind of groupings and perform the same role in the sentence, and in fact might refer to one single individual. Moreover, we also know that we could carry on adding details about this friend more or less ad infinitum by using devices such as *and, that, which,* etc., running the risk of boring our listener to tears! We also know that the crucial word in these groupings is *friend,* or *she* if we have already referred to this person earlier in the conversation. This kind of structural grouping is called a **Phrase**, and in the examples above, we are dealing with a **Noun-Phrase**, as the main or central element (the head) of this phrase is a noun (or pronoun). In fact, all languages in the world are structured in this way, and are made up of sentences which consist of at least a **Noun-Phrase** (NP) and a Verb-Phrase (VP), as in [$_{NP}$Paul] [$_{VP}$sings], which in turn may optionally contain other phrases or even whole sentences, as (d) in the examples above shows.

This knowledge – that languages are structure-dependent – is a crucial aspect of all human languages that has many implications; it is a **principle** of Universal Grammar which explains many of the operations we routinely perform on language. For example, when we ask a question in English, we change the canonical (i.e. basic) order of the sentence (Subject–Verb–Object in English):

Your cat is friendly
Is your cat | friendly?

The way in which we do that is not based on the linear order of the sentence, but is structure-dependent. We do not move the first verb we encounter, or, say, the third word in the sentence, rules which would work in the above example, but would generate ungrammatical sentences in the following example:

The cat who is friendly is ginger
*Is the cat who friendly is ginger?
*Who the cat is friendly is ginger?

The correct answer is of course, *Is the cat who is friendly ginger?*, where the second *is* is moved to the beginning of the sentence. Note that there is no immediately obvious reason why this should be the case; computers would have no problems dealing with either of the two artificial rules above. In fact, computers find it considerably more difficult to apply a rule that is based on a hierarchical structure, as is the case in this natural-language example. As Cook and Newson (1996, p. 8) put it, 'Movement in the sentence is not just a matter of recognising phrases and then of moving the *right* element in the *right* phrase: movement depends on the structure of the sentence'. In our example, the *is* that moves is the one belonging to the main clause, not the one in the relative clause.

The same restrictions apply to passive sentences. The sentence, *The car hit the girl*, can be made into a passive by raising the object Noun-Phrase to the subject position, *The girl was hit by the car*. Notice that it is the whole Noun-Phrase that is moved to the front; it could just as well have been *Lisa*, or *The girl with the blue trousers*, or *The girl who won first prize in the creative writing competition*. French passive constructions work in exactly the same way: *L'enfant chatouille le nounours* (the child tickles the teddy) becoming *Le nounours est chatouillé par l'enfant* (the teddy is tickled by the child). In fact:

> structure-dependency can therefore be put forward as a universal principle of language: whenever elements of the sentence are moved to form passives, questions, or whatever, such movement takes account of the structural relationships of the sentence rather than the linear order of words.
>
> (Cook and Newson, 1996, p. 11)

The movement we have just described is another Universal Grammar principle, called **Move** α. Universal Grammar contains many such principles. One further example of a universal principle found in all languages is the **A over A condition**, which limits the application of rules to a small sub-set of the logical possibilities. If a category (such as Noun-Phrase) includes as part of its structure another instance of the same category (i.e. another Noun-Phrase) then any rule that mentions 'Noun-Phrase' has to be construed as referring to the more inclusive instance (Smith, 1999). So the sentences:

Harry stirred the stew and the pudding.
Harry stirred the stew that tasted of turnips.

can give rise to the following questions and answers:

What did Harry stir?
– *the stew and the pudding*
– *the stew that tasted of turnips.*

but not to:

> *What did Harry stir the stew and – ?*
> *What did Harry stir – and the pudding?*
> *What did Harry stir the stew that tasted of – ?*
>   (from Smith, 1999, p. 64)

Lastly, according to this theory, the syntactic categories used in language, both lexical and functional, also form part of our Universal Grammar endowment, and do not have to be learnt. Universal Grammar includes a universal inventory of categories that the child selects from on the basis of the input, as not all languages will necessarily make use of all categories or their features. According to White, there are three potential sources of cross-linguistic variation relating to functional categories:

i.   Languages can differ as to which functional categories are realized in the grammar. On some accounts, for example, Japanese lacks the category Det [Determiner] (Fukui and Speas, 1986).
ii. The features of a particular functional category can vary from language to language. For instance, French has a gender feature, while English does not.
iii. Features are said to vary in strength: a feature can be strong in one language and weak in another, with a range of syntactic consequences. For example, Infl [Inflection] features are strong in French and weak in English . . ., resulting in certain word-order alternations between the two languages.
                                                                 (White, 2003, p. 10)

We will come back to these sources of variation shortly. Before doing so, let us define in more detail what is meant by these functional categories.

3.3.1.1   Functional categories

Functional categories★ are perhaps best explained by contrast to lexical categories, which we are already familiar with. What we call lexical categories are groups such as nouns, verbs, adjectives, etc., that is, so-called 'content words' that carry a specific meaning. The kind of items we are now turning

---

★The term 'functional' is used in a number of different senses in linguistics. Crystal (1991, pp. 145–7) offers definitions of a range of traditional meanings of the term, as in 'functional grammar', etc. In Chapter 5 below, we ourselves use the term in a more traditional way. In this chapter, however, we follow current usage among Universal Grammar theorists. As defined by these theorists, functional categories have been playing an important part in Universal Grammar-based language acquisition studies since the beginning of the 1990s, and have been influential in accounting for some aspects of child grammars, and more recently of second language learners' grammars.

our attention to are grammatical words or 'function' words, such as determiners (e.g. *the, my*, etc.) and complementizers (e.g. *whether*), or grammatical morphemes such as plural *-s*, past tense *-ed*, etc. Another way of conceptualizing the difference between lexical and functional categories is in terms of an open class of language items, and a closed class of items. An open class (a lexical category) is one to which you can add new items quite freely; for example, in the lexical categories Noun or Verb, words such as *e-mail, microchip, to e-mail, to computerize*, etc., are being added all the time. A closed class (a functional category) is one to which items cannot easily be added, but which instead has a fixed number of members that does not vary. For example, you cannot add new determiners or new past-tense morphemes to a language, in the straightforward way in which you can add new nouns or new adjectives.

In itself, this distinction between content words and functional items is not by any means new to linguistics. However, recent theory claims that these 'functional' items, whether words or morphemes, also have phrases attached to them in the same way as 'lexical' words do. In fact, these functional phrases are organized in the same way as any other phrase, with the function word or morpheme as head of that phrase. We will therefore have Determiner Phrases (DP), and Complementizer Phrases (CP), with determiners such as *the* or complementizers such as *whether* as their heads, and also Inflection Phrases (IP) made up of Tense Phrases (TP) and Agreement Phrases (AgrP), which carry tense and agreement markers such as past tense *-ed* or third-person singular *-s* in English. The structure of these functional phrases is basically the same as that of lexical phrases, and they can be represented in the same way.

In Chomsky's most recent work on Universal Grammar (Chomsky, 1995, 2000, 2002), called the Minimalist Program, he suggests that the language faculty consists of a computational procedure, which is virtually invariant across languages, and a lexicon (Chomsky, 2000, p. 120). The principles proposed in the Minimalist Program are 'still more powerful and abstract in their effects on language knowledge' (Cook, 1997, p. 259), but probably the biggest challenge to current thinking proposed by Chomsky's Minimalist Program concerns parameters. Instead of being linked to specific principles and contained in the structural part of the grammar, parameters would now be contained within the lexicon. In fact, in this view, languages are different from one another only because their lexicons are different, and all that language acquisition involves is the learning of the lexicon.

In this view, the abstract principles underlying all human languages will already be specified in the computational module, and the task facing children (or second language learners) is therefore to learn the lexicon of the language around them, as well as the settings of the parameters applying to that language. This idea is known as the 'lexical parameterization hypothesis', and it suggests that the parameters are contained primarily in the functional categories. For example, the functional category Agr, which governs agreement phenomena, contains a gender feature in languages such as French or Italian, but not in others such as English.

3.3.2   Parameters

The structure-dependency principle that we discussed earlier seems common to all languages, as they are all organized hierarchically in terms of phrases (Noun-Phrases, Verb-Phrases, Prepositional-Phrases, etc.). From a Universal Grammar perspective, such a principle would form part of the computational module and will therefore not have to be learnt. However, we also know that all languages do not behave in the same way in terms of their structural properties. This is where parameters come in. Let us now turn our attention to an often-discussed example of a parameter, also to do with language structure, which is going to determine one of the ways in which languages can vary. This particular parameter is called the **head parameter**. (For more detailed analyses of both the structure-dependency principle and the head parameter, *see*, for example, Towell and Hawkins, 1994; Cook and Newson, 1996; Herschensohn, 2000; Hawkins, 2001).

The head parameter deals with the way in which phrases themselves are structured. It applies to phrases headed by both lexical and functional categories. Each phrase has a central element, called a **head**; in the case of a Noun-Phrase, the head is the noun, in the case of a Verb-Phrase it is the verb, in the case of a Determiner-Phrase, it is the determiner, and so on. One dimension along which languages vary is the position of the head in relation to other elements inside the phrase, called complements. For example, in the Noun-Phrase, *(the) girl with blue trousers*, the head-noun *girl* appears to the left of the complement *with blue trousers*; in the Verb-Phrase, *hit the girl*, the head *hit* appears to the left of its complement *the girl*; similarly, in the Prepositional-Phrase, *with blue trousers*, the head *with* is on the left of its complement *blue trousers*; in the Complementizer-Phrase, *whether he is too old*, the complement *he is too old* follows the head *whether*. In fact, English is a **head-first** language, because the head of the phrase always appears before its complements.

Japanese, on the other hand, is a **head-last** language, because the complements precede the head within the phrase. The following example is taken from Cook and Newson (1996):

E wa kabe ni kakatte imasu
(picture wall on is hanging)
'The picture is hanging on the wall.'
The head verb *kakatte imasu* occurs on the right of the verb complement *kabe ni*, and the *post*position *ni* (on) comes on the right of the PP complement *kabe*.

(Cook and Newson, 1996, p. 14)

Japanese is a head-last language, and all Japanese phrases will be ordered in that way. So, the head parameter tells us how the head and its complements are ordered in relation to one another in a given language, and it has two possible settings: head-first (like English), or head-last (like Japanese).

From an acquisitional point of view, what this means is that children, equipped with Universal Grammar, do not need to discover that language is structured into phrases, as this principle forms part of the blueprint for language in their mind. They also 'know' that all phrases in the language they are learning are going to be consistently ordered in relation to the head. The only task remaining is to learn which parameter setting actually applies in the language that the child is learning. (In this case, is it head-first or head-last?) In theory, the only input the child needs in order to set the head parameter to the correct value is one example of one phrase, and the child will then automatically 'know' the internal structure of all other phrases. In this view, the task facing children is considerably simpler than if they had to work out for themselves the extremely complex and abstract structure of natural language, and if they also had to discover the order of constituents within each type of phrase. Moreover, they only need minimal exposure on the basis of which they are able to make wide-ranging generalizations that affect different parts of the syntax of the language they are learning. In fact, Radford (1997, p. 22) claims that 'young children acquiring English as their native language seem to set the **head parameter** at its appropriate *head-first* setting from the very earliest multiword utterances they produce (at around age 18 months), and seem to know (tacitly, not explicitly, of course) that English is a *head-first* language'.

Remember also the puzzle that we posed in Section 3.2.2, when we asked how children could possibly figure out the precise relationships that apply between reflexives such as *himself* and their Noun-Phrase antecedents, in English? The answer offered by Universal Grammar theory to this problem is that universal principles, the Binding principles, and their associated parameters stating which binding domains are possible (the Governing Category parameter), are pre-existing in the child's language module, and only need to be 'set' in a certain way to generate this particular bit of language-specific knowledge. For example, in English, the reflexive must be bound within a local domain, which means that in the sentence, *Mark wanted Tom to treat himself,* *himself* can only refer to Tom and not to Mark. In other languages which allow long distance binding, such as Chinese for example, *himself* could refer to either Tom or Mark. In other words, what is a highly complex area of grammar is reduced to the simple matter of picking the appropriate binding domain out of a restricted set of possibilities, making the task considerably more straightforward for the young child (for further details, *see* Schachter, 1996; Herschensohn, 2000; Hawkins, 2001).

In line with the newer thinking of the Minimalist Program, let us now illustrate parametric variation for a functional category, Inflection (Infl, or I). Inflection is the functional category that contains the tense and agreement features of verbs (tense, person, number; whence its name, as these features are often realized through an inflectional paradigm). Just as nouns and verbs can head NPs and VPs, Infl can also head an Inflectional-Phrase (IP). Features associated with functional categories can be either weak or strong, with implications for syntactic properties of that language. For example, Infl in English is *weak*, whereas in French it is *strong*. This parametric variation (+/– strong) means that in languages like French, in which the features are strong, finite verbs have to move to the I position for feature checking (i.e. to 'collect' their tense, number and agreement features), as shown in Fig. 3.1.

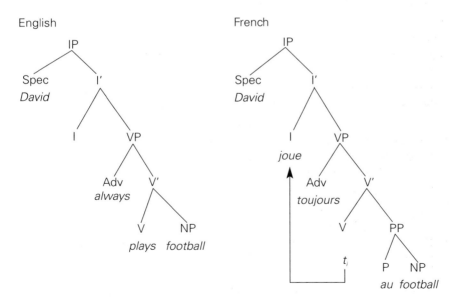

Fig. 3.1 Parametric variation for a functional category in English and French

In languages like French, therefore, within an Inflectional-Phrase (IP), the finite verb has to rise to the I position to pick up tense and agreement features. In languages like English, the verb remains in VP. This parametric variation in feature strength has important consequences for other areas of grammar, and explains a number of word order differences between French and English, which otherwise have very similar structures. These differences are summarized below:

	English	**French**

Declaratives	*Patrick reads the newspaper*
	  S V O
		Patrick lit le journal
		  S V O

Adverb-placement	*Patrick often reads the*
	  S A V
	newspaper
	  O
		Patrick lit souvent
		  S V A
		le journal
		  O

Negation	*Patrick doesn't read the*
	  S neg V
	newspaper
	  O
		Patrick (ne) lit pas
		  S V neg
		le journal
		  O

Questions	*Does he read the newspaper?*
	        S V
		Lit-il le journal?
		  V S
		(pronominal subjects only)

Within this view of learning, all learners have to do is set the parameter to either weak or strong, on the basis of the input (French or English), and all these properties will be in place. (For fuller treatments, *see* Herschensohn, 2000; Hawkins, 2001; White, 2003.)

According to Chomsky, 'a language is not, then, a system of rules, but a set of specifications for parameters in an invariant system of principles of Universal Grammar'. He proposes a network metaphor for the whole 'language faculty':

> We can think of the initial state of the faculty of language as a fixed network connected to a switch box; the network is constituted of the principles of language, while the switches are the options to be determined by experience. When the switches are set one way, we have Swahili; when they are set another way, we have Japanese. Each possible human language is identified as a particular setting of the switches – a setting of parameters, in technical terminology. If the research program succeeds, we should be able literally to deduce Swahili from one choice of settings, Japanese from another, and so on through the languages that humans can acquire. The empirical conditions of language acquisition require that the switches can be set on the basis of the very limited information that is available to the child. Notice that small changes in switch settings can lead to great apparent variety in output, as the effects proliferate through the system. These are the general properties of language that any genuine theory must capture somehow.
>
> (Chomsky, 2000, p. 8)

In conclusion to this section, it is important to point out that one main reason for viewing functional categories as the site of parametric variation comes from first language acquisition studies. In this model, children learning their mother tongue have to learn the lexicon of their language, which means learning both the lexical categories contained in it, and the functional categories, with their associated parameters. It has been claimed that children go through a stage of having acquired the lexical categories, but not the functional ones (for a detailed discussion of this phenomenon, *see* Radford 1990, 1996). Around the two-word stage, sometimes also termed the telegraphic stage for the obvious reason that the child's language contains almost exclusively 'content' words, children show no surface evidence of having acquired functional categories. Their language is devoid of such elements as determiners or tense markings, and this phase has sometimes been termed the 'pre-grammatical' stage for that reason (e.g. *play ball, dolly drink, daddy garden,* etc.). From this theoretical viewpoint, the explanation is that the underlying functional categories, which control much surface 'grammar', have not yet been acquired. There is also evidence suggesting that children suffering from the specific language impairment may have a faulty functional categories system. (For a discussion of these controversial issues, *see* Clahsen, 1996; Van der Lely, 1996; Herschensohn, 2000; Lorenzo and Longa, 2003.)

But let us now turn specifically to the way in which Universal Grammar explains language acquisition data.

3.4   Universal Grammar and first language acquisition

So, what is the evidence in the child acquisition literature for the Universal Grammar viewpoint: do children indeed build phrase structure by applying principles and setting parameters in the way we have described above?

Before we can deal with this question, we need to first examine in more detail the structure of phrases (*see* Towell and Hawkins, 1994, pp. 61–8; Hawkins, 2001, pp. 13–16). So far, we have only mentioned heads and complements, and we have not explained in any detail the hierarchical structure of phrases. We have seen already that the world's languages are made up of phrases that have an invariant structure consisting of a head category (the core element of the phrase) and of complements that optionally modify the head. Another type of modifier – also optional – is called a **specifier**, as shown in the example of a Noun-Phrase in English given below (Fig. 3.2). Here, the head noun *holiday* is modified by its complement *in the Caribbean Islands*, and the grouping *holiday in the Caribbean Islands* is itself modified by the specifier, *my mother's*.

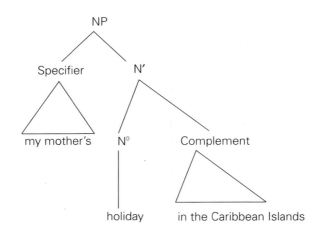

Fig. 3.2 [NP**my mother's holiday in the Caribbean Islands**] [VP*was fantastic*]

It is claimed in Universal Grammar theory that the same underlying structural configuration of head, complement and specifier applies to all phrases in a given language. The following examples show how this works in English for the Verb-Phrase (Fig. 3.3), the Adjectival-Phrase (Fig. 3.4) and the Prepositional-Phrase (Fig 3.5).

All phrases are organized in this hierarchical manner, with an optional Specifier modifying an X′, itself consisting of an X⁰ (the head) modified by an optional complement, where X can be any of the head-categories: N⁰ (noun), V⁰ (verb), A⁰ (adjective), P⁰ (preposition), D⁰ (determiner), INFL⁰

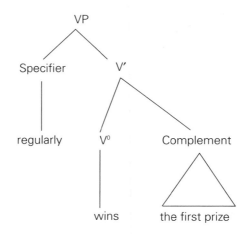

Fig. 3.3 [NP*My brother*] [VP**regularly wins the first prize**]

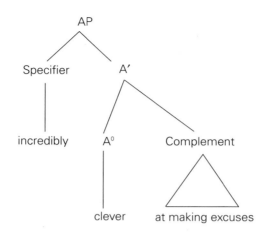

Fig. 3.4 *She became* [AP**incredibly clever at making excuses**]

(inflection). (The notation X', X⁰ is used to indicate the different levels in the hierarchical structure of phrases, with X⁰ representing the head element on its own, X' representing the unit 'head-element + complement' and so on.) The only possible variant is the situation of head, specifier and complement in relation to one another. Thus in a language such as English, the general configuration illustrated in Figures 3.2–3.5 above can be summed up as shown in Fig. 3.6) (Towell and Hawkins, 1994, p. 64).

In this case, in all types of phrase, the specifier typically precedes the head element, and the complement follows it. However in languages such as

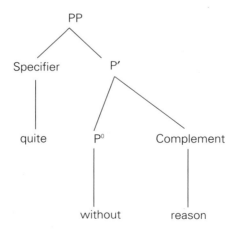

Fig. 3.5 *He did this* [PP**quite without reason**]

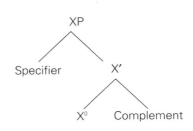

Fig. 3.6 Summary of the hierarchical structure of phrases shown in English in Figures 3.2–3.5

Japanese, Turkish and Burmese, both specifier and complement precede the head (Fig. 3.7) (Hawkins, 2001, p. 15).

Following this pattern, a literal translation of the examples given above would be *my mother's in the Caribbean Islands holiday, incredibly at making excuses clever,* and *quite reason without.*

The last possible ordering that is found in natural languages comprises head followed by both complement and specifier (Fig. 3.8).

This would give rise to the following re-ordering of our examples: *holiday in the Caribbean Islands my mother's, clever at making excuses incredibly,* and *without reason quite.* This configuration is found in languages such as Malagasy, Gilbertese and Fijian (Hawkins, 2001, p. 15).

In terms of first language acquisition, what does this mean? Remember that we have said that the structure of phrases is an invariant principle of Universal Grammar. Children would therefore know that sentences are

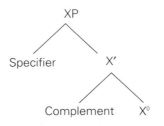

Fig. 3.7 Both specifier and complement precede the head in languages such as Japanese

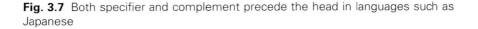

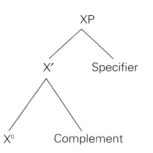

Fig. 3.8 The last possible ordering found in natural languages

made of phrases which consist of (specifier)–head–(complement), and would not have to work this out. However, they would not know the precise ordering of these elements that is found in their own language; that is, they would have to set the head parameter on the basis of language input. Notice, though, that the number of possibilities is constrained, as there are only two possible settings: specifiers either precede or follow X' categories, and complements either follow or precede X^0 categories (Hawkins, 2001, p. 16).

There is indeed evidence from first language acquisition research that children have set the head parameter as early as the two-word stage (Radford, 1997, p. 22), and that they 'know how to project [i.e. construct] productively X^0 categories into X' categories, and X' categories into XP categories' (Towell and Hawkins, 1994, p. 65), at least as far as lexical categories are concerned. This is shown in the examples below, taken from Radford (1990, cited in Towell and Hawkins, 1994, p. 66):

	X^0	*Complement*		
	cup	tea	(N')	'a cup of tea'
	ball	wool	(N')	'a ball of wool'
	open	box	(V')	'open the box'
	get	toys	(V')	'get my toys'
(put)	in	there	(P')	'put it in there'
(get)	out	cot	(P')	'I want to get out of the cot'

	Specifier	X'		
	Mummy	car	(NP)	'Mummy's car'
	Hayley	dress	(NP)	'Hayley's dress'
	Dolly	hat	(NP)	'Dolly's hat'
	Daddy	gone	(VP)	'Daddy has gone'
	Hayley	draw (boat)	(VP)	'Hayley is drawing (a boat)'
	Paula	play (with ball)	(VP)	'Paula is playing (with a ball)'

Radford suggests on the basis of this type of evidence that:

> the initial grammars formulated by young children show clear evidence of the
> acquisition of a well-developed set of symmetrical lexical category systems, in
> that young children at the relevant stage (typically between the ages of 20 and
> 23 months +/- 20%) seem to 'know' how to project head nouns, verbs, prep-
> ositions and adjectives into the corresponding single-bar and [XP] categories.
> (Radford, 1990, p. 81, cited in Towell and Hawkins, 1994, p. 66)

Universal Grammar theory would predict this to be the case, as the result
of the general principle underlying phrase-structure. It would also predict
that children have to set the parameters for the particular language they are
exposed to in order to learn the linear ordering of constituents within the
phrase; because this has to be learnt on the basis of language input rather
than being 'inbuilt', it might appear later in the production of children, who
have to work out what that order is. In fact, Tsimpli has argued this to be
the case when studying the early development of young children in a range
of first languages (1991, quoted in Towell and Hawkins, 1994, p. 66). For
example, she found utterances produced by children learning French
exhibiting the following orders: Spec X^0; X^0 Spec; Spec X^0 Comp; X^0 Spec,
showing that the order is variable at this stage and the parameter not yet
consistently set to the correct value for French.*

There is also evidence that the kind of parametric variation of functional
features which we have illustrated earlier (strong vs. weak Infl) is acquired
in children in a cluster-like fashion. That is to say, when French children
start to project IP (e.g. when they are using inflected verbs), all properties
linked to it fall into place, that is, the verb rises to I, past adverbs, negators,
etc. We thus find children with French as their first language producing
sentences in which IP has not been projected and the verb is therefore non-
finite and has not moved from its VP-internal position, and simultaneously
producing sentences in which IP has been projected and the verb is therefore finite and has moved, for example:

Pas aller dodo (no go bed)   *bébé va pas dodo* (baby goes not bed)

---

*Although we will see later that all languages are not uniformly directional and French is a
case in point. Languages appear to have a canonical order of constituents within the phrase
that will apply to all phrase types; that is, if the Noun-Phrase exhibits a
Specifier–N^0–Complement order, so will all other phrases in that language (VP, AP, PP,
etc.). However, some languages such as French have a canonical order that has exceptions:
the French clitic object pronoun appears before the Verb, giving the VP a
Specifier–Complement–V^0 order. French children acquire this construction relatively late,
and seem initially to rely on the canonical order for such constructions.

What we do not find, however, are sentences in which non-finite verbs have risen past adverbs or negators, for example *bébé aller pas dodo* (baby go not bed), or in which the finite verb does not rise, for example *bébé pas va dodo* (baby not goes bed) (Pierce, 1992).

This simplified account has enabled us to see, with the help of a concrete example, the kinds of predictions a Universal Grammar approach enables us to make in the context of children acquiring their mother tongue. This kind of account has been advanced to account for the rapid, effortless and uniform acquisition of the extremely abstract and complex system that language is:

> The **principles and parameters** model of acquisition enables us to provide an explanation for why children manage to learn the relative ordering of heads and complements in such a *rapid* and *error-free* fashion. The answer provided by the model is that learning this aspect of word order involves the comparatively simple task of setting a binary parameter at its appropriate value. This task will be a relatively straightforward one if UG tells the child that the only possible choices are for a language to be uniformly *head-first* or uniformly *head-last*. Given such an assumption, the child could set the parameter correctly on the basis of minimal linguistic experience.
>
> (Radford, 1997, p. 22)

How far can such an approach enlighten our understanding of second language acquisition, a phenomenon which shares some similarities with first language acquisition, but which is also different in many ways?

3.5 Universal Grammar and second language acquisition

3.5.1 Theoretical relevance of Universal Grammar to second language learning

The above sections should have made clear what the appeal of the Universal Grammar model has been in the field of first language acquisition, but it might not be so obvious at first sight what its usefulness might be in the field of second language acquisition. However, as Universal Grammar is a theory of natural languages, claiming it plays no part in second language acquisition would mean claiming that second languages are not natural languages.

We need to go back to the developments that took place in the 1970s, which we outlined in Chapter 2. Remember that a major impetus for second language acquisition research then was the discovery that first and second language acquisition was similar in many ways. For example, we outlined similarities in the development of a number of English morphemes and of English negative and interrogative structures in first and second language acquisition. Not only do children learning negative (or interrogative) constructions in their first language go through well-defined stages, but their productions are also unlike the language around them. In first language acquisition, the explanation that generated most enthusiasm, and therefore a wealth of theoretical and empirical work, was that there was some kind of language blueprint in the brain. This is the work we have summarized so far in this chapter.

If, as we have seen, second language learners also go through fairly rigid stages when acquiring certain constructions in the second language, which are unlike both their first language and the second language they are exposed to, and which are not unlike the stages children go through, then a similar explanation is surely worth investigating. From a theoretical point of view, however, the situation is even more complicated than is the case for first language acquisition. It is complicated by a number of factors, such as:

- second language learners are cognitively mature
- second language learners already know at least one other language
- second language learners have different motivations for learning a second language (language learning does not take place in order to answer the basic human need to communicate).

These points have important implications that need to be addressed. In fact, even if the Universal Grammar hypothesis is correct for first language learning, there are still a number of logical possibilities concerning its role in SLL.

Second languages are not Universal Grammar-constrained

Second languages are not constrained by Universal Grammar principles and parameters, and they do not behave like natural languages.

Second languages are Universal Grammar-constrained

- Full access: the whole of Universal Grammar is available to second language learners, in the same way as it is to first language learners. Within this view, there are different hypotheses about the initial grammars of second language learners, which we will review shortly.
- Partial access: some parts of Universal Grammar are not available any longer. For example, functional features that are not realized in the first

language (such as strong Infl or gender, for English first language learners of other languages which possess these features), cannot be acquired. Within this view, second language grammars are Universal Grammar-constrained, that is, they do not violate principles and parameters, but learners might not be able to reset parameters, and therefore operate with first language settings for some parts of the new language.

It is obvious straightaway that the situation is rendered more complicated by the presence of the first language and its relationship with the second language acquisition process. Moreover, different modules of Universal Grammar might play different roles in second language acquisition; for example, Universal Grammar could be split into principles and lexicon, which in turn would be split into lexical categories and functional categories, which in turn contain functional features that are parameterized. Each of these levels could be hypothesized to have a different role to play in the acquisition process. In fact, recent second language acquisition studies increasingly adopt hypotheses which address such complications; for example, examining whether functional features are available or not, even if the rest of Universal Grammar is assumed to be available (Clahsen, 1996; Herschensohn, 2000; Hawkins, 2001, 2003; White, 2003).

3.5.3   Principles and parameters in second language acquisition

3.5.3.1   The head-parameter

Let us return to the first examples that we used to illustrate first language acquisition, namely the structure dependency principle and the head parameter.

First, there seems to be no evidence in second language grammars that learners ever violate the structure dependency principle. From the very onset of second language development, learners seem to know that the second language will be hierarchically structured in terms of phrases, rather than linearly ordered.

Second, we saw that there are two possible settings for the head parameter, head-first and head-last. Both French and English are head-first languages, that is, the head precedes its complements. However, in French, although all phrases normally exhibit this order, there is one instance when this order changes (Towell and Hawkins, 1994, p. 68; Hawkins, 2001, pp. 11–12). This is in the case of unstressed object pronouns, as exemplified below:

1. *Le chat* [$_{VP}$*mange* [$_{NP}$*la souris*]] (the cat eats the mouse)
2. *Le chat* [$_{VP}$[$_{NP}$*la*] *mange*] (the cat it eats = 'the cat eats it')

In Verb-Phrases in French where the complement is a full Noun-Phrase (1), the head verb precedes its complement as normal; however, when the complement is an unstressed pronoun (2), the head verb follows it. Note that in English, the head direction is the same whether the complement is a full NP or a pronoun.* From an acquisitional point of view, we have seen that children need minimal evidence in order to set the head-direction parameter, as all phrases in a given language normally follow the same order. For French children, there is ample evidence in the language around them that French is head-first. We would therefore expect French children to set the parameter early on (and we saw in Section 3.4 that children do this, as early as the two-word stage), and to always place the head before its complement. This is in fact the case, and children produce utterances such as *Le chat mange la*, before going through a stage of omitting the pronoun altogether *Le chat mange Ø*, and later still inserting it in its target position *Le chat la mange*. (Clark, 1985; Hamann *et al.*, 1996).

If this developmental sequence is indeed because French children have set the head-parameter and have thereafter to accommodate this particular structure, which seems to go against it, then we should expect the same to happen for second language learners of French, as the task facing them is exactly the same. If Universal Grammar is available to them, they would also find ample evidence in French for setting the head-direction parameter.

> In fact, the stages of development that L1 English speakers go through in acquiring this pattern in L2 French are very similar to the stages that child L1 learners of French go through in acquiring it. Following an initial stage where learners leave object pronouns postverbally in the position occupied by full noun phrases, e.g. *Le chien a mangé les*, 'The dog has eaten them' (Zobl 1980; Clark 1985), they go to a stage of omission of the pronoun: *Le chien a mangé Ø* (Adiv 1984; Schlyter 1986; Véronique 1986) before eventually acquiring preverbal object pronouns: *Le chien les a mangés*.
>
> (Towell and Hawkins, 1994, p. 69)

It is interesting to note that French learners of English as a second language do not have problems in acquiring object pronouns in English, and do not

---

*In fact, this is not a violation of this parameter setting, but it occurs because unstressed pronouns in French cliticize on to the verb (i.e. attach themselves to the verb). In other words, object pronouns originate after the verb as expected given that French is head-first, and subsequently move to a pre-verbal position.

go through a stage of preposing the pronoun (*the cat it eats*) nor through a stage of omitting the pronoun (Zobl, 1980). This is to be expected if we assume that, on the basis of ample evidence in English that it is head-first, second language learners set the head direction parameter early on and apply it consistently.

It is important to note at this stage that, because both French and English are head-first languages, we cannot say whether these observations are due to the fact that second language learners reset the parameter to its correct value, or simply transfer their first language parameter value. What is interesting, however, is that French learners do not transfer the idiosyncratic property of French for pronoun placement.

In order to know whether the head-parameter can be reset, it is necessary to investigate the acquisition of, say, a head-first language by learners whose first language is head-last. Flynn (1983, 1984, 1987) studied the role of this parameter in Japanese learners of English. (We have already seen that Japanese is a head-last language.) She concludes 'that, from the earliest stages of acquisition, Japanese speakers learning English as a Second Language (ESL), are able to acquire the English value of the head-direction parameter' (Flynn, 1996, p. 135).

The evidence presented here therefore seems to suggest that, in the case of the head-parameter at least, second language learners have access to Universal Grammar in the same way as children do. We have to be careful, however, not to draw hasty conclusions on the basis of evidence relating to one structure only, and we have to bear in mind that other explanations that do not involve Universal Grammar might be possible, and have indeed been put forward.

3.5.3.2   Strong or weak Infl

We have discussed earlier that functional categories are now thought to be the primary location for parametric variation (although headedness is an exception as it applies to both lexical and functional categories), and we used the example of the strength of Infl in French and English, respectively.

Remember that in French, Infl is strong and forces the verb to rise past, for example, adverbs, negators, etc., unlike in English where Infl is weak and the verb remains within the verb-phrase. French learners of English therefore have to reset the Infl parameter to [−strong], and English learners of French have to reset it to [+strong]. Several studies have investigated this property (*see* White, 2003, for a review). Yuan (2001) studied the acquisition of Chinese (weak I) by French (strong I) and English (weak I) learners. He found that all learners, regardless of their first language or their proficiency level, realized the ungrammaticality of verb-raising in Chinese, suggesting that they were able to reset this parameter. Another study by White (1992), however, found somewhat different results. She studied the acquisition of verb-raising in questions, negatives and adverb placement, in French learners of English as a second language. Her learners (beginners) seemed to have realized that English has weak I in the context of questions and negatives, but not in the context of adverbs. Learners rejected sentences such as:

Like you pepperoni pizza?
The boys like not the girls

with a high degree of accuracy, but not:

Linda takes always the metro

which they accepted to a considerable extent.

White argues this might be because we are dealing with two different parameters underlying these properties. For further details, *see* White (2003, pp. 129–32). The results to date on this particular parameter are somewhat inconclusive. The Universal Grammar framework, however, enables researchers to develop clear hypotheses of this type about second language acquisition issues.

3.5.3.3   Current debates and hypotheses about parameter resetting

As we have seen, one of the recent developments in the context of the Minimalist Program has been the importance given to functional categories as the location of parametric variation. In first language acquisition research, this has given rise to intense debates about whether children in the early stages only have access to lexical categories and lack functional categories, which would explain the telegraphic nature of their early utterances (i.e. the fact that children's early utterances contain content words exclusively, and no function words, e.g. *daddy go*; *mummy hat*). More specifically, the debate centres on whether functional categories are available from the start but are not in evidence because of external factors (e.g. for pragmatic reasons: the Continuity hypothesis (Weissenborn, 1992; Penner and Weissenborn, 1996); whether they mature over time, that is, come 'on line' at specific ages: the Maturation hypothesis (Haegeman, 1996; Harris and Wexler, 1996); or whether children 'build' their grammar gradually as they learn the lexicon of their language and project the relevant structure: the 'structure-building' approach (Radford, 1990, 1996). For a discussion of these issues, see Atkinson (1996).

Similar debates about what is termed the **Initial State** (the subconscious linguistic representations second language learners have at the onset of SLL) are also taking place in second language acquisition. Some researchers have argued that functional categories are also absent in the very early stages of adult second language acquisition (Vainikka and Young-Scholten, 1996a, 1996b, 1998; Hawkins, 2001; White, 2003; Myles, in press a), this phenomenon manifesting itself by a lack of morphological markings and of syntactic movement. Other researchers, however, have argued that functional categories are indeed present in the early stages in child second language (Lakshmanan, 1993; Lakshmanan and Selinker, 1994; Grondin and White, 1996) and also in adult second language (Schwartz and Eubank, 1996; Schwartz and Sprouse, 1996; Schwartz, 1998), and that the lack of morphological markings is not a syntactic issue. Some recent accounts argue for a structure-building approach to second language development (Herschensohn, 2000; Hawkins, 2001). The debate is likely to go on for some time, complicated by the fact that functional categories themselves are not yet very clearly defined in Universal Grammar theory.

What is becoming increasingly clear within the Universal Grammar framework is that the question which has generated so much research over the last 15 years or so – namely, whether Universal Grammar is available to second language learners or not – is now being replaced by more focused questions about which sub-components of Universal Grammar might be available or not to the second language learner, how Universal Grammar interacts with other modules involved in language learning, and the role played by the first language settings. Principles are generally thought to be available, as second language learners do not seem to produce interlanguages that violate them, and most of the work has concentrated on testing the availability of parameters, with as yet somewhat inconclusive results. However, recent book length treatments of the second language acquisition of syntax within this framework reflect considerable advances in attempts to understand the role of Universal Grammar within second language acquisition (Herschensohn, 2000; Hawkins, 2001; White, 2003).

In a review, White suggests:

> that L2 learners often develop IL [interlanguage] grammars that are different from the grammars of NSs [native speakers] but that are nevertheless constrained by UG, and that this is due, in part, to properties of the L2 input interacting with UG and the L1 grammar. Many questions remain to be answered, including the question of why some learners 'fossilize' with these divergent IL grammars, whereas others successfully attain a nativelike grammar; why some parameters are successfully reset, whereas others are not, why

positive L2 input is only sometimes successful as a trigger for grammar change.

(White, 1996, p. 115)

3.5.4   Empirical evidence

After having illustrated, in the context of second language acquisition, how to apply a Universal Grammar framework, taking the example of one principle (structure-dependency) and of two parameters (head-direction and strength of Infl), we can now turn to the reassessment of the theoretical positions we outlined in Section 3.5.1.

As we have already mentioned before, which aspects of Universal Grammar might be available and which not, is the subject of much debate. The various theoretical positions have to attempt to reconcile somewhat contradictory facts about the second language acquisition process:

- Learners do not seem to produce 'wild' grammars, that is, grammars that would not be constrained by Universal Grammar. Does that suggest that at least principles of Universal Grammar are available to them?
- Learners produce grammars that are not necessarily like either their first language or their second language. Does this suggest that parameter settings other than those realized in their first or second languages are available to them?
- Some principles and parameters seem to be unproblematic to reset (e.g. the head parameter), others more difficult, or even impossible (e.g. subjacency). Why?

3.5.4.1   Hypothesis 1: no access to Universal Grammar

The view that Universal Grammar is no longer available to second language learners is still very much alive. Proponents of this position argue that there is a 'critical period' for language acquisition during children's early development, and that adult second language learners have to resort to other learning mechanisms. The reasons for adopting such a position are several (for a review, *see* Bley-Vroman, 1989), but perhaps the most convincing one is the commonsense observation that immigrant children generally become native-like speakers of their second language, whereas their parents rarely do. For example, an influential study (Johnson and Newport, 1989) found a correlation between age of arrival in the USA and native-like judgements on a number of grammatical properties of English. Immigrants who had arrived in the States before the age of seven years performed in a native-like way, and the older learners were on arrival, the more errors they made in the test. The correlation was not equally strong for all grammatical properties investigated, however, and some researchers who have critically evaluated their data have argued it does not mean that the adult grammars are not Universal Grammar-constrained (Hawkins, 2001; White, 2003).

Studies adopting this position tend to focus on differences between first and second language acquisition, and on differences in the end result of the acquisition process. For example, in an extensive study of the acquisition of negation in French and German by first and second language learners, Meisel (1997, p. 258) concludes, 'I would like to hypothesize that second language learners, rather than using structure-dependent operations constrained by UG, resort to linear sequencing strategies which apply to surface strings'. Meisel therefore claims that one of the most fundamental principles of Universal Grammar (structure-dependency) is not available to second language learners any more. It must be said, however, that most studies conducted within a generative framework would argue very strongly that second language grammars are Universal Grammar-constrained.

3.5.4.2   Hypothesis 2: full access to Universal Grammar

Full access/no transfer: Flynn (1996) adopts this position. That is, she argues that Universal Grammar continues to underpin SLL, for adults as well as children, and that there is no such thing as a critical period after which Universal Grammar ceases to operate. If it can be shown that learners can acquire principles and/or parameter settings of the second language, which differ from those of their first language, she claims, the best interpretation is the continuing operation of Universal Grammar. She goes on to review a range of empirical work with second language learners moving from a language such as Japanese to English (Flynn, 1996, pp. 134–48). Thus, for example, we have already met her claim that adult Japanese learners of English as a second language can successfully reset the head-direction parameter (i.e. from head-last to head-first). She also claims that similar learners can instantiate principles that do not operate in Japanese, such as the Subjacency principle (which controls *wh*-movement in English; i.e. the way in which we move the *wh*-phrase to the beginning of the sentence); and can acquire functional categories, supposedly non-existent in Japanese. Flynn concludes her review thus:

It appears that L2 learners do construct grammars of the new TLs [target languages] under the constraints imposed by UG; those principles of UG carefully investigated thus far indicate that those not instantiated or applying vacuously in the L1 but operative in the L2, are in fact acquirable by the L2 learner.

We are thus forced to the conclusion that UG constrains L2 acquisition; the essential language faculty involved in L1 acquisition is also involved in adult L2 acquisition.

(Flynn, 1996, pp. 150–1)

Other researchers who believe that Universal Grammar is still available to second language learners include Thomas (1991), on the basis of work on the acquisition of reflexive binding, and White *et al.* (1992), on the basis of work on *wh*-movement as well.

Full transfer/full access: this model also believes that second language learners have full access to Universal Grammar principles and parameters, whether or not they are present in the learners' first language (Schwartz and Sprouse, 1994, 1996). But in this view, second language learners are thought to transfer all the parameter-settings from their first language in an initial stage, and subsequently to revise their hypotheses when the second language fails to conform to these first language settings. Learners then develop new hypotheses that are constrained by Universal Grammar. In this view, Universal Grammar is accessed via the first language in a first stage, and directly thereafter when the second language input cannot be accommodated within the first language settings. Studies which support the full transfer or full access hypothesis include Yuan (1998), Slabakova (2000) and Haznedar (2001); for a review of these studies, *see* White (2003).

Full access/impaired early representations: several researchers also believe that learners can reset parameters to the second language values, but that initially, learners are lacking functional categories altogether. The **Minimal Trees** approach (Vainikka and Young-Scholten, 1996b, 1998) has been highly influential and forms the starting point for a number of recent accounts of the development of syntax (*see below*): only lexical categories are projected initially, which transfer from the first language. Functional categories develop later, but are not transferred from the first language. A similar approach is that of Eubank (1996) and is called the **Valueless Features** hypothesis. In this view, both lexical and functional categories are transferred early on (with a short stage in which only lexical projections are present), but functional categories lack values such as tense, agreement, etc., and are present as syntactic markers only (i.e. inflections may be lacking, but the syntactic operations linked to these categories will be in place).

These views have much in common with the approaches we will review next (and we will discuss empirical evidence about impaired functional categories in that section), but crucially their belief is that all parameters can be reset.

3.5.4.3   Hypothesis 3: Partial access

No parameter resetting: proponents of this position claim that learners only have access to Universal Grammar via their first language. They have already accessed the range of principles applying to their first language, and set parameters to the first language values, and this is the basis for their second language development. Other principles and parameter settings are not available to them, and if the second language possesses parameter settings that are different from those of their first language, they will have to resort to other mechanisms in order to make the second language data fit their internal representations. These mechanisms will be rooted in general problem-solving strategies, rather than being Universal Grammar-based. Bley-Vroman claims:

> Thus, the picture of the difference between child language development and foreign language learning as advocated here is the following:
>
> *Child language development*   *Adult foreign language learning*
> A. Universal Grammar   A. Native language knowledge
> B. Domain-specific learning procedures B. General problem-solving systems
>
> This approach has attempted to account for the phenomena of transfer, and of the differences in the outcome of the learning process in L2 acquisition compared to L1 acquisition.
>
> (Bley-Vroman, 1989, p. 51)

Schachter is also a supporter of the indirect access hypothesis, which she combines with the notion of a critical period for second language acquisition. In a recent review (Schachter, 1996), she cites a number of studies of adult second language learners, claiming these show failure to acquire principles which are absent from the learners' first languages, and/or failure to reset particular parameters. For example, she cites her own work with Korean first-language learners of English as a second language, who performed randomly in grammaticality judgement tests of *wh*-movement. In English, *wh*-movement is allowed, but is restricted by the Subjacency principle (the extracted *wh*-word can move only across certain structural boundaries). In Korean, there is no *wh*-movement, so the Subjacency principle is presumably not operative. If all the principles of Universal

Grammar are still available to the learner, the absence of this particular principle from their first language should not matter, and Subjacency should still be acquirable in English as a second language. Schachter claims that the Korean subjects' failure to recognize *wh*-movement problems reflects the non-availability to them of Universal Grammar principles that were not already operative in their first language; that is, that Universal Grammar principles are accessible only as they have taken shape in the first language.

Schachter does accept that Universal Grammar may be available for child second language learners, but argues that there is a critical period (or periods) for the successful acquisition of second language principles and/or parameter settings, if these have not been operative in the learner's first language. She calls this critical period a Window of Opportunity, and argues that child second language learners pass through different Windows for different modules of the target language (Schachter, 1996, p. 188). In support, she cites a study by Lee (1992) that tested Korean-English bilinguals on a particular parameter, the Governing Category parameter (GC), which is set differently in the two languages involved. (As we have seen already, this parameter has to do with the binding of items such as reflexives; the English reflexive must refer to the subject within its own clause, while in Korean it may refer to a more remote subject: Schachter, 1996, p. 178.)

In Lee's study, the Korean learners of English were of different ages; the youngest and oldest subjects had not acquired the English setting for the GC parameter, while the older children had apparently succeeded in doing so. Schachter (1996, p. 187) concludes that these findings show the Window of Opportunity not yet operative for the youngest learners, but available to the older children. As far as adult learners are concerned, she concludes that 'UG . . . fails to shed light on adult L2 acquisition – either in terms of a biological perspective on maturation or in terms of the known linguistic achievements of adult L2 learners'. Instead, she believes, the only principles and parameter settings easily available to the adult second language learner are those already activated in the course of first language learning.

Impaired functional features: lastly, we will briefly review two approaches which believe that second language grammars are Universal Grammar-constrained, but that not all parameter settings will be available to learners. Second language learners will therefore try to accommodate the second language grammar within the settings they already have. The **Modulated structure building** hypothesis (Hawkins, 2001) argues that learners start with 'minimal trees' (as described above), that is, lexical projections determined by the first language. Functional projections develop gradually, with first language functional features transferring on to the second language, but only when the relevant syntactic representation has been sufficiently elaborated to instantiate the property in question. Hawkins and Chan (1997) argued that functional features cannot be reset in the second language. For example, Cantonese learners of English studied by Hawkins and Chan failed to acquire properties linked with *wh*-movement, which does not exist in Cantonese. They argue that learners re-analyse the input to make it fit their first language settings. In an alternative view, **Constructionism** 'proposes that the L2er uses a coalition of resources – a UG template (including, for example, a limited set of parameters, a small inventory of null anaphora, universal principles), first-language transfer, primary linguistic data, its mediation in social discourse (input and intake) and instructional bootstrapping – to construct the L2 vocabulary and grammar' (Herschensohn, 2000, p. 220).

What all these accounts crucially have in common is that they believe that second language acquisition is **Universal Grammar-constrained**, but that access to parametric options is unlike first language acquisition.

As we can see, there is much overlap between the approaches we have briefly reviewed here, and they might be better presented as a continuum. It is useful, however, to separate them in this way, as they adopt different positions on the issues that are currently at the core of debates in generative second language acquisition. For example, they have different views on the Initial State, on the role of the first language, on the possibility of parameter resetting, on the Steady State (the final stable state), or on the role of non-Universal Grammar constrained mechanisms.

Recent work has generated new and more detailed hypotheses about which particular aspects of Universal Grammar might be transferred from the first language. For example, the availability or not of functional categories at the onset of second language acquisition has been the focus of much debate. Like first language learners, second language learners also go through a phase of using uninflected verbs initially, gradually introducing inflected forms into their grammar (Hyams, 1996; Wexler and Harris, 1996; Ionin and Wexler, 2000). But whereas in first language acquisition, 'the realisation or not of verbal inflection is not a random occurrence in early child language, but it is rather systematically linked to syntactic development' (Herschensohn, 2001), in second language acquisition the evidence is less clear, with some researchers arguing for such links and others not (White, 1996; Prévost and White, 2000; Sorace, 2000; Franceschina, 2001; Herschensohn, 2001; Myles, in press a). In other words, researchers have been investigating the role played by functional features in second language acquisition, both from the point of view of their availability (in parallel with discussions in first language acquisition theory), but also from the point of view of the transfer or not of first language functional features, and of the possibility of resetting parameters linked with verb morphology. (For fuller discussion of these questions, see Herschensohn, 2000; Hawkins, 2001; Myles, in press a.)

Table 3.1 (taken from White, 2003, p. 270) summarizes some of these issues.

To round off this section, it is fair to say that the argument concerning access to Universal Grammar in SLL is not concluded, and that strong defenders of all these positions can still be found. Often, they seem to be arguing about the best technical interpretation of admittedly indirect and tantalizing evidence, often gathered through grammaticality judgement tests, etc. Research in this area seems to have shifted from the initial question of the availability versus non-availability of Universal Grammar, towards a more modular view of language and the language faculty, with Universal Grammar itself being modular (Smith and Tsimpli, 1995). As a result, the questions that studies in second language acquisition have been addressing are becoming more focused, testing the availability of sub-modules of Universal Grammar rather than Universal Grammar itself.

Table 3.1   L2 acquisition and UG: initial to steady state

	UG-impaired		UG-constrained		
	Global impairment	Local impairment	No parameter resetting	Full access (without transfer)	Full transfer, full access
Initial state	?	L1 grammar + inert features	L1 grammar	UG	L1 grammar
Development	Pattern matching; separate constructions	Some L2 properties acquirable; features remain inert	No parameter resetting	Parameter setting directly to L2 values	Parameter resetting (L1 to Ln)
Final outcome	Grammar essentially different from native-speaker grammars. L2-like grammar not attainable	L2-like grammar not attainable	L1-like grammar L2-like grammar not attainable	L2-like grammar	L2-like grammar possible but not inevitable

(*Source*: White, 2003, p. 270)

3.6   Evaluation of Universal Grammar-based approaches to second language acquisition

Universal Grammar is a well-established theory of language, which has been highly influential in many areas of linguistic research, including language acquisition research. In this section, we aim to evaluate its particular contribution to our understanding of second language acquisition.

3.6.1   The scope and achievements of the Universal Grammar approach

It is important to remind ourselves in this section that Universal Grammar is a theory which aims to describe and explain human language. As such, even if its prime concern is not second language acquisition, it is nonetheless directly relevant to the study of second languages, which are assumed to be natural languages. Second language acquisition researchers, in order to understand the interlanguage system, need to understand what constrains formal language systems generally.

In evaluating Universal Grammar, however, we must remember that it is a **linguistic theory**, with its own aims and objectives, and not a **learning theory**. Although one of Chomsky's stated objectives mentioned earlier on in this chapter is to understand how knowledge of language is acquired, and how knowledge of language is put to use, most of the work to date has focused on his first question: What constitutes knowledge of language? These questions are related though, and language acquisition data, both first and second, has increasingly been used to refine and test hypotheses about the nature of human language. Additionally, the Universal Grammar descriptive framework has been hugely influential in helping researchers to draw up sophisticated hypotheses about a range of issues which are central to our understanding of second language acquisition, such as the exact nature of the language system (the learner system as well as the first and second language systems), the interplay between the first and second language in second language learners, the linguistic knowledge learners bring to the task of second language acquisition, etc.

As a general theory of language therefore, the scope of Universal Grammar is potentially very broad. It would be fair to say, however, that Universal Grammar research has been primarily concerned with the description and explanation of the formal system underlying language. Moreover, its focus has been primarily morphosyntax, and other aspects of the linguistic system have received much less attention. (Although this is changing, and phonology, morphology and more recently the lexicon have been the source of renewed interest, other areas such as semantics, pragmatics and discourse are still largely ignored.) The Universal Grammar contribution to our understanding of the acquisition of morphosyntactic properties in second language acquisition has been outstanding, and will no doubt feed into a comprehensive second language acquisition theory when it comes of age. Its scope does not include a theory of processing, or a theory of learning. It has very little to say about what triggers development in either first or second language acquirers. It is a property theory and not a transition theory, and must therefore be evaluated as such.

3.6.2   The Universal Grammar view of language

The Universal Grammar view of language has been very influential since the 1950s, but not uncontroversial. The Universal Grammar approach views language as a mental framework, underlying all human languages. In so doing, it focuses on some aspects of language and not others. Until very recently as we have seen, syntax was the privileged object of study. Universal Grammar is only concerned with the sentence and its internal structure, rather than any larger unit of language. Work at the level of smaller units (words, morphemes, phonemes) has also been primarily concerned with structure and how different elements relate to one another. This is one of the major criticisms of work in this tradition; it studies language somewhat clinically, in a vacuum, as a mental object rather than a social or psychological one. Moreover, it separates language knowledge and language use rigidly, and some linguists disagree with this dichotomy, as we will see in the next chapter.

Following from this, the methodologies used by Universal Grammar theorists have sometimes been criticized for not being representative of reality. The theory is preoccupied with the modelling of linguistic competence, and the study of naturalistic performance is not seen as a suitable window into mental representations of language (Towell and Hawkins, in press). However, tapping the underlying linguistic representations of second language learners is even more difficult than in the case of native speakers, as second language representations are less stable. We have seen (Chapter 1), that grammaticality judgement tests (in which subjects – learners or native speakers – have to decide on the grammaticality of sentences presented to them), are thought to be the most appropriate methodology to access native speakers' intuitions about their native language, and that native speakers usually agree about what is grammatical or ungrammatical in their language. Second language learners' intuitions, however, are much more likely to be unstable, and therefore less reliable. We have seen in earlier sections how often data on second language competence deriving from grammaticality judgement tests is disputed and reinterpreted. (For a discussion of this problem, *see* Sorace, 1996; Chaudron, 2003.)

Grammaticality judgement tests have often been relied on in second language acquisition studies, as without them it can be very difficult to get evidence about subtle grammatical properties, which might not be present in learners' spontaneous output (e.g. violations of subjacency, or of binding conditions). However, Universal Grammar theorists have taken criticisms about the lack of reliability of second language judgements seriously, and recent work in this tradition has used a range of elicitation techniques, from matching sentences to pictures, (semi-) spontaneous productions, sentence completion and others, as witnessed for example by current issues of *Second Language Research*. Using a range of elicitation techniques makes any consistent findings much stronger. The problem of drawing inferences about mental representations from such data nonetheless remains.

Despite of these criticisms, Universal Grammar has been highly influential as a theory of language, and is probably the most sophisticated tool available for analysing language today, whether native or second languages.

3.6.3   The Universal Grammar view of language acquisition

When applied specifically to the context of second language acquisition, how successful can the Universal Grammar theory claim to be?

Universal Grammar-based approaches to second language acquisition have been criticized for exactly the same reasons as the theory itself. It has left untouched a number of areas that are central to our understanding of the second language learning process. First, linguistically, this approach has in the past been almost exclusively concerned with syntax. Even if recent interest in phonology, morphology and the lexicon should redress the balance somewhat, semantics, pragmatics and discourse are excluded. Second, the Universal Grammar approach has been exclusively concerned with documenting and explaining the nature of the second language linguistic system. The social and psychological variables that affect the rate of the learning process are beyond its remit and therefore ignored.

Bearing the above in mind, there is little doubt that the Universal Grammar approach to research into second language acquisition has been highly influential and fruitful, and has generated a wealth of studies that have greatly enhanced our understanding of second language morphosyntactic development. It has been very useful as a tool for linguistic analysis, enabling researchers to formulate well-defined and focused hypotheses that could then be tested in empirical work. This powerful linguistic tool has been useful in describing not only the language produced by learners, but also the language to be acquired as well as the first language of the learner. The work carried out by second language acquisition researchers within this framework is also feeding into our more general understanding of human language.

This approach has also been useful, not only in establishing some of the facts about second language acquisition, but also meeting with some success in explaining those facts. For example, it has enabled second language researchers to draw up a principled view of language transfer or cross-linguistic influence, in terms of principles and parameters. As we have seen, for example, researchers have been able to test empirically whether parameters can be reset.

3.6.4   The Universal Grammar view of the language learner

The Universal Grammar approach is only interested in the learner as the possessor of a mind that contains language; the assumption is that all human beings are endowed with such a mind, and variations between individuals are of little concern to Universal Grammar theorists. The emphasis is very much again here on language as the object of study, rather than on the speaker or learner as a social being, and the focus is on what is universal within this mind.

Overall, there is little doubt that the Universal Grammar approach to second language research meets the criteria for a good theory as defined in Chapter 1, by making clear and explicit statements of the ground it aims to cover and the claims it makes, by having systematic procedures for theory-evaluation, by attempting to explain as well as describe at least some second language phenomena, and finally by engaging increasingly with other theories in the field. As one of the most active and developing theories, it can be expected to continue to make highly valuable contributions to the field.

4

Cognitive approaches to second language learning

The acquisition of grammar is the piecemeal learning of many thousands of constructions and the frequency-biased abstraction of regularities within them.

(N.C. Ellis, 2003, p. 67)

4.1 Introduction

In Chapter 3, we outlined the work of second language acquisition researchers who are interested in the development of second language grammars from a purely linguistic point of view. In that view, second language learning (SLL) is seen as different from other kinds of learning, and a formal description of the linguistic systems involved (be they the first language, the second language or the learner's interlanguage) is seen as crucial to our understanding of the SLL task. Universal Grammar-based researchers put the emphasis firmly on the **language** dimension of SLL, and see language as a separate module in the mind, distinct from other aspects of cognition. Universal Grammar, as we have discussed, is primarily a **property theory**.

The second language acquisition researchers we are about to consider now, on the other hand, put more emphasis on the **learning** component of SLL, that is, they are interested in **transition theories**. They view SLL as just one instantiation (i.e. working example) of learning among many others, and they believe that we can understand the second language acquisition process better by first understanding how the human brain processes and learns new information. The focus here is still very much on the learner as an individual (unlike the work of social theorists we will examine later), but, unlike Universal Grammar theorists who draw their hypotheses from the study of linguistic systems, the

hypotheses they are investigating come from the field of cognitive psychology and neurology, and from what we know about the acquisition of
complex procedural skills in general.

Remember the distinction we have already discussed, between linguistic
competence and linguistic **performance**. We said in Chapter 3 that
Universal Grammar theorists were interested primarily in competence, that
is, in the linguistic system underlying second language grammars, and in its
construction. They are not centrally concerned with how learners access
this linguistic knowledge in real time, or in the strategies they might employ
when their incomplete linguistic system lets them down, or why some individuals are substantially better than others at learning other languages. For
cognitive theorists, on the other hand, these are central issues.

The dichotomy between linguists who believe that language is a separate
innate module in the mind, and linguists who believe that language is just
another form of information which is processed using general mechanisms,
is of course somewhat caricatural. You will find researchers who believe that
there is a language-specific module for first language acquisition, but that
the learning of second languages is different and relies on general cognitive
mechanisms (*see* Bley-Vroman, 1989). You will also find that, even for first
language acquisition, some researchers believe that some aspects of
language acquisition are innate and other aspects not, for example
Butterworth and Harris:

> In some respects, both the claims of Piaget and Chomsky are correct. There
> is evidence that acquisition of some aspects of language, notably syntax, are
> independent of other aspects of cognitive development . . . At the same time,
> however, there is no doubt that full understanding of a great deal of language
> requires other, more general, cognitive abilities.
>
> (Butterworth and Harris, 1994, p. 124)

Some authors leave the question open:

> Related to this issue is that of the extent to which language acquisition
> depends upon innate language-specific principles. For example, it is not clear
> whether the way in which young children relate words to features of the world
> is constrained by specific innate limitations on the types of hypotheses which
> can be generated, or on more general principles such as 'attach words to
> whole objects in the first instance', or some combination of these.
>
> (Harley, 1995, pp. 381–2)

As the above examples make clear, the question of the specificity and
innateness of the language faculty is far from resolved, in both the first and
second language acquisition fields, and the opposition between cognitivists

and innatists should be seen more in terms of the two ends of a continuum rather than a dichotomy. Even within frameworks concentrating firmly on the processing component of language learning, such as Pienemann's Processability Theory, which we will review shortly, the possibility of an innate linguistic module is not rejected outright; the author does not pronounce himself, and deals exclusively with the growth of the computational mechanisms required to process second languages. These two approaches are increasingly seen as complementary rather than conflictual.

Cognitive theorists fall into two main groups:

- The theorists we will review first in this chapter, such as Pienemann, or Towell and Hawkins (1994), who believe that language knowledge might be 'special' in some way, but who are concerned to develop transition or processing theories to complement property theories such as Universal Grammar or Lexical Functional Grammar.
- Theorists such as N.C. Ellis, MacWhinney, or Tomasello, who do not think that the separation between property and transition theories is legitimate, as they believe that you can explain both the nature of language knowledge and how it is processed through general cognitive principles. In fact, they do not generally make the distinction between competence and performance, as they see these as being one and the same thing. In this view, the learner is seen as operating a complex processing system that deals with linguistic information in similar ways to other kinds of information.

For ease of presentation, we will say that the first group of linguists belong to **processing** approaches, and the second group to **emergentist** or **constructionist** approaches.

Processing approaches, as their name indicates, investigate how second language learners process linguistic information, and how their ability to process the second language develops over time. They are focused primarily on the computational dimension of language learning, and might or might not believe that language is a separate innate module.

Constructivist or emergentist views of language learning share a usage-based view of language development, which is driven by communicative needs, and they refute the need to posit an innate, language specific, acquisition device. They include approaches known as emergentism, connectionism or associationism, constructivism, functionalism, cognitivism, Competition Model, etc. (for overviews *see* Tomasello, 1992, 2003; Plunkett, 1998; MacWhinney, 1999; Tomasello and Brooks, 1999.) 'They emphasize the linguistic sign as a set of mappings between phonological forms and conceptual meanings or communicative intentions' (N.C. Ellis, 2003, p. 63). Learning in this view is seen as the analysis of patterns in the language input, and language development is seen as resulting from the billions of associations which are made during language use, and which lead to regular patterns that might look rule-like, but in fact are merely associations. 'Constructivists believe that the complexity of language emerges from associative learning processes being exposed to a massive and complex environment' (N.C. Ellis, 2003, p. 84). Many researchers within emergentist frameworks believe that language develops as learners move from the learning of exemplars (words, formulae) that are committed to memory; from these, regularities emerge, giving rise to slot-and-frame patterns, such as *all-gone* + referent or *I can't* + verb. As more and more of these formulae develop, they are compared and analysed, regularities extracted and applied elsewhere. This phenomenon is well documented in early first language acquisition (Pine and Lieven, 1993, 1997; Pine *et al.*, 1998), and many emergentist first language acquisitionists believe it drives the acquisition process (Tomasello, 1992, 2003; Elman *et al.*, 1996; MacWhinney 1999). 'The children are picking up frequent patterns from what they hear around them, and only slowly making more abstract generalisations as the database of related utterances grows' (Ellis, 2003, p. 70). Verbs have been found to be particularly productive in allowing children to make abstract generalizations about their argument structure on the basis of the formulaic sequences they appear in (Goldberg, 1999). In second language acquisition, chunks are also very common in the early stages, and learners have been shown to gradually analyse them into their constituents (Vihman, 1982; Raupach, 1984; Robinson, 1986; Hickey 1993; Weinert, 1995; Mitchell and Martin 1997; Myles *et al.*, 1998, 1999; Myles and Mitchell, 2003). N.C. Ellis (2003) has also argued that these processes of chunking (i.e. moving from unanalysed chunks to abstract generalizations) are central to second language acquisition.

This chapter is divided into two main sections. The first one, entitled **Processing approaches**, investigates the work of psycholinguists who have analysed the second language acquisition of procedural skills from a range of perspectives. We will be concentrating in most detail on **information-processing** approaches, and on Pienemann's (1998) **processability theory**.

The second section investigates approaches that study the acquisition of language from the **constructionist** or **emergentist** point of view. In this school, the (second) language is acquired through usage, by extracting pattern and regularities from the input, and building ever-stronger associations in the brain. We will focus in particular on the **connectionist**

approach, which applies computer modelling to investigate this process.

Before moving on, it is important to stress we have had to be highly selective in this chapter. The field of cognitive linguistics is vast and expanding fast, and we have focused here on what we perceive as the main **theoretical paradigms** used to investigate the process of SLL. We have therefore ignored important developments that have focused on the investigation of a range of factors that might affect this process (i.e. speed it up or slow it down). Researchers recently have investigated in some detail the psychological constraints underlying SLL, such as the role of memory, of noticing and attention, of implicit or explicit learning and of individual differences (e.g. motivation, aptitude, intelligence, etc.), and their pedagogical implications. (For recent accounts, *see* Hulstijn, 2001, 2003; Robinson, 2001, 2002, 2003; DeKeyser, 2003; Dörnyei and Skehan, 2003.) For the moment, we refer the reader to these detailed reviews; we revisit some of these concepts in later chapters.

4.2   Processing approaches

The approaches we will review here all have in common the fact that they are interested in the way in which the brain's processing mechanisms deal with the second language. The first approach, information processing, investigates how different memory stores (short-term memory (STM); long-term memory (LTM) – declarative and procedural) deal with new second language information, and how this information is automatized and restructured through repeated activation. The second approach, processability theory, looks more specifically at the processing demands made by various formal aspects of the second language, and the implications for learnability and teachability of second language structure.

4.2.1   Information-processing models of second language learning

The work we will be discussing under this heading originates from information-processing models developed by cognitive psychologists, which have then been adapted to the treatment of language processing, both first and second language. First, we examine McLaughlin's (1987, 1990) information-processing model. Second, we will turn our attention to Anderson's Active Control of Thought (ACT*) model (1983, 1985), paying particular attention to O'Malley and Chamot's (1990) application of the model in the field of learner strategies and to Towell and Hawkins' (1994) application to the development of fluency.

4.2.1.1   McLaughlin's information-processing model

> In general, the fundamental notion of the information-processing approach to psychological inquiry is that complex behaviour builds on simple processes.
>
> (McLaughlin and Heredia, 1996, p. 213)

Moreover, these processes are modular and can therefore be studied independently of one another. Table 4.1 summarizes the main characteristics of such an approach.

Table 4.1   Some characteristics of the information-processing approach

Humans are viewed as autonomous and active
The mind is a general-purpose, symbol-processing system
Complex behaviour is composed of simpler processes; these processes are modular
Component processes can be isolated and studied independently of other processes
Processes take time; therefore, predictions about reaction time can be made
The mind is a limited-capacity processor

(*Source*: McLaughlin and Heredia, 1996, p. 214)

When applied to SLL, this approach can be summarized as follows:

> Within this framework, second language learning is viewed as the acquisition of a complex cognitive skill. To learn a second language is to learn a *skill*, because various aspects of the task must be practised and integrated into fluent performance. This requires the automatization of component sub-skills. Learning is a *cognitive* process, because it is thought to involve internal representations that regulate and guide performance ... As performance improves, there is constant restructuring as learners simplify, unify, and gain increasing control over their internal representations (Karmiloff-Smith 1986). These two notions – automatization and restructuring – are central to cognitive theory.
>
> (McLaughlin, 1987, pp. 133–4)

Automatization (McLaughlin 1987, 1990; McLaughlin and Heredia 1996) is a notion based on the work of psychologists such as Shiffrin and Schneider (1977), who claim that the way in which we process information may be either controlled or automatic, and that learning involves a shift from controlled towards automatic processing. Applied to SLL, such a model works as follows.

Learners first resort to **controlled processing** in the second language. This controlled processing involves the temporary activation of a selection of information nodes in the memory, in a new configuration. Such processing requires a lot of attentional control on the part of the subject, and is constrained by the limitations of the **short-term memory**. For example, a beginner learner wanting to greet someone in the second language might activate the following words: *good morning how are you?* Initially, these words have to be put together in a piecemeal fashion, one at a time (assuming they have not been memorized as an unanalysed chunk).

Through repeated activation, sequences first produced by controlled processing become **automatic**. Automatized sequences are stored as units in the **long-term memory**, which means that they can be made available very rapidly whenever the situation requires it, with minimal attentional control on the part of the subject. As a result, automatic processes can work in parallel, activating clusters of complex cognitive skills simultaneously. So, in the above example, once a learner has activated the sequence *good morning how are you?* a large number of times, it becomes automatic, that is, it does not require attentional control. However, once acquired, such automatized skills are difficult to delete or modify.

Learning in this view is seen as the movement from controlled to automatic processing via practice (repeated activation). When this shift occurs, controlled processes are freed to deal with higher levels of processing (i.e. the integration of more complex skill clusters), thus explaining the incremental (step by step) nature of learning. It is necessary for simple sub-skills and routines to become automatic before more complex ones can be tackled. Once our learner has automatized *good morning how are you?*, he or she is free to deal with the learning of more complex language, as the short-term memory is not taken up by the production of this particular string.

This continuing movement from controlled to automatic processing results in a constant **restructuring** of the linguistic system of the second language learner. This phenomenon may account for some of the variability characteristic of learner language. Restructuring destabilizes some structures in the interlanguage, which seemed to have been previously acquired, and hence leads to the temporary reappearance of second language errors. Restructuring is also the result of exemplar-based representations becoming rule-based (McLaughlin and Heredia, 1996). As we suggested earlier, second language learners often start by memorizing unanalysed chunks of language, which will later be analysed and give rise to productive rules (Wong-Fillmore, 1976; Weinert, 1995; N.C. Ellis 1996a, 1996b; Myles *et al.*, 1998, 1999; Wray and Perkins, 2000; Wray, 2002). For example, a learner might first memorize a question as an unanalysed chunk, for example *have you got a pet?*, without having a productive rule for interrogatives, involving inversion. When this learner starts generating interrogatives that are not rote-learned chunks, he or she might produce an alternative, uninverted form, such has *you have pet?*

This account is especially convincing in its explanation of the vexed issue of **fossilization**, which is so well documented in second language acquisition studies. As we saw in Chapter 1, fossilization refers to the fact that second language learners, unlike first language learners, sometimes seem unable to get rid of non-native-like structures in their second language despite abundant linguistic input over many years. Fossilization in this model would arise as a result of a controlled process becoming automatic prematurely, before it is native-like. As we have seen, automatic processes are difficult to modify as they are outside the attentional control of the subject. Thus they are likely to remain in the learner's interlanguage, giving rise to a stable but erroneous construction. However, this general idea does not explain why some structures seem much more likely to fossilize than others.

4.2.1.2   Anderson's ACT* model

Another processing model from cognitive psychology, which has also been applied to aspects of SLL, is Anderson's (1983, 1985) ACT* model. This model is not dissimilar from McLaughlin's. It is more wide-ranging, and the terminology is different, but practice leading to automatization also plays a central role. It enables **declarative knowledge** (i.e. knowledge *that* something is the case) to become **procedural knowledge** (i.e. knowledge *how* to do something). One of the major differences is that Anderson posits three kinds of memory: a working memory, similar to McLaughlin's short-term memory and therefore tightly capacity-limited, and two kinds of long-term memory – a declarative long-term memory and a procedural long-term memory. Anderson believes that declarative and procedural knowledge are different kinds of knowledge that are stored differently.

But, before outlining the way in which the different kinds of memories work and interact, let us illustrate with a simple example what is meant by declarative and procedural knowledge. If you are learning to drive, for example, you will be told that if the engine is revving too much, you need to change to a higher gear; you will also be told how to change gear. In the early stages of learning to drive, however, **knowing that** (declarative knowledge) you have to do this does not necessarily mean that you **know how** (procedural knowledge) to do it quickly and successfully. In other words, you go through a declarative stage before acquiring the procedural knowledge linked with this situation. With practice, however, the mere noise of the engine getting louder will trigger your gear changing, without you even having to think about it. This is how learning takes place in this view: by declarative knowledge becoming procedural and automatized.

Anderson's (1983) application of his model to first language acquisition has been criticized for insisting that all knowledge starts out in declarative form (DeKeyser, 1997). This is clearly problematic in the case of first language learners, as Anderson has accepted in answering some of these criticisms. With respect to language learning, Anderson does not claim that all knowledge needs to start as declarative knowledge any longer (Anderson and Fincham, 1994; MacWhinney and Anderson, 1986). However, other applications, such as to the learning of algebra, geometry or computer programming, have been very successful. Indeed, it is the comparability of the teaching or learning of second languages in instructional environments with the teaching or learning of complex skills such as algebra that has attracted the attention of second language acquisition researchers. Because Anderson's model is a general cognitive model of skill acquisition, it can be applied to those aspects of SLL that require proceduralization and automatization (Raupach, 1987; O'Malley and Chamot, 1990; Schmidt, 1992; Towell and Hawkins, 1994; Johnson, 1996).

Let us illustrate with an example how the notions of declarative and procedural knowledge could apply to SLL. If we take the example of the third person singular -*s* marker on present tense verbs in English, the classroom learner might initially know, in the sense that she has consciously learnt the rule, that *s/he* + Verb requires the addition of an -*s* to the stem of the verb. However, that same learner might not necessarily be able to consistently produce the -*s* in a conversation in real time. This is because this particular learner has declarative knowledge of that rule, but it has not yet been proceduralized. After much practice, this knowledge will hopefully become fully proceduralized, and the third person -*s* will be supplied when the context requires it. This dichotomy between, on the one hand, knowing a rule, and on the other, being able to apply it when needed, is all too familiar to second language learners and teachers.

According to Anderson, the move from declarative to procedural knowledge takes place in three stages (Anderson, 1985, p. 232, cited in Towell and Hawkins 1994, p. 203):

1. **The cognitive stage**: a description of the procedure is learnt.
2. **The associative stage**: a method for performing the skill is worked out.
3. **The autonomous stage**: The skill becomes more and more rapid and automatic.

In the examples outlined above, in the cognitive stage, the learner would learn that the clutch pedal has to be pushed down and the gear lever moved to the correct position, or, in the case of the language example, that an -*s* must be added to the verb after a third person subject. In the associative stage, the learner would work out how to do it, that is, how to press the pedal down and how to get the gear lever in the correct position, or how to add an -*s* when the context requires it. In other words, the learner learns to associate an action (or a set of actions) with the corresponding declarative knowledge. In the autonomous stage, our learner's actions (changing gear or adding an -*s*) become increasingly automatic, to the point that the corresponding declarative knowledge may even be lost; in other words, our learner might not be able to explain or even be conscious of what they are doing.

In the same way as with McLaughlin's model, we can also see how this model would explain the step-by-step nature of learning. When tasks become proceduralized, they are accessed automatically, without having to resort to the working memory, which is limited in its processing capacity. Therefore, new declarative knowledge can be attended to and thereafter proceed through the associative and eventually autonomous stages.

Once it has become autonomous, proceduralized knowledge presents similar advantages and disadvantages to McLaughlin's automatized knowledge. It is available quickly and efficiently, and does not make many demands on the working memory; it will be difficult to modify, however, and will be applicable only to the situation that gave rise to it. The process will also need time and the same routine will have to be activated successfully a large number of times, in order to become proceduralized. Each time the procedure is applied successfully, it is strengthened and thereafter called upon more easily. To illustrate this shift from declarative to procedural knowledge in the context of SLL, Anderson himself speculated:

> When we learn a foreign language in a classroom situation, we are aware of the rules of the language, especially just after a lesson that spells them out. One might argue that our knowledge of the language at that time is declarative. We speak the learned language by using general rule-following procedures applied to the rules we have learned, rather than speaking directly, as we do in our native language. Not surprisingly, applying this knowledge is a much slower and painful process than applying the procedurally encoded knowledge of our own language. Eventually, if we are lucky, we can come to know a foreign language as well as we know our native language. At that point, we often forget the rules of the foreign language. It is as if the class-taught declarative knowledge had been transformed into a procedural form.
>
> (Anderson, 1980, p. 224)

Here, we see the basic suggestions that the learner's speech becomes more fluent as more knowledge becomes proceduralized, and is therefore accessed more quickly and efficiently. We can also see how, as knowledge becomes proceduralized, the working memory is freed to work on higher level knowledge.

Johnson (1996) has pursued the application of Anderson's model to explicit classroom instruction, and many teaching traditions operate on principles compatible with the model. However, most contemporary theorists of SLL, from whatever perspective, would not now agree with the implied position taken by Anderson (1980), that all or most of second language grammar is initially learnt through the conscious study and application of explicit rules. Even for classroom learners, there is a consensus that much grammar learning takes place without conscious awareness, whether by the operation of a specific language module, or by general cognitive processes. Some information-processing theorists have responded to this problem by suggesting that the 'declarative knowledge' component can be subdivided into conscious and unconscious parts (Bialystok, 1991). Others have argued that information-processing models are most helpful in explaining more peripheral strands in SLL. In following sections we see how Anderson's model has been applied to two such strands: to the application of learning strategies to the SLL problem, and to the development of second language fluency.

4.2.1.3   Application of ACT* to learning strategies

This section will examine how the ACT* model has been applied to the field of language learning strategies, by researchers such as O'Malley and Chamot (1990). Learning strategies are procedures undertaken by the learner, in order to make their own language learning as effective as possible. They may include:

> focusing on selected aspects of new information, analysing and monitoring information during acquisition, organizing or elaborating on new information during the encoding process, evaluating the learning when it is completed, or assuring oneself that the learning will be successful as a way to allay anxiety.
>
> (O'Malley and Chamot, 1990, p. 43)

Learning strategies must not be confused with communication strategies, although there is some overlap; their focus is on facilitating learning, whereas communication strategies are used in order to overcome a specific communicative problem (*see* further discussion in Chapter 6). Learning strategies can be classified into three categories, as exemplified in Table 4.2 (O'Malley and Chamot 1990, p. 46).

Table 4.2   Classification of learning strategies

Generic strategy classification	Representative strategies	Definitions
Metacognitive strategies	Selective attention	Focusing on special aspects of learning tasks, as in planning to listen for key words or phrases
	Planning	Planning for the organization of either written or spoken discourse
	Monitoring	Reviewing attention to a task, comprehension of information that should be remembered, or production while it is occurring
	Evaluation	Checking comprehension after completion of a receptive language activity, or evaluating language production after it has taken place
Cognitive strategies	Rehearsal	Repeating the names of items or objects to be remembered
	Organization	Grouping and classifying words, terminology, or concepts according to their semantic or syntactic attributes
	Inferencing	Using information in text to guess meanings or new linguistic items, predict outcomes or complete missing parts
	Summarizing	Intermittently synthesizing what one has heard to ensure the information has been retained
	Deducing	Applying rules to the understanding of language
	Imagery	Using visual images (either generated or actual) to understand and remember new verbal information
	Transfer	Using known linguistic information to facilitate a new learning task
	Elaboration	Linking ideas contained in new information, or integrating new ideas with known information
Social or affective strategies	Co-operation	Working with peers to solve a problem, pool information, check notes or get feedback on a learning activity
	Questioning for clarification	Eliciting from a teacher or peer additional explanation, rephrasing or examples
	Self-talk	Using mental redirection of thinking to assure oneself that a learning activity will be successful or to reduce anxiety about a task

(*Source*: O'Malley and Chamot, 1990, p. 43)

In the view of O'Malley and Chamot:

> learning strategies are complex procedures that individuals apply to tasks; consequently, they may be represented as procedural knowledge which may be acquired through cognitive, associative, and autonomous stages of learning. As with other procedural skills at the different stages of learning, the strategies may be conscious in early stages of learning and later be performed without the person's awareness.
>
> (O'Malley and Chamot, 1990, p. 52)

Thus, strategies have to be learnt in exactly the same way as other complex cognitive skills. A good language learner will be a learner who has proceduralized the strategies described in Table 4.2. Remember that before a skill is proceduralized, it will have to compete for working memory space with other aspects of the task in hand; as the working memory has strictly limited capacity, learning strategies which have not yet been fully proceduralized might not be applied because of competing demands.

An obvious pedagogical implication of such a view is that second language learners would benefit from being taught learning strategies. If learning strategies are a skill, then they can be taught, with the advantage that they will become proceduralized more quickly, therefore freeing working memory space for other aspects of learning. A problem raised by O'Malley and Chamot is that the teaching of strategies will involve a considerable investment of time and effort in order to be effective (before the skills taught can become proceduralized), and we therefore need long-term studies investigating the effect of strategy teaching. Their own research does suggest some positive effect of strategy teaching on vocabulary development, listening comprehension and oral production.

O'Malley and Chamot (1990, p. 217) sum up the general benefits of applying cognitive theory to the field of second language acquisition as follows:

- Learning is an active and dynamic process in which individuals make use of a variety of information and strategic modes of processing.
- Language is a complex cognitive skill that has properties in common with other complex skills in terms of how information is stored and learnt.
- Learning a language entails a stagewise progression from initial awareness and active manipulation of information and learning processes to full automaticity in language use.
- Learning strategies parallel theoretically derived cognitive processes and have the potential to influence learning outcomes in a positive manner.

O'Malley and Chamot are clear, however, that such an approach does not concern itself with the language learning route followed by learners. It deals exclusively with the rate of learning and how learning strategies can influence it:

> The cognitive theory described in this book is largely a theory of learning processes and not a theory that specifies precisely what is learned, what content will be easiest (or most difficult) to learn, or what learners will select to learn at different stages of development or levels of mastery of a complex skill.
> (O'Malley and Chamot, 1990, p. 216)

4.2.1.4   ACT* and fluency development in second language acquisition

A number of researchers continue to investigate how to operationalize the concepts underlying automaticity and its acquisition in the context of second language acquisition (Schmidt, 1992; Johnson, 1996; DeKeyser, 2001; Segalowitz, 2003). We refer the reader to these works for insightful overviews, and we will concentrate here on one illustration of the application of psychological models to the development of fluency. We will outline how Towell and Hawkins (1994) have incorporated aspects of the ACT* model into their overall model of SLL, in order to account for fluency development.

Towell and Hawkins (1994) reject the idea that Anderson's model can account for all aspects of SLL, notably the acquisition of 'core' grammatical knowledge. They have used models of natural language processing, such as those of Anderson and of Levelt (1989), primarily in order to explain how grammatical knowledge becomes transformed into fluent performance in the second language. Their model (shown here as Figure 4.1) attempts to integrate how learners learn the second language system with how they learn to use the system. In order to explain why certain grammatical structures appear before others, and why learners go through fairly rigid stages in their acquisition of second languages, they resort to a Universal Grammar approach. In order to understand how learners use this grammatical knowledge in increasingly efficient ways (hopefully!), Towell and Hawkins (1994) appeal to an information-processing account.

As can be seen from Fig. 4.1, the internally derived hypotheses about second language structure (shaped by Universal Grammar and the first language) are stored in different ways in the mind at different stages of the learning process. In a first stage, a hypothesis will be stored in the declarative long-term memory (controlled). (In Towell and Hawkins' (1994) account, declarative knowledge may be implicit or explicit, and the learner

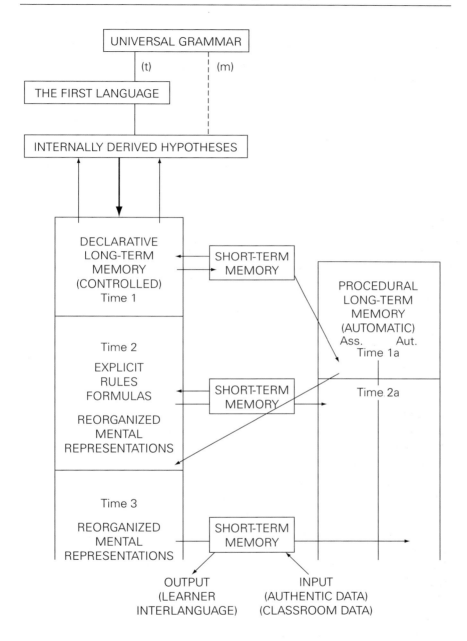

UNIVERSAL GRAMMAR

(t)   (m)

THE FIRST LANGUAGE

INTERNALLY DERIVED HYPOTHESES

DECLARATIVE
LONG-TERM
MEMORY
(CONTROLLED)
Time 1

SHORT-TERM
MEMORY

PROCEDURAL
LONG-TERM
MEMORY
(AUTOMATIC)
Ass.   Aut.
Time 1a

Time 2

EXPLICIT
RULES
FORMULAS

SHORT-TERM
MEMORY

Time 2a

REORGANIZED
MENTAL
REPRESENTATIONS

Time 3

REORGANIZED
MENTAL
REPRESENTATIONS

SHORT-TERM
MEMORY

OUTPUT
(LEARNER
INTERLANGUAGE)

INPUT
(AUTHENTIC DATA)
(CLASSROOM DATA)

Fig. 4.1   A model of second language acquisition (*Source*: Towell and Hawkins, 1994, p. 248)

will not normally have any conscious analysed knowledge of such Universal Grammar-derived hypotheses.) When put to use, this kind of internally derived knowledge will give rise to a production stored in the procedural long-term memory, initially in 'associative' form (i.e. under attentional control from the learner). The hypothesis may then be revised and cause some reorganization of the declarative knowledge, which will then give rise to other revised productions. Eventually, after successive reorganizations, these productions will become autonomous (i.e. automatized and free from attentional control) and are stored as such in the 'autonomous' part of the procedural memory. This model allows Towell and Hawkins (1994, pp. 250–1) to make a number of specific claims concerning different kinds of learning:

Internally derived hypotheses about second language structure, if confirmed by external data, will give rise to a production which will be stored in procedural memory, first in associative form and eventually in autonomous form.

Formulae, that is, form–function pairs which have been learnt as routines (e.g. *What's your name?* produced in the absence of a generative rule for the formation of interrogatives) can be stored in the procedural memory at the associative level, before going back to declarative memory for reanalysis under controlled processes, and can finally be stored as an autonomous procedure when all stages of analysis and re-analysis have been completed.

Explicit rules (e.g. verb conjugations) can be learnt and stored as proceduralized knowledge. As such, they will only be recalled as a list of verb-endings. But, if they can feed back to the declarative memory in order to undergo a controlled process of analysis by interacting with internally derived hypotheses, they might eventually also give rise to autonomous productions available for language use.

Learning strategies facilitate the proceduralization of mechanisms for faster processing of linguistic input. They are incorporated in the information-processing part of the model, without having to interact with internal hypotheses.

This model attempts to reconcile internal, Universal Grammar-derived hypotheses about second language structure with what actually happens to these hypotheses during the processes of language learning and language use. It thus represents an ambitious attempt to link together linguistic and cognitive approaches to the study of SLL.

4.2.2   Theories of second language processing

The next two approaches we will review focus on the factors controlling the way in which second language learners process the linguistic input. These are: Processability theory; discussed (along with its pedagogical implications) in sections 4.2.2.1–4.2.2.2 and the Perceptual Saliency approach; discussed in Section 4.2.2.3.

There are other models that analyse in detail the way in which learners process the input. For example, Carroll's (2000) Autonomous Induction theory aims to provide a comprehensive second language acquisition model in which the role played by input processing is central. We refer to this model elsewhere (in Chapter 6) and will not therefore review it here.

4.2.2.1   Processability theory

Like Towell and Hawkins, the Processability theory outlined by Pienemann (1998, 2003) also claims we need to use both a theory of grammar and a processing component in order to understand second language acquisition. However, it focuses on the acquisition of the procedural skills required for processing the formal properties of second languages. The theory of grammar used in the illustration of the theory, titled Lexical Functional Grammar (Kaplan and Bresnan, 1982), also differs from the Chomskyan theory we have considered in Chapter 3, but the details need not concern us here. Suffice it to say that Lexical Functional Grammar, unlike Universal Grammar, is a theory of grammar that attempts to represent both linguistic knowledge and language processing within the same framework. Unlike Universal Grammar, which is exclusively a theory of linguistic knowledge, Lexical Functional Grammar aims to be psychologically plausible, that is, to be in line with the cognitive features of language processing.

Processability theory aims to clarify how learners acquire the computational mechanisms that operate on the linguistic knowledge they construct. Pienemann believes that language acquisition itself is the gradual acquisition of these computational mechanisms, that is, the procedural skills necessary for the processing of language. It is limitations in the processing skills at the disposal of learners in the early stages of learning which prevent them from attending to some aspects of the second language.

The processing challenge facing learners within this framework is that they must learn to exchange grammatical information across elements of a sentence. (This process of sharing grammatical information is called 'feature unification' within the Lexical Functional Grammar model.)

In other words, the unification of lexical features, which is one of the main characteristics of LFG, captures a psychologically plausible process that involves (1) the identification of grammatical information in the lexical entry, (2) the temporary storage of that information and (3) its utilisation at another point in the constituent structure.

(Pienemann, 1998, p. 73)

Thus, language users have to ensure that a verb and its subject have the same number feature, or that a noun and its article have the same gender, number and case features, in languages where this is appropriate. For example, the sentence *Peter walk a dogs* is ungrammatical because *walk* and *Peter* do not have the same person and number feature (third person singular), and *a* and *dogs* also do not share the same number feature. In SLL, the ability to match features across elements in a sentence develops gradually. The basic logic behind Processability theory is that learners cannot access hypotheses about the second language that they cannot process. They are claimed to have a Hypothesis Space, which develops over time according to the following hierarchy of processing resources (Pienemann, 1998, p. 87):

- Level 1: lemma access; words; no sequence of constituents.
- Level 2: category procedure; lexical morphemes; no exchange of information – canonical word order.
- Level 3: phrasal procedure; phrasal morphemes.
- Level 4: simplified S-procedure; exchange of information from internal to salient constituent.
- Level 5: S-procedure; inter-phrasal morphemes; exchange of information between internal constituents.
- Level 6: Subordinate clause procedure.

The hierarchical nature of this list arises from the fact that the procedure of each lower level is a prerequisite for the functioning of the higher level: a word needs to be added to the L2 lexicon before its grammatical category can be assigned. The grammatical category of a lemma is needed before a category procedure can be called. Only if the grammatical category of the Head phrase is assigned can the phrasal procedure be called. Only if a phrasal procedure has been completed and its value is returned can Appointment Rules determine the function of the phrase. And only if the function of the phrase has been determined can it be attached to the S-node and sentential information be stored in the S-holder.

(Pienemann, 1998, p. 80)

What this means in practice is that learners will be able to share information across elements in a sentence in gradually less local domains. Initially, they will not be able to produce any structures that require the matching of second language grammatical information using syntactic procedures; for example, to mark both nouns and articles within a noun-phrase as +feminine (until Level 3: phrasal procedure) or to match person in subject and verb (Level 4: inter-phrasal information exchange). We can represent this visually (Fig. 4.2) by suggesting that learners will gradually move 'up' the structure, first accessing words, then their syntactic category, then joining them in a phrase, etc., all the way up the tree.

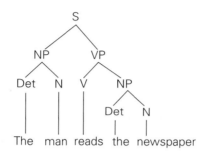

Fig. 4.2   Learners gradually move 'up' the structure of a sentence

The predictions for acquisition will therefore be as follows (Pienemann, 1998, pp. 83–6):

- During the first stage, no language-specific procedures can take place. The learner has no syntactic information about the second language lexical item, and is only able to map conceptual structures onto individual words and fixed phrases.
- Once lexical items have been assigned a grammatical category lexical morphological markers can be produced (but no grammatical information can be exchanged yet). At this stage too, because learners cannot exchange grammatical information, they will rely, for the mapping of semantic roles onto surface form, on procedures that do not require this. For example, they might rely on strictly serial word order (e.g. action + agent + patient).
- Phrasal procedures are developed which enable the sharing of information at phrase level, that is, between a Head and its modifiers. No information can be exchanged yet across phrases.
- Once phrasal procedures are present, Appointment Rules and the S-procedure can be developed. This means that the functional destination of phrases can be determined and phrases can be assembled into sentences, with each phrase playing a clear function within the sentence as a whole (e.g. subject of S).

- Once the syntactic information at the level of the sentence is available for processing by learners, subordinate clauses can develop.

Pienemann (1998) applied his model to a range of developmental phenomena that have been observed in second language acquisition, in both morphology and syntax, and across languages (German, English, Swedish, Japanese). We will review here his explanation of the well-documented acquisition of word order in German, based on the findings of the ZISA project (Zweitspracherwerb Italienischer, Spanischer und Portugiesischer Arbeiter; see Meisel *et al.*, 1981). This project worked with Italian, Spanish, Portuguese and later Turkish first language (Clahsen and Muysken, 1986) learners of German in an untutored setting (they were all migrant workers). One of the major findings was that there is a clear developmental route in the acquisition of German word order (a complex and much-studied feature of the German language), found in both naturalistic and classroom learners.

The developmental stages that Pienemann and colleagues describe are as follows:

- Stage 1: Canonical Order (SVO)
  Die kinder spielen mimt ball (= the children play with the ball)
  Learners' initial hypothesis is that German is SVO, with adverbials in sentence-final position.

- Stage 2: Adverb preposing
  Da kinder spielen (= there children play)
  Learners now place the adverb in sentence initial position, but keep the SVO order (no verb–subject inversion yet).

- Stage 3: Verb separation
  Aller kinder muß die pause machen (= all children must the pause have)
  Learners place the non-finite verbal element (here *machen*) in clause-final position.

- Stage 4: Verb-second
  Dann hat sie wieder die knoch gebringt (= then has she again the bone brought)
  Learners now place the finite verb element (*hat*) in sentence-second position, resulting in verb–subject inversion.

- Stage 5: Verb-final in subordinate clauses
  Er sagte daß er nach hause kommt (= he said that he to home comes)
  Learners place the finite verb (*kommt*) in clause-final position in subordinate clauses.

Processability Theory accounts for these stages as follows:

- Stage 1: Strict SVO order. This does not involve any feature unification and therefore corresponds to Level 2 of the processing hierarchy.
- Stage 2: Adverb preposing. The adverb is topicalized, according to the saliency principle (more about this later); there is still no exchange of grammatical information.
- Stage 3: Verb separation. For this split-verb construction to occur, both parts of the verb have to be unified, that is, the participle value of the main verb and the auxiliary entry. This exchange of information occurs across constituent boundaries. However, the non-canonical position involved is perceptually salient (it is in final position).
- Stage 4: Verb second. This rule involves the unification of the feature requiring inversion of the verb and its subject across V and another phrase, and cannot rely on saliency principles.
- Stage 5: Verb-final in subordinate clauses. In the Lexical Functional Grammar framework, features of embedded clauses that distinguish them from main clauses are acquired after word order constraints in the main clause have been acquired.

We can see from the above explanation of the stages that they are due primarily to the hierarchy of processing procedures that Pienemann has outlined, in terms of the exchange of grammatical information. This is the main principle of his theory. He also relies, however, on a second principle, that of **perceptual saliency**, a widely used concept in cognitive psychology. The feature of perceptual saliency that Pienemann resorts to in the explanation of the stages above, is that the beginning and end of stimuli are easier to remember and therefore to manipulate. This means that learners will first be able to move elements from inside to outside the sentence, that is, to sentence-initial or sentence-final positions, then from outside to inside before being able to move elements within the sentence. This notion of perceptual saliency has also been used by others, as we shall see below. Before we do that, however, we need to outline one further aspect of Pienemann's theory which has attracted interest because of its potential pedagogical implications: his **Teachability hypothesis**.

4.2.2.2   Teachability

Pienemann developed his Processability theory in order to explain the well-documented observation (*see* Chapter 2) that second language learners follow a fairly rigid **route** in their acquisition of certain grammatical structures. This notion of route implies that structures only become 'learnable' when the previous steps on this acquisitional path have been acquired. For Pienemann, at any given point in time, learners can only operate within their Hypothesis Space, which is constrained by the processing resources they have available to them at that time. This has led him to develop his **Teachability hypothesis** (Pienemann 1981, 1987, 1989, 1998), in which he considers the pedagogical implications of the learnability or processability model, and draws precise conclusions about how some structures should be taught.

The predictions of the Teachability hypothesis are as follows:

- Stages of acquisition cannot be skipped through formal instruction.
- Instruction will be most beneficial if it focuses on structures from 'the next stage' (Pienemann, 1998, p. 250).

A number of empirical studies have provided some support for this hypothesis (*see* Pienemann, 1998, for details) but possibly its most interesting aspect is the attempt to establish a link between learning and teaching. This is a refreshing development, as second language acquisition researchers rarely attempt to assess the pedagogical implications of their research (though there are important exceptions such as R. Ellis, 1990, 1991; Cook, 2001).

4.2.2.3   Perceptual saliency

The Perceptual Saliency approach (Andersen, 1984, 1990; Slobin, 1985) argues that human beings perceive and organize information in certain ways, and that it is the perceptual saliency of linguistic information that drives the learning process forward.

This approach is largely based on the work of Slobin in the 1970s and 1980s, culminating with the publication of a cross-linguistic collection of child language development studies starting in 1985. Slobin argues that the similarity in linguistic development across children and across languages is because human beings are programmed to perceive and organize information in certain ways. It is this perceptual saliency that drives the learning process, rather than an innate language-specific module:

I believe that we do not know enough yet about the LMC* [Language Making Capacity] to be very clear about the extent to which it is specifically

*Language Making Capacity: Slobin's version of Chomsky's LAD (Language Acquisition Device).

tuned to the acquisition of language as opposed to other cognitive systems, or the degree to which LMC is specified at birth – prior to experience with the world of people and things, and prior to interaction with other developing cognitive systems.

(Slobin, 1985, pp. 1158–9)

Slobin has devised, added to and refined over the years a number of **operating principles** which guide children in their processing of the linguistic strings they encounter. His operating principles have been adapted to SLL by Andersen (1984, 1990), and we will review this work shortly. Pienemann's processibility or teachability theory also draws on the notion of perceptual saliency as we have already seen.

4.2.2.4   Operating principles and first language acquisition

Slobin's (1973, 1979, 1985) operating principles are based on the claim that 'certain linguistic forms are more "accessible" or more "salient" to the child than others' (Slobin, 1979, p. 107). The 1979 edition of his book, *Psycholinguistics,* lists five operating principles and five resulting universals; these are different from linguistic universals in that they are cognitive rather than linguistic in nature, and they characterize the way in which children perceive their environment and try to make sense of it and organize it. These early principles are as follows (Slobin 1979, pp. 108–10):

Operating Principle A: pay attention to the ends of words.

Operating Principle B: there are linguistic elements that encode relations between words.

Operating Principle C: avoid exceptions.

Operating Principle D: underlying semantic relations should be marked overtly and clearly.

Operating Principle E: the use of grammatical markers should make semantic sense.

Language acquisition universals are predicted from these principles in the following way:

Universal 1 (based on principles A and B): For any given semantic notion, grammatical realizations as postposed forms will be acquired earlier than realizations as preposed forms.

Universal 2 (based on C): the following stages of linguistic marking of a semantic notion are typically observed: (1) no marking; (2) appropriate marking in limited cases; (3) overgeneralization of marking; (4) full adult system.

Universal 3 (based on D): the closer a grammatical system adheres to one-to-one mapping between semantic elements and surface elements, the earlier it will be acquired.

Universal 4 (based on E): when selection of an appropriate inflection among a group of inflections performing the same semantic function is determined by arbitrary formal criteria (e.g. phonological shape of word stem, number of syllables in stem, arbitrary gender), the child initially tends to use a single form in all environments.

Universal 5: semantically consistent grammatical rules are acquired early and without significant error.

By 1985, the list of operating principles had reached the number of 40, and they had become much more sophisticated, using evidence from first language acquisition in a range of languages. However, the above examples suffice to give us a picture of the approach adopted.

4.2.2.5   Operating principles in second language acquisition

In second language acquisition, operating principles have been investigated by Andersen (*see* Andersen, 1984, 1990, 1991; Andersen and Shirai, 1994). Andersen's principles are based on those of Slobin, but are then adapted to the learning of second languages (Andersen, 1990, pp. 51–63).

The one-to-one principle: an interlanguage system should be constructed in such a way that an intended underlying meaning is expressed with one clear invariant surface form (or construction). Example:

> Learners of German initially maintain an SVO word order in all contexts, in spite of the fact that German word order is not so consistent (Clahsen, 1984).

The multifunctionality principle: (a) where there is clear evidence in the input that more than one form marks the meaning conveyed by only one form in the interlanguage, try to discover the distribution and additional meaning (if any) of the new form; (b) where there is evidence in the input that an interlanguage form conveys only one of the meanings that the same form has in the input, try to discover the additional meanings of the form in the input. Example:

The one-to-one principle means that learners of English will often start with just one form for negation (e.g. *no the dog; he no go*), but once this form has been incorporated into their interlanguage, they are able to notice other forms and differentiate the environment in which they occur.

The principle of formal determinism: when the form–meaning relationship is clearly and uniformly encoded in the input, the learner will discover it earlier than the other form–meaning relationships and will incorporate it more consistently within his interlanguage system. In short, the clear, transparent encoding of the linguistic feature in the input forces the learner to discover it. Example:

> If we consider the example of English negation above, the learner will be driven from the use of a single form to the use of multiple forms because the distribution of such forms in English is transparent (e.g. *don't* is used in preverbal environments, *not* with noun phrases, adverbs, etc.).

The principle of distributional bias: if both X and Y can occur in the same environments A and B, but a bias in the distribution of X and Y makes it appear that X only occurs in environment A and Y only occurs in environment B, when you acquire X and Y, restrict X to environment A and Y to environment B. Example:

> In Spanish, punctual verbs (e.g. *break*) occur mainly in the preterite form, and verbs of states (e.g. *know*) mainly in the imperfect form, making the preterite much more common in the input. Second language learners of Spanish reproduce this bias, and acquire the preterite form earlier.

The relevance principle (based on Bybee, 1985, and presented by Slobin, 1985, in the following way): if two or more functors apply to a content word, try to place them so that the more relevant the meaning of a functor is to the meaning of the content word, the closer it is placed to the content word. If you find that a notion is marked in several places, at first mark it only in the position closest to the relevant content word. Example:

> Andersen's (1991) research on the second language acquisition of Spanish verb morphology broadly supports the prediction that aspect should be encoded before tense, as it is most relevant to the lexical item it is attached to (the verb), and that tense would be next since it has wider scope than aspect, but is more relevant to the verb than subject–verb agreement, which would be last.

The transfer to somewhere principle: a grammatical form or structure will occur consistently and to a significant extent in the interlanguage as a result of transfer if and only if (1) natural acquisitional principles are consistent with the first language structure or (2) there already exists within the second language input the potential for (mis)generalization from the input to produce the same form or structure. Furthermore, in such transfer preference is given in the resulting interlanguage to free, invariant, functionally simple morphemes that are congruent with the first and second languages (or there is congruence between the first language and natural acquisitional processes) and [to] morphemes [which] occur frequently in the first and/or the second language. Example:

> Unlike English learners of French who follow English word order for the placement of French clitic (i.e. unstressed) object pronouns and produce sentences like *Camille lit le* (target: *Camille le lit;* Camille **it** reads), French learners of English do not follow the French word order for clitic placement (i.e. they never produce *Camille it reads* in English as a second language). This is because no model for such transfer is available in the input, whereas French provides a model for post-verbal placement of objects in the case of lexical noun-phrases (as in *Camille lit le journal;* Camille reads **the newspaper**).

The relexification principle: when you cannot perceive the structural pattern used by the language you are trying to acquire, use your native language structure with lexical items from the second language. Example:

> Japanese learners of English sometimes use Japanese SOV word order in English in the early stages, with English lexical items.

In a detailed review of both first and second language acquisition of tense and aspect, Andersen and Shirai conclude that the data can best be explained by just three principles (relevance, congruence and one-to-one):

> Learners restrict use of verb morphology such as past/perfective, progressive, and imperfective to a small subset of the verbs to which the morphology could be attached in fluent adult native speakers' language use. We attribute this early conservative use of verb morphology to adherence to (a) the Relevance principle (which guides learners to look for morphological marking relevant to the meaning of the verb), (b) the Congruence Principle (which guides learners to associate verb morphology with verb types most congruent with the aspectual meaning of the verb inflection), and (c) the One to One Principle (which causes learners to expect each newly discovered form to have one and only one meaning, function, and distribution).
>
> (Andersen and Shirai, 1994, pp. 151–2)

What all the approaches we have reviewed so far in this chapter have in common is that they apply models of processing to the SLL context. They do not generally have a great deal to say about the linguistic system that learners are constructing. By and large, they leave the task of analysing the language rules underlying second language productions to linguists interested in the formal properties of those systems, that is, property theorists. What they are primarily interested in is the way in which the input is processed, given various constraints that operate on learners, and how these constraints change over time, that is, a transition theory. The 'emergentist' linguists we are going to review next do not make this distinction between the formal linguistic system and processing mechanisms; they believe the two grow together and are inextricably linked.

4.3 Connectionism

The **connectionist** (previously known as associationist) approach to learning has been around for some time, but advances in computer technology have given it a new breath of life. Since the mid-1980s especially, there has been a growing number of studies applying a connectionist framework to the general study of memory and learning. More recently, connectionism has been applied to SLL.

Connectionism, or parallel distributed processing likens the brain to a computer that would consist of **neural networks**: complex clusters of links between information nodes. These links or connections become strengthened or weakened through activation or non-activation, respectively. Learning in this view occurs on the basis of associative processes, rather than the construction of abstract rules. In other words, the human mind is predisposed to look for associations between elements and create links between them. These links become stronger as these associations keep recurring, and they also become part of larger networks as connections between elements become more numerous. When applied to the learning of language, connectionism claims that learners are sensitive to regularities in the language input (i.e. the regular co-occurrence of particular language forms) and extract probabilistic patterns on the basis of these regularities. Learning occurs as these patterns become strengthened by repeated activation.

> Connectionism attempts to develop computationally explicit parallel distributed processing (PDP) models of implicit learning in well-understood, constrained, and controllable experimental learning environments. The models allow the assessment of just how much of language acquisition can be done by extraction of probabilistic patterns of grammatical and morphological regularities. Because the only relation in connectionist models is strength of association between nodes, they are excellent modelling media in which to investigate the formation of associations as a result of exposure to language.
>
> (N.C. Ellis and Schmidt, 1997, p. 153)

An example of a connectionist network is shown as Fig. 4.3.

The connectionist approach differs strikingly from the accounts we have reviewed so far, as it does not believe that the learning of rules underlies the construction of linguistic knowledge, but rather that this happens through the associative processes we have just described. This goes against much that the linguists we have been reviewing up to now believe in, namely that language is a set of modules (syntax, morphology, phonology) with an accompanying lexicon, and that the task facing language learners is to extract rules from the language around them in order to build up their own mental set of those rules, as well as learning the lexicon which will then fit into the slots made available by the grammar. Saying, as connectionists do, that learning is not rule-governed, but is based on the construction of associative patterns, is a fundamental departure from most currently held views. Connectionism is seen as an alternative to symbolic accounts of language acquisition: rule-like behaviour does not imply rule-governed behaviour (N.C. Ellis, 1996b, p. 364).

Connectionism is thus the computer modelling of the constructivist or emergentist views of language learning that we introduced at the beginning of this chapter. It is a transition theory that aims to explain how these associative patterns emerge in learners. Whereas property theories characterize the language that learners develop, connectionism attempts to model the dynamic acquisition of that language. If language learning is all about

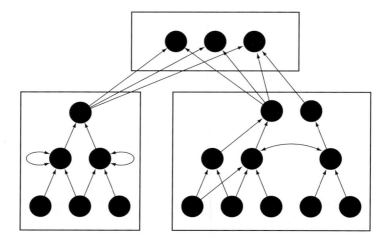

Fig. 4.3   A complex network consisting of several modules (arrows indicate the direction of flow of excitation or inhibition) (*Source*: Elman *et al.*, 1996, p. 51)

the building of billions of associations and the extraction of patterns resulting in rule-like behaviour, how do these come about? Connectionism provides the computational tools for exploring the conditions under which
emergent properties arise (N.C. Ellis, 2003, p. 84).

4.3.1   Connectionism and first language acquisition

Researchers working within this framework have been testing their
hypotheses by designing computer models that are analogous to the kind of
neural networks which become established within the human mind as
learning takes place. These models create networks on the basis of the input
(linguistic or otherwise) they receive. The computer is then presented with
novel input, and the output of the model is compared to natural (human)
output. Let us illustrate what is meant with a concrete example, taken from
the pioneering work of Rumelhart and McClelland (1986).

These researchers devised a computer model to simulate learning the
regular versus irregular past tense in English, on the basis of associative
patterns. It is well known that children go through three phases in the
acquisition of irregular past tenses in English. In a first phase, they produce irregular past tense forms correctly (e.g. *went, fell*); in a second
phase, they overgeneralize the regular past tense ending to irregular verbs
(e.g. *goed, falled*); in a third phase they supply irregular forms correctly
again. This pattern is usually explained by claiming that children start by
rote-learning a few common past-tense forms (many of the common
verbs in early child language are irregular, e.g. *go, eat, fall, throw, sleep,
come, give*, etc.), and only later extract from the linguistic input the rule
that the past tense is most commonly formed by adding *-ed* to the verb.
Children then apply this general rule to all verbs indiscriminately, before
being able to allow exceptions.

Rumelhart and McClelland's simple learning model involved a computer
that generalized on the basis of stored examples. This reproduced closely
the way in which children acquire the past tense in English, including the
typical U-shaped curve of learning for irregular verbs. Although this early
model was criticized (Pinker and Prince, 1988), it has given rise to many
further studies in recent years, which have addressed some of the criticisms
(MacWhinney and Leinbach, 1991; Plunkett and Marchman, 1991; N.C.
Ellis and Schmidt, 1997; Hahn and Nakisa, 2000). The application of the
model has now also been extended beyond the remit of morphology, to
phonology, prosody, syntax and the lexicon (Elman *et al.*, 1996; N.C. Ellis,
1998, 2003; Plunkett, 1998; Allen and Siedenberg, 1999; MacWhinney,
1999; Christiansen and Chater, 2001).

4.3.2   Connectionism and second language acquisition

In second language acquisition, there are far fewer studies using the connectionist model to date, but a number of researchers have explored connectionism recently (Sokolik, 1990; Soklik and Smith, 1992; N.C. Ellis and Schmidt, 1998; Gair, 1998; Kempe and MacWhinney, 1998; MacWhinney, 1999, 2001; Taraban and Kempe, 1999; Ellis, 2001, 2003). We will concentrate here on two studies: that of Sokolik and Smith (1992) and that of N.C. Ellis and Schmidt (1997). For fuller reviews of this approach, *see* Ellis (2003) or chapters in Robinson (2001).

Sokolik and Smith (1992) investigated the assignment of gender to French nouns using a connectionist framework. In French, nouns are marked for gender, either masculine or feminine, with little semantic basis for gender assignment. However, noun endings represent a good clue to their gender, with, for example, nouns ending in *-ette* or *-tion* being feminine, and nouns ending in *-eur* or *-on* being masculine. Although noun endings are not a foolproof way of determining gender, they are nonetheless predictive, and young French-speaking children have been shown to assign gender to novel nouns as well as nonsense nouns on the basis of these regularities. In fact, children learning French as a first language do not seem to have much problem with gender assignment, which is thought to be acquired by the age of three (Clark, 1985). Gender assignment for second language learners, on the other hand, seems to remain problematic for a substantial period of time.

Sokolik and Smith devised a computer-based connectionist-type network model that learnt to identify correctly the gender of a set of French nouns. The model was then able to generalize from that learning experience and assign gender to previously unstudied nouns with a high degree of reliability. The model assigned gender by relying solely upon the orthography of the noun itself, to the exclusion of any other clues such as adjective or pronoun agreement, or semantic clues. In other words, the computer seemed to be able to assign gender accurately to novel nouns on the basis of the regularities (associative patterns) it had 'observed' in the input.

Learning in this view is thought to take place as the strength of given interconnections between nodes increases as the associative patterns are repeated over time. What is important to remember from this type of account is that the learner does not extract rules and then apply them (in this case the fact that gender assignment in French is not random but obeys certain orthographic and phonetic rules), but merely registers associative patterns that become strengthened with use:

We have outlined a relatively simple model that is capable of learning the gender of a large set of French nouns. It accomplished this without relying on article or adjective agreement, without knowledge of noun meaning, and without being programmed with (or inferring) explicit morphological or phonological rules of gender formation. Rather it 'learned' that certain features (in this case, orthographic) of French nouns are correlated with particular genders. Based only on this information, it was able to classify at a high rate of reliability the gender of nouns it had never before encountered. These studies provide evidence that gender can in principle be assigned during relatively low-level perceptual analysis without the application of explicit rules.

(Sokolik and Smith, 1992, p. 50)

The difference between first language learners, who do not seem to encounter problems with gender assignment, and second language learners, who persist in making gender assignment errors at advanced stages, is explained by changing two of the variables in the model. First, whereas the computer model assigned first language learners a zero state of connectivity (they have not formed any associative patterns yet and are therefore starting as a blank slate), it assumed that second language learners come to the task with some pre-existing pattern of connectivity that interferes with the task in hand. Second, this particular model also assigned a lower learning rate to second language learners, to reflect the researchers' belief that children seem to be better language learners than adults. With these variables built into the programme, Sokolik and Smith were able to simulate the development of gender assignment in both first and second language learning.

If the acquisition of gender assignment can be explained quite successfully using a connectionist model (though *see* Carroll, 1995, for a critique), it could be argued that it is not representative of rules of grammar generally. The computer had only to assign gender; the accompanying agreement features were not part of the study. If we now turn to (arguably more complex) morphosyntactic rules, what have connectionist models to offer?

N.C. Ellis and Schmidt (1997) investigated the claim made by Rumelhart and McClelland (1986) that a connectionist model reproduced very closely the way in which children acquire the past tense in English (discussed above) and the counter claim made by Pinker (1991), who argued that only irregular verbs are retrieved from an associative memory (the kind of connectionist network we have described). For Pinker, regular verbs are produced as a result of a suffixation rule (i.e. a symbolic rule rather than merely an associative pattern).

Using an artificial language in a laboratory situation, so that exposure and proficiency could be monitored closely, N.C. Ellis and Schmidt (1997) investigated the adult acquisition of plural morphology. Half of the plurals were regular, that is, shared the same affix, and half were irregular. Frequency was also a variable built into the study, with half the plurals being five times more frequent than the other half. Exactly the same input was fed into a simple connectionist model. They found that the results obtained from their connectionist model accurately mirrored their human data, and they conclude that associative mechanisms are all that are needed in order to explain the acquisition of plural morphology, and that we do not need the hybrid system suggested by Pinker (1991) in which the regular would be rule-governed and the irregular associative: 'These effects are readily explained by simple associative theories of learning. It is not necessary to invoke underlying rule-governed processes' (N.C. Ellis and Schmidt, 1997, p. 152).

4.4   Evaluation of cognitive approaches to second language learning

In conclusion, it is clear that a wealth of second language studies have been carried out recently from the angle of cognitive psychology. The methods used as well as the questions asked differ substantially from more traditional second language acquisition studies which stem directly from the field of linguistics, or from a more socially-oriented approach.

4.4.1   The scope and achievements of cognitive approaches

There is no doubt that we have learnt much from cognitive approaches about the role of processing mechanisms in second language acquisition. We understand better, for example, how these mechanisms develop over time, or why fossilized structures can be so difficult to eradicate, even if we do not understand yet why some structures fossilize and not others.

The scope of cognitivists' research varies widely, from the application of general models of language processing, to studies using computers in order to simulate the acquisition of discrete grammatical phenomena. More generally, as we have seen in the introduction, some cognitivists see their field of enquiry as being specifically the processing mechanisms and how they develop in SLL. They believe that we also need a property theory in order to understand the linguistic system, which will complement the transition theory they are developing. Others, adopting an emergentist or connectionist view of learning, see their field of enquiry as the whole process of language learning, as they do not separate the development of processing from the development of the linguistic system.

4.4.2   Cognitivists' view of language

Processing theorists we have reviewed do not say much about the nature of language itself; they are concentrating on the study of the processing constraints operating in second language acquisition. It does not mean to say that they do not incorporate a linguistic theory in their overall model of second language acquisition, such as Lexical Functional Grammar in the case of Pienemann, or Universal Grammar in the case of Towell and Hawkins.

However, as we have just seen, the view of language in emergentism or connectionism differs fundamentally from views of language reviewed so far. Learning in this view occurs on the basis of associative processes, rather than the construction of abstract rules. Connectionists believe that the human mind is predisposed to look for associations between elements and create neural links between them. These links become stronger as these associations keep recurring, and they also become part of larger networks as connections between elements become more numerous. Language in this view is seen as a set of probabilistic patterns that become strengthened in the brain of the learner through repeated activation.

Methodologically, connectionist researchers have tended to rely on controlled laboratory research, often involving experiments with artificial languages or small fragments of real languages. This is partly because computer simulations are only able to deal with small, well-contained samples, and also because the connectionist approach stems directly from the field of psychology, where such a degree of control is common. From one point of view, that of control of extraneous variables, this can be seen as an advantage:

> Laboratory research offers a number of important advantages over research conducted with L2 learners in classrooms or with uninstructed, so-called natural learners: control of the language and the target structures to be learned, control of exposure, control of instruction (explanation), control of tasks, and control of response measurement.
>
> (Hulstijn, 1997, pp. 139–40)

However, the controlled nature of laboratory research can also be seen as a disadvantage. It is questionable how far you can isolate variables that would be interacting in a natural context, and therefore how far results obtained in that way actually mirror what happens in real life with real languages. Moreover, because of the highly controlled nature of laboratory experiments, the questions being asked tend to be very specific and local, with the resulting danger of ignoring how different aspects of the learning process might interact. Connectionists have tended to concentrate on simple, discrete, language phenomena: 'However, the more controlled the design and the more specific the learning task, the more we bear the risk of not studying L2 acquisition any more, but only participants' capacity to carry out some kind of cognitive puzzle' (De Graaff, 1997, p. 272).

Having said that, studies recently have been drawing on corpus linguistics in order to estimate the input 'real' learners learning 'real' languages have had, and to compare their performance to that of a connectionist simulation of the acquisition of some properties (e.g. in German and Russian: Kempe and MacWhinney, 1998). Nonetheless, connectionist models overall have often been criticized for their rather clinical and fragmentary view of language, ignoring social and linguistic phenomena.

Moreover, connectionist models are not in a position yet to adequately explain what the mental grammar of the learner consists of, and what constrains learners' hypotheses about the language system, although they are clearly attempting to do just that. But at the moment, the developmental route followed by second language learners, or the acquisition of highly complex linguistic phenomena, are not convincingly explained by such approaches.

4.4.3   Cognitivists' view of language learning

As we have seen throughout this chapter, cognitivists investigate primarily the development of processing in second language learners. In order to do that, psychologists make use of laboratory techniques to measure accurately performance indicators such as length of pauses, priming effects, etc. Linguists, on the whole, tend to apply linguistic analysis techniques to the study of second language learners' productions or intuitions, though they tend to consider language outside of the mechanisms underlying its use.

Both methodologies have their advantages and disadvantages. We have seen earlier how laboratory studies have the benefit of being able to control in a precise way the variables under study. This very fact can also be seen as a disadvantage, as it assumes one can study discrete aspects of language in isolation, without taking account of the interaction between the different language modules.

The ultimate goal of any second language acquisition model, that of better understanding the second language acquisition process overall, has undoubtedly been much enriched by studies of the cognitive processes involved. It is clear that our understanding of how second language learners use and process language has greatly increased, and the development of fluency for example has received well-deserved attention. Cognitive approaches have also been able to enlighten us on what processes are involved in the speeding up of the acquisition process; we should in due course be able to draw pedagogical implications from such findings.

Eventually, both linguistic and cognitive theories will surely feed into a comprehensive model of second language acquisition, encompassing both linguistic and cognitive development.

4.4.4   Cognitivists' view of the language learner

Cognitivists, like the linguists reviewed in Chapter 3, are concerned primarily with the individual, and do not view the learner as a social being. But they are interested in the learner's mind, as a processor of information rather than in the specificity of the linguistic information it contains.

Additionally, a distinctive feature of connectionist approaches resides in the links they attempt to build with neurology and even neurobiology. Connectionists believe that we have to study learning within the actual architecture of the brain, and make use of neurological information. As Ellis and Schmidt put it:

> The advantages of connectionist models over traditional symbolic models are that (a) they are neurally inspired, (b) they incorporate distributed represen-tation and control of information, (c) they are data-driven with prototypical representations emerging as a natural outcome of the learning process rather than being prespecified and innately given by the modellers as in more nativist cognitive accounts, (d) they show graceful degradation as do humans with language disorders, and (e) they are in essence models of learning and acquisition rather than static descriptions. Two distinctive aspects of the con-nectionist approach are its strong emphasis on general learning principles and its attempt to make contact with neurobiological as well as cognitive phenomena.
>
> (N.C. Ellis and Schmidt, 1997 p. 154)

We will certainly hear a lot more about processing approaches to second language acquisition. Recent models have made well-developed proposals for integrating linguistic and cognitive dimensions, even if much research remains to be done (Towell and Hawkins, 1994; Pienemann, 1998; Carroll, 2000). The connectionist approach is an exciting and promising new avenue for research. Especially within the field of first language acquisition, there have been important developments recently. However, at present, the models which have been applied to the study of second language acquisition have tended to be concerned with the acquisition of relatively simple (and often artificial) data, somewhat removed from the richness and complexity of natural languages and language learning contexts, and much more research needs to take place before connectionist simulations of SLL give us a more comprehensive picture of the processes involved in learning in real situations.

5
Functional/pragmatic perspectives on second language learning

You won't understand adult language acquisition if you don't understand discourse activity.

(Perdue and Klein, 1993, p. 263)

5.1 Introduction

Where do grammars come from? In Chapter 3, we encountered theorists whose main concern was this particular question, and who have argued that because of its complexity as a formal system, the natural grammar of human language cannot be learnt in its entirety, from scratch, by each individual human being, but must at least to some extent be innate. We went on to examine the work of a range of second language acquisition researchers who see as their central interest the understanding of how this inbuilt system and associated processing mechanisms develop in second language learners.

In this chapter, we review the work of researchers who adopt a broadly functional or pragmatic approach to the study of learners' interlanguage development. Rather than making the formal linguistic system their starting point, these researchers are centrally concerned with the ways in which second language learners set about making meaning, and achieving their personal communicative goals. They argue that the great variety of interlanguage forms produced by second language learners cannot be sensibly interpreted unless we pay attention also to the speech acts that learners are seeking to perform, and to the ways they exploit the immediate social, physical and discourse context to help them make meaning. Further, it is argued that these meaning-making efforts on the part of learners are a driving force in ongoing second language development, which interacts with the development of formal grammatical systems.

The reader should note that the term 'functional' is being used here in a different sense from the way it is used in recent Chomskyan theory, discussed in Chapter 3. Here, we follow the definition offered by Rispoli (1999, p. 222), 'Functionalism in linguistics is the explication and explanation of grammatical structure in which semantic and pragmatic constructs are integral'. Theoretical linguists who have adopted this perspective in varying degrees include Givón (1979, 1985), Halliday (1985) and Van Valin (1992). These particular 'functionalist' linguists are mentioned here because they have all taken a serious interest in language acquisition, and we will see some of their influence on second language learning (SLL) work later in the chapter. (It should be noted that the chapter does not deal with the development of second language pragmatics, which are considered independently from the development of second language grammar; these are surveyed in detail by Kasper and Rose, 2003.)

We begin the chapter with a brief consideration of the place of this kind of functionalist analysis in research on first language acquisition. Next, we examine some small-scale functionalist case studies of SLL, selected to illustrate key issues and principles of this approach. We then review a major research programme of the European Science Foundation, which examined SLL by adult immigrants in a range of European countries, and look at some recent studies that have followed more focused lines of inquiry into the development of interlanguage means for encoding the notion of 'past time'. Lastly, we evaluate the overall contribution so far of this tradition to our understanding of second language development.

5.2   Functional perspectives on first language development

Researchers studying child language have been interested for many years in the meanings that children are trying to convey, the possible relationship between developments in children's messages and developments in the formal systems through which they are expressed. Table 5.1 is drawn from one of the best-known 1970s child language studies, already referred to in Chapter 1 (Brown, 1973); here, we see children's two-word utterances being interpreted as expressing a range of semantic relations. For example, in Brown's data the utterance 'Daddy hit' is interpreted not as an expression of the formal syntactic relationship Subject + Verb, but as a combination of semantic categories of 'Agent' (or 'doer') plus 'Action'. As the examples show, the child's language at this point is lacking in function words and overt morphological markers of case, tense, number, etc. This is one key reason why it has been suggested that formal categories devised to describe the mature adult system may not be useful at this developmental stage. Some researchers in this tradition have argued essentially 'that syntactic categories develop as prototypes based on semantic information' (Harley, 1995, p. 371). Others who believe that formal syntactic categories have an independent origin have nonetheless accepted that interactions between syntactic, semantic and pragmatic information are vital in driving forward first language acquisition (*see* survey by Ninio and Snow, 1999).

Budwig (1995) produced a useful survey of broadly functionalist approaches to the study of child language development. She brought together a wide range of perspectives on the relationship between form and function in child language, and on development in this relationship over time. She has divided them into four main 'orientations' (Budwig, 1995, pp. 3–13): cognitive orientation, textual orientation, social orientation and multifunctional orientation.

Table 5.1   Eleven important early semantic relations and examples

Relation	Example
Attributive	'big house'
Agent–Action	'Daddy hit'
Action–Object	'hit ball'
Agent–Object	'Daddy ball'
Nominative	'that ball'
Demonstrative	'there ball'
Recurrence	'more ball'
Non-existence	'all-gone ball'
Possessive	'Daddy chair'
Entity + Locative	'book table'
Action + Locative	'go store'

Source: Brown, 1973

5.2.1   Cognitive orientation

Cognitive orientation can be exemplified by the work of Slobin (1985), which we have already referred to in Chapter 4. Slobin proposes the existence of a 'basic child grammar', in which children construct their own form–function relationships to reflect a child's-eye view of the world. For example, Slobin suggests, on the basis of cross-linguistic comparisons regardless of the particular target language that is being acquired, that 'one of the opening wedges for grammar is the linguistic encoding of a scene in which an *agent* brings about a *change of state* in an *object*' (Budwig, 1995, p. 10).

5.2.2   Textual orientation

As far as textual orientation is concerned, 'the issue of central importance is the extent to which particular linguistic devices are employed to help organize stretches of discourse both intrasententially and across broader stretches of text' (Budwig, 1995, p. 11). At the level of discourse, functional linguists are interested in how both vocabulary and grammar (e.g. connectives such as *and/but/whereas*, deictic elements such as *this/that*, pronoun systems, etc.) are deployed to create textual cohesion across sequences of clauses and sentences (*see* Halliday 1985, Chapter 9). In child language studies, functionally oriented research concerned with textual matters has examined topics such as the systems used by older children to establish cohesion in narratives (Karmiloff-Smith, 1987). The following example is drawn from a study of children's gradual acquisition of the different discourse functions of determiners:

Time 1	C:	Isabelle gave a talk about her rabbit and Alexia will give a talk about the tortoise
	E:	About which tortoise?
	C:	. . . the tort . . . well, hers, and well . . . not only hers . . . well . . . the tortoises, about all the tortoises
Time 2	E:	You remember that Isabelle gave a talk about her rabbit and Alexia gave one about the tortoise?
	C:	Yes
	E:	About which tortoise?
	C:	About the animal, the tortoise (shrugs shoulders as if it were quite obvious)

(Karmiloff-Smith, 1979, pp. 222–3, author's translation from original French)

At Time 1, when child C is aged 7 years 9 months, she has difficulty distinguishing the deictic and generic functions of the definite article; by Time 2, when child C is aged 9 years 2 months, generic functions are used without any difficulty.

5.2.3   Social orientation

Functionalist child language research with a social orientation is interested in relationships between the development of children's formal language system, and aspects of their social world. Some of this work examines the speech acts that children perform, and their relationships with lexical or grammatical choices (*see* Ninio and Snow (1999, pp. 353–60) for a recent overview). For example, Deutsch and Budwig (1983) re-analysed some of the data gathered by Brown (1973), arguing that expressions involving first-person possessive determiners (*my pencil*) consistently expressed different speech acts from expressions involving the child's own name (*Adam pencil*) – the first group were **indicative** ('That's my pencil'), whereas the second group were **volitional** ('I, Adam, want a pencil').

Other work looks much more broadly at the social context within which children interact, and the types of speech events in which they are engaged, and seeks to link these wider influences to linguistic development. A striking example is the work of Ochs (1988), on the acquisition of Samoan, where she argues for a link between children's acquisition of inflectional morphology, and socially patterned variation in adults' usage. The specific example analysed by Ochs concerns the acquisition of ergative case marking.* In Samoan, ergative case marking is optional, and rare in women's domestic talk. Samoan children seem to acquire this feature much later than do children learning other ergative languages, such as Kaluli, for example. This social orientation on child language acquisition is revisited more fully in Chapter 8.

5.2.4   Multifunctional orientation

The functional approaches to child language studies that have been outlined briefly pay attention, respectively, to the relations between grammatical development and prototype events; between grammar, pragmatics and text organization; and between grammar and the social world. Budwig (1995, p. 13) cites the work of Gee or Gerhardt as an example of work on child language that seeks to integrate the study of these different sets of relationships in a multifunctional orientation (Gee and Savasir, 1985; Gerhardt, 1990). For example, Gerhardt studied the use of the forms *will*

---

*'Ergative' languages are those in which 'the subject of an intransitive verb [S] receives the same treatment (morphological and/or syntactic) as the object of a transitive verb [O], while the subject of a transitive verb [A] receives different treatment' (Van Valin, 1992, p. 16). Take for example, pairs of sentences such as:

1   *The boy [A] opened the door [O]*
     Subject + Transitive verb + Object
2   *The door [S] opened*
     Subject + Intransitive verb

In an ergative language, O and S (in our two sentences, 'the door') will be marked with the same case ('ergative'), while A ('the boy') will be marked with a different case ('absolutive'). This contrasts with 'accusative' languages (such as Russian, for example), where A and S are marked with the same 'nominative' case, and O is marked with a different case ('accusative').

and *gonna* by three-year-old children, and argues that they are used in different discourse contexts, to express different speech acts:

> *Gonna* appears in discourse in which the children were planning and organising; it implies a more distant intention to act in a particular way. In contrast, *will* appears in the context of ongoing cooperative peer play, and refers to an immediate intentional stance.
>
> (Budwig, 1995, p. 13)

In her own longitudinal research, Budwig (1995) examines the self-reference forms (*I, me, my, Own Name,* etc.) used by a group of two-year-old children to express the semantic notions of **agentivity** and **control**, and also seeks to explain variability in usage in terms of the different pragmatic functions that are being expressed. For example, at 20 months, Megan used the three forms *I, my* and *Meggie* for self-reference; *my* was seen as expressing high agentivity (*my open that*), while *Meggie* expressed mid or low agentivity (*Meggie swinging*) and *I* was used typically for mental state verbs (*I wanna wear that*). There were also differences in usage that could be related to pragmatic function, for example *my* typically appeared in disputes over control of objects: (*my cups!* said as Megan grabs cups from another child). Over time, however, Megan extended the use of *I* to perform a wider range of functions and her use of *my* and *Own Name* became more target-like.

Budwig's 1995 study is typical of recent research on form–function relationships in child language. It has a number of characteristics that are also found in much SLL research in the functional tradition:

- Her data comprises longitudinal case studies of a small number of individual children; her prime concern is to trace the evolving patterns of relationships between language form and function over time.
- That is, her research is interested in the evolving developmental process, rather than in end states; acquisition is viewed as a slow, incremental business, and researchers are especially interested in the **first emergence** of new forms.
- She is concerned to link different levels of analysis of learner language (e.g. paying attention to intonation as a signal of pragmatic function) and she is concerned to collect data from a variety of social settings, for example peer interactions as well as caretaker–child interactions, in the interest of accessing a wide range of pragmatic functions.

In conclusion, Budwig reviews possible factors that may drive children forward to continually reorganize their systems of form–function relationships along the documented developmental path: linguistic maturation; cognitive development; encounters with target input; and communicative need. As yet, she argues, child language data do not offer definitive support to any one theoretical position: 'the specific mechanisms guiding the reorganization process are . . . quite vague' (Budwig, 1995, p. 197). We will review below the efforts of functionalist SLL researchers to address the same fundamental problem.

5.3   Early functionalist studies of second language learning

In Chapter 2, we have already reviewed the emergence during the 1970s of the concept of **interlanguage** in second language research (Corder, 1967; Selinker, 1972). This involved a major shift away from viewing learner language essentially as a defective version of the target language, or as a mixture of first and second language, as the earlier tradition of **contrastive analysis** had done, towards viewing it as an organic system with its own internal structure.

5.3.1   Pragmatic vs syntactic modes of expression

Within interlanguage research, functionalist approaches to the study of second language communication and development soon appeared. Dittmar (1984) presents a re-analysis of data collected for an earlier, grammar-oriented study of adult first-language Spanish migrants' second language of German. This is a cross-sectional study of learners at a very elementary level, who make little use of the morphology of standard German, and typically express semantic concepts like temporality and modality either lexically or through contextual inference, rather than through grammatical encoding.

For example, the following learner utterance, involving code switching between German and Spanish (in parentheses), was interpreted in context as expressing a promise:

> *Ich morgen /a/ España /y/ sage bei dir: zuruck España, eine /botella de coñac/ bei dir*
> I tomorrow to Spain and say with you: back Spain, one bottle of cognac with you
> 'I am going to Spain tomorrow and promise to bring back a bottle of cognac for you'
>
> (after Dittmar, 1984, p. 243)

Here, the only explicit reference to future time is expressed in the lexical item *morgen* (tomorrow); modality and the notion of 'promising' have to be inferred from context; the inflected second-person pronoun *dir* seems to be produced as part of an unanalysed chunk, *bei dir*, etc. Dittmar argues that the interpretation of data like this is helped by the theoretical distinction drawn by Givón (1979) between pragmatic and syntactic 'modes of expression'. Givón has argued that both informal speech and learner speech (whether first or second language) convey meaning through a relatively heavy reliance on context, whereas more formal styles of language rely on more explicit language coding, with reduced dependence on contextual meaning. For Givón, these **pragmatic** and **syntactic** 'modes' are the ends of a continuum, rather than discrete categories; he interprets language acquisition, language change and language variation in terms of movement along this continuum.

Table 5.2 shows the main features of the pragmatic and syntactic modes proposed by Givón. Dittmar (1984) argues that the conversational talk of his elementary adult learners shows many characteristics of the pragmatic mode. In particular, he argues that their utterances are typified by a **theme–rheme** (or topic–comment) structure, delineated by a single intonation curve, rather than by a grammar-based subject–predicate structure. Typical examples from his German interlanguage data are:

ich alleine – nicht gut
I alone – not good

immer arbeite – nicht krank
always work(ing) – not ill

ich vier Jahre – Papa tot
I four years – father dead

Table 5.2   Pragmatic and syntactic modes of expression

Pragmatic mode	Syntactic mode
Topic–comment structure	Subject–predicate structure
Loose conjunction	Tight subordination
Slow rate of delivery (under several intonation contours)	Fast rate of delivery (under a single intonation contour)
Word order is governed mostly by one *pragmatic* principle: old information goes first, new information follows	Word order is used to signal *semantic* case functions (though it may also be used to indicate pragmatic–topicality relations)
Roughly one-to-one ratio of verbs to nouns in discourse, with the verbs being semantically simple	A larger ratio of nouns over verbs in discourse, with the verbs being semantically complex
No use of grammatical morphology	Elaborate use of grammatical morphology
Prominent intonation-stress marks the focus of new information; topic intonation is less prominent	Very much the same, but perhaps not exhibiting as high a functional load, and, at least in some languages, totally absent

(Source: Givón, 1979, p. 98)

However, Dittmar's analysis in this early study was somewhat impressionistic, and the issue of how learners' utterances might move on from topic–comment structure to conventional target language sentence syntax was not addressed in detail. Altogether, although this study appealed to the theoretical framework of Givón, by showing that learners start at the pragmatic end of the continuum, it did not yet offer any very rigorous test of it, as it does not tell us what happens after these very early stages. (In later work, e.g. that of the P-MoLL Project investigating modality in learner varieties of German, Dittmar adopted a longitudinal case study approach, and performed a variety of more detailed form-to-function and function-to-form analyses; *see* various papers in Dittmar and Reich, 1993.)

5.3.2   Form-to-function analysis

Some other early functionalist studies did take a longitudinal approach, for example the year-long case study conducted by Huebner (1983) of a Hmong first language speaker, Ge, learning English as a second language. Ge arrived as an adult in Hawaii with no English (but bilingual in two topic-prominent languages, Hmong and Lao) and was contacted within a few weeks by Huebner, who audio-recorded informal conversations with him at three-week intervals. Ge was working full time in a garden centre, and attended no language classes. Huebner studied a number of forms in Ge's interlanguage where development was apparent, all of them important for the management of information in discourse.

For example, Huebner studied the changing functions of the form *is(a)* in Ge's interlanguage, over time. This form served initially as a general marker for topic–comment boundaries, and developed over time into a copula (as in standard English). Initially, therefore, *is(a)* was used in many 'ungrammatical' environments:

ai werk everdei, + *isa woter da trii*
'As for the work I do everyday, it involves watering the plants' (Huebner, 1983, p. 74)

The course of development evident in Ge's use of the *is(a)* form was not straightforward. From using it frequently as a topic boundary marker, he moved to much less frequent use of the form, in both grammatical and ungrammatical environments, according to the norms of Standard English (SE). Finally, Ge 'gradually and systematically re-inserted the form in SE grammatical environments' (Huebner, 1983, p. 205), that is, where it performed the copula function.

Huebner describes similar patterns of development for the evolution of the functional distribution of the article form *da*. Thus, he identified all possible contexts for production of *da*, and examined its actual frequency distribution over time. This analysis showed that:

> Ge's use of the article *da* shifts from an almost SE one but one which is dominated by the notion of topic, to one in which the form marks virtually all noun phrases. From that point, Ge's use of *da* is first phased out of environments which share no common feature values with SE definite noun phrases, followed by those environments that share one of the two feature values with SE definite noun phrases.
>
> (Huebner, 1983, p. 130)

Huebner's study thus provides further evidence that early learner utterances may be characterized by topic–comment organization; 'the rules governing various aspects of the interlanguage grammar were influenced by the structure of discourse' (Huebner, 1983, p. 203). He also documents the complexity of development in Ge's interlanguage, arguing that apparent variability is caused by gradual, systematic shifts in function for particular forms, which may include apparent 'backtracking' away from target language norms. Lastly, his study illustrates the need to pay attention to more than one level of language to make sense of interlanguage development. In order to pinpoint the functions of the forms *isa* and *da*, his analyses begin at the level of discourse or pragmatics and move to an examination of syntax and morphology.

An important limitation of his study, however, lies in the fact that the languages in which Ge was already fluent (Lao and Hmong) are both topic-prominent languages. Therefore, Huebner recognizes that it is impossible to tell whether the topic–comment structure found in Ge's early English interlanguage is the product of first language transfer, rather than a more universal characteristic of learner language. Another limitation concerns the small number of sub-systems actually studied; Huebner (1983, p. 210) can only speculate on possible linkages across the interlanguage system as a whole. Finally, of course, Huebner's work has all the limitations of a single-subject case study (Huebner, 1983, p. 209).

5.3.3   Function-to-form analysis: a fuller test of Givón

Another longitudinal case study conducted by Sato (1990), working with two first-language Vietnamese boys Thanh and Tai, also drew on the theoretical contrast proposed by Givón between pragmatic and syntactic modes of expression. However, Sato was critical of much earlier work in this functionalist or textual tradition, on the grounds of vagueness in the operationalization and identification of topic–comment structures in learner language (Sato, 1990, pp. 29–39). Indeed, she questioned the opposition between topic–comment and subject–predicate patterns, which second language acquisition researchers have borrowed from Givón (*see* Table 5.2):

> Topic–comment structure, the most extensively studied feature to date, has proved difficult to analyze and the available results cannot be interpreted as strong evidence of the existence of topic–comment *as opposed to* subject–predicate structure. This is not to argue that topic–comment structure does not characterize the pragmatic mode. Rather, it seems to be the case that analysis has not gone very much beyond sentence-based, NP-focused quantification, where syntactic, semantic, and pragmatic dimensions of topic–comment structure have been inappropriately conflated.
>
> (Sato, 1990, pp. 45–6)

Sato argues that for the purposes of interlanguage research, Givón's framework must be adapted in a variety of ways. Her own study did not pursue the topic–comment problem further. Instead, it was designed to explore the extent to which her subjects' interlanguage moved from **parataxis** (adapted from Givón's 'pragmatic mode of expression') to **syntacticization** (from Givón's 'syntactic mode'). These concepts are re-defined by Sato (1990, pp. 51–2) as follows:

- Parataxis: extensive reliance on discourse-pragmatic factors in face-to-face communication and minimal use of target language (TL) morphosyntactic devices in expressing propositions. Discourse-pragmatic factors include shared knowledge between interlocutors, collaboration between interlocutors in the expression of propositions, and the distribution of propositional content over a sequence of utterances rather than within a single utterance.
- Syntacticization: the process through which the use of morphosyntactic devices in IL increases over time, while the reliance on discourse-pragmatic context declines.

Sato's two subjects were brothers in their early teens, who had arrived in the USA as 'boat people' and had been fostered in a white American family. They attended school, but received no specialist English as a second language instruction there. Over a period of 10 months, Sato collected informal conversational data from the boys at weekly intervals. An example of talk between Sato (C) and Thanh (Th), in Sato's phonemic transcription, is given below (Sato, 1990, p. 125):

Th1:   tudeị aị ga muvi ɪn də ɪn də sku /
        'Today [I *got*] a movie in school'
C: You saw a movie?
Th2:   tu au yæ
        '[For] two hours, yeah'
C: of what?
Th3:   muvi – ts əh (hʌv) yu si muvi / (1 sec. pause)
        '[A] movie – (unclear) you [seen this] movie?'
Th4:   ɔnli bɔn pipol æn deị faịt /
        'People only [made of bone] *were* fighting'
Th5:   pipol ɔnli bɔn
        'People [who were] only [made of] bone'
C: Skeletons?

The recorded speech of Thanh and Tai was divided into 'utterances' on the basis of phonological criteria ('an utterance being defined as a sequence of speech under a single intonation contour bounded by pauses', Sato, 1990, p. 58). To explore the nature and degree of parataxis or syntacticization, Sato concentrated on a **function-to-form** analysis of their IL talk. She first explored all means used by the boys to express **past time reference**, and second, examined the linguistic encoding of semantic **propositions**, both simple and complex. (A propositional utterance was defined as one that 'expressed at least one argument and a predication about that argument', Sato, 1990, p. 94.) We now look at how Sato applied this approach to the development of these two areas of grammar.

5.3.3.1   Thanh and Tai: the expression of past time reference

As far as past time reference was concerned, Sato found that over the 10 months, there was little development from a paratactic mode of expression in the direction of syntax. Throughout, the boys typically expressed past time either adverbially, or through inference from the discourse context. A few irregular past tense forms (*bought, came*) appeared in time, but the regular -*ed* inflection was never detectable.

Sato's findings are in line with many other studies, which show that inflected past-tense verb forms are slow to develop for naturalistic learners; 10 months was just too short a time for syntacticization to take place in this domain. (Ongoing research on the expression of past time has shown that this is an area where formal instruction can make a great difference to the rate of acquisition; *see* Section 5.6 below.) Sato points out how seldom the absence of formal past tense markers caused any communication difficulties for Thanh and Tai (i.e. there was little **communicative pressure** to include these). She also points out the necessity of a multi-level perspective on this issue; regular past-tense inflections were not phonologically very salient in the TL input that the boys were receiving. Another complication was the fact that in the boys' own speech, because of first language phono-logical influence, realizations of syllable-final consonant clusters remained distant from the English target.

5.3.3.2   Thanh and Tai: the encoding of propositions

As far as propositional encoding was concerned, Sato (1990, p. 93) hypoth-esized that parataxis would involve:

- a predominance of non-propositional speech (i.e. a large proportion of non-propositional utterances)
- a low proportion of multi-propositional utterances
- extensive reliance on interlocutor collaboration in the production of propositions
- little use of connective morphology in expressing inter-propositional relations.

On this dimension, syntacticization would appear through:

- an increase in propositional speech
- an increase in multi-propositional utterances
- a decrease in reliance on interlocutor collaboration
- an increase in the use of connective morphology (Sato, 1990, p. 93).

The actual results did not fit the expected pattern, however. From the beginning of the study, Thanh and Tai were found to be producing a high proportion of (single-) propositional utterances, with little need of scaffold-ing by their interlocutors; Sato attributes these findings to their relative 'cognitive maturity', compared with the younger subjects studied in first language acquisition research and some child second language acquisition research (such as Hatch, 1978). Multi-propositional utterances were rare, however, and simple juxtaposition was the most important means of linking them; both learners were only beginning to use a variety of logical connec-tors other than *and*. (Table 5.3 shows some examples of what Sato calls 'paratactic precursors' for various target language constructions, from the speech of Tai.)

Where multi-propositional utterances were produced, many of them involved a small set of memorized phrases or 'chunks' as the starting point. The expressions /ai dono, hi dono, ai tin, hi sei, yu sei/ (I don't know, he

Table 5.3   Paratactic precursors of different TL constructions (examples from Tai)

Precursors	Examples
Infinitival complement	hi wan mi go fɔtbæk he-want-me-go-fullback 'He wanted me to [play] fullback'
WH-complement	noʷ ai̯ pɪkɪdau̯? wʌt stɔri no-I-pick-it-out-what-story- ai̯ wa æn ši rid mi I-want-and-she-read-me 'No I pick out which story I want and she reads it to me'
Relative clause	tan hi sei̯ ə – də piβɫ dei̯ sɪktin dei̯ kæn go tu mvi aːr Thanh-he-say-the-people-they-sixteen-they- can-(?)-go-to-movie-R' 'Thanh says that people who are sixteen can go to R-rated movies'
Adverbial clause	wi wɔkin ai̯ sɔ də di dɛd we-walking-I-saw-the-deer-dead 'When we were walking, I saw the dead deer'

(*Source*: Sato, 1990, p. 111)

don't know, I think, he say, you say) were found in around 25% of all such utterances. Sato argues here that particular lexical–semantic items may form important 'entry points' to aspects of TL syntax, another example of the general need for multi-level analysis.

Though Sato's study is once more small scale, it has been treated at some length, because it raises a number of important theoretical issues for functionalist research in SLL:

- She critiques and seeks to clarify the Givón distinction between pragmatic and syntactic modes of expression (though her own predictions about the relationship between parataxis and syntacticization are not fully borne out).
- In her work on past time reference and propositional encoding, she offers a clear example of function-led analysis (in contrast with e.g. Huebner, who started with particular forms identified in the English interlanguage of his subject Ge, and tried to track the changing functions they expressed).
- She demonstrates important interrelationships between different levels of language (phonology, lexis and grammar), in particular highlighting the potential importance of particular chunks or lexical items as entry points into new syntactic patterns.

- She highlights the need to take account of second language learners' level of cognitive maturity, and offers a reminder of the limitations of conversational interaction as a 'driver' for syntactic development, because communication problems in this context can so routinely be solved through discourse–pragmatic means.

5.4   Functionalism beyond the case study: the European Science Foundation project

The functionalist research studies that we have reviewed up to this point have been small-scale case studies of one or two learners, and typically involving just one source language and one target language (Spanish–German, for Dittmar, 1984; Hmong–English, for Huebner, 1983; Vietnamese–English, for Sato, 1990). In small-scale work of this kind, the personal characteristics of the learner, as well as individual patterns of social encounters with the target language and its users, may affect the rate or route of second language development, and these individual effects are not 'averaged out'. In studies involving single pairs of languages, it is also not possible to determine how far the particular characteristics of the learner's interlanguage are the product of first language influence.

In this section we turn to a major project on the second language acquisition of adult migrants, which brought a functionalist perspective to bear on the problem of second language acquisition on a much larger scale. Authoritative overviews can be found in volumes authored or edited by the project directors (Klein and Perdue, 1992; Perdue, 1993a, 1993b, 2000). The project was funded from the European Science Foundation over a period of six years (1982–1988) and involved research teams in five European countries. These teams worked with groups of adult migrants, both men and women, who were acquiring one of five target languages (English, German, Dutch, French and Swedish). The migrants spoke a range of first languages, so that ten language pairs in all were explored, in the following pattern:

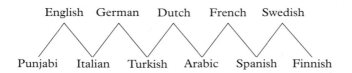

In the end, a total of 21 learners contributed substantially to the research. When selecting the participants, care was taken to avoid people currently attending language classes, as the aim was to study naturalistic development. The research teams kept in contact with the participants over a period of 2.5 years, by means of regular tape-recorded or video-recorded encounters. The participants undertook a varied range of tasks that were repeated regularly, including informal conversation, picture description, role-plays (e.g. of service encounters such as interviews with housing officials) and re-telling the story of a silent Charlie Chaplin film.

5.4.1   Aims and findings of the European Science Foundation project

One aim of the project was to produce a comprehensive account of both the rate and the route of naturalistic interlanguage development among adult learners. Another aim was to document the characteristics of native speaker–non-native speaker communication, and to identify internal and external factors on which the rate and degree of success of the acquisition process might depend. Perdue and Klein (1993, pp. 266–9) argue very explicitly for a functional approach, as the basis for a theory of second language acquisition that is independent of theoretical linguistics. Like Sato and others, they argue that only a broad pragmatic approach can capture the changing means used by the learner to express notions such as **temporality**. They therefore aim to provide a complete, contextualized account of the origins of more narrowly linguistic means for encoding time reference (verb morphology to do with tense and aspect). Similarly, they argue that structuring within learners' utterances has its basic origins in the wish:

> to refer to persons or objects . . . Speakers do not learn – for example – N-bar structure. They learn to refer with varying means under varying conditions, and *the result of this acquisitional process is what theoretical linguists like to call N-bar structure.*
>
> (Perdue and Klein, 1993, p. 269; emphasis in original)

Drawing especially on the Charlie Chaplin narratives, Klein and Perdue (1992) argue that through a functional analysis, three developmental levels in the basic organization of learners' utterances could be identified across all the linguistic groups that were studied. These were:

- Nominal utterance organization (NUO)
- Infinite utterance organization (IUO)
- Finite utterance organization (FUO).

The three types of utterance organization are distinguished as follows:

> In NUO, utterances are extremely simple and mainly consist of seemingly unconnected nouns, adverbs and particles (sometimes also adjectives and participles). What is largely missing in NUO is the structuring power of verbs – such as argument structure, case role assignment, etc. (hence, 'preverbal utterance organisation' might be a better term). This is different in IUO: The presence of verbs allows the learner to make use of the different types of valency which come with the (non-finite) verb; it allows, for example, a ranking of the actants of the verb along dimensions such as agentivity, and the assigning of positions according to this ranking. At this level, no distinction is made between the finite and non-finite component of the verb; such a distinction, which is of fundamental importance in all languages involved in this study, is only made at the level of FUO, which is not attained by all our learners. Transition from NUO to IUO and from there to FUO is slow and gradual, and the coexistence of several types of utterance organisation as well as backsliding is not uncommon.
>
> (Klein and Perdue, 1992, p. 302)

The infinite utterance organization level is exemplified in an extract from a Charlie Chaplin film retelling by one of the first-language Punjabi learners of English, when Charlie Chaplin escapes from a police van:

(1) *back door stand the policeman? right?*
(2) *she pushin policeman . . .*
(3) *charlie and girl and policeman put on the floor*
(4) *car gone . . .*
(5) *charlie get up first*
(6) *he say daughter/ sorry +*
     he pickup girl + charlie +
(7) *say 'go on*
(8) *this time nobody see you'*
(9) *policeman get up*
(10) *charlie hittin the head*

(Klein and Perdue, 1992, p. 76)

At all levels of proficiency, the European Science Foundation team argue that learner utterances were produced under a range of competing constraints, **pragmatic**, **semantic** and **phrasal**. In proposing pragmatic constraints on the form of learner utterances, Klein and Perdue revisit the issue of topic–comment structure, originally proposed by Givón as typical of the pragmatic communication mode. They re-label and redefine the concepts of topic and comment as **topic** and **focus**, as follows:

> Very often, a statement is used to answer a specific question, this question raising an alternative, and the answer specifying one of the 'candidates' of that

alternative. For example, the question 'Who won?' raises an alternative of 'candidate' persons – those who may have won on that occasion – and the answer specifies one of them. . . . Let us call 'focus' that part of a statement which specifies the appropriate candidate of an alternative raised by the question, and 'topic' the remainder of the answer.

(Klein and Perdue, 1992, pp. 51–2)

They also suggest that a pragmatic constraint operates on learner utterances, which provides that the focus element in an utterance should normally come last (e.g. *Charlie* [topic] *get up first* [focus]).

The main semantic constraint has to do with the notion of **control**. For verbs which associate with more than one 'actant' (or argument),

a semantic asymmetry is observed in that one actant has a higher, and the other(s) a lower degree of control over the situation . . . This asymmetry is a continuum ranging from clear 'agent–patient' relations down to cases of real or intended possession.

(Klein and Perdue, 1992, p. 340)

The proposed semantic constraint on utterance structure is that the actant with highest control (the 'controller') should be mentioned first. Again, in the Charlie Chaplin example, we see this exemplified for two-place verbs, such as *push, hit*.

These two constraints, **Focus last** and **Controller first**, are said to interact with phrasal constraints that basically specify the range of syntactic resources available at a given developmental level, and their permitted sequences. Of course, these constraints are sometimes in competition (as when the 'controller' is 'in focus'), and Klein and Perdue (1992, p. 303) see these conflicts as 'a major germ of development'.

5.4.2   Basic learner variety

An important descriptive claim of the European Science Foundation project is that all the learners in the study, irrespective of language background, developed a particular way of structuring their utterances that seemed to represent a 'natural equilibrium' between the various phrasal, semantic and pragmatic constraints. This they termed a 'basic variety', mainly characterized by a small number of phrasal patterns, which were:

(a) NP1 – V – (NP2)
(b) NP1 – Cop –   {NP2}
                              {Adj}
                              {PP}
(c) V – NP2.

In these phrases, NP2 must be lexical, whereas NP1 may be represented by a personal pronoun or an empty element. All patterns could be preceded or followed by adverbials of time or space; verbs are not inflected (i.e. are non-finite); 'Focus last' and 'Controller first' apply throughout. This basic variety was exemplified for English in the first Chaplin example above. Another example of basic variety German is given in another Chaplin example (here the source language is Italian). It must be emphasized that, lexis apart, the researchers see the basic variety as 'remarkably impermeable to the specifics of source language and target language' (Perdue and Klein, 1993, p. 257).

(1) *jetzt charlie komme in eine restaurant*
     'now Charlie come in a restaurant'
(2) *und essen*
     'and eat'
(3) *und wann is fertig + *chiama**
     'and when is ready + (calls)'
(4) *eine polizei komme*
     'a police come'
(5) *und charlie sage*
     'and Charlie say'
(6) *"bezahle"*
     ' "pay"'
(7) *charlie sage de polizei*
     'Charlie say the police'
(8) *"bezahle was alles ich esse"* [this is repeated, with slight variants]
     ' "pay what all I eat"'
(9) *und die polizei jetzt bezahle*
     'and the police now pay'
(10) *nicht charlie + die polizei*
     'not Charlie + the police'
(11) *und fort brauchen die charlie*
     'and away bring the Charlie'
(12) *und jetzt komme eine auto*
     'and now come a car'
(13) *und charlie *sale**
     and Charlie (leaves)'

                                    (Klein and Perdue, 1992, pp. 152–3)

5.4.3 Development beyond the basic variety

Before arriving at the basic variety, the learners have passed through a pre-basic variety, which is largely noun-based; one noun is related to another through topic and focus organization, and temporality, etc., are inferred from context. All learners in the study appeared to achieve the basic variety, and some then fossilized, that is, did not grammaticize their productions any further.

Others, however, did progress beyond the basic variety; the most important indicator of this development was the acquisition of 'finiteness', that is, the gradual appearance of verb inflections (tense marking preceding aspect marking, irregular forms preceding regular ones). Parallel developments were identified in the pronoun system, in the acquisition of focalization devices such as cleft structures (*is not the man steal the bread, is the girl*, Klein and Perdue, 1992, p. 321) and of means for subordination (*they think about one house for live together*, Klein and Perdue, 1992, p. 322). Some learners made considerable progress towards TL syntactic norms, and the researchers conclude that they can see no reason in principle why second language learners cannot achieve these in full. However, first language background was now seen as influencing at least the rate of progress beyond the basic variety, and possibly as affecting the degree of ultimate success.

But what drives development? If the basic variety is effective for everyday communication, why move beyond it? At varying times, the European Science Foundation researchers propose somewhat different answers to this question. When discussing the acquisition of temporality they review two possible factors promoting the gradual development of verb inflection:

- the subjective need to sound and to be like the social environment
- concrete communicative needs.

At this point, they argue that:

> Our observations about development beyond the basic variety clearly indicate that the first factor, the subjective need to sound and be like the social environment, outweighs the other factor, the concrete communicative needs. Learners try to imitate the input, irrespective of what the forms they use really mean, and it is only a slow and gradual adaptation process which eventually leads them tò express by these words and constructions what they mean to express in the target language.
>
> (Klein *et al.*, 1993, p. 112)

However, Perdue and Klein elsewhere give priority to 'communicative needs in discourse' (Perdue and Klein, 1993, p. 261); 'acquisition is pushed by the communicative tasks of the discourse activities that the learner takes part in' (Perdue and Klein, 1993, p. 262). This is argued not only with reference to the acquisition of the basic variety, but also with reference to some post-basic features. However, it is recognized that learners cannot attend to all their communicative needs at once, and that 'you have to work

new items and rules in' (Perdue and Klein, 1993, p. 265); at particular
times, particular interlanguage rules will become 'critical', that is, open to
change and reorganization.

(It is worth comparing the European Science Foundation team's views
on this point with those of Dittmar, who argues that the shift from pragmatic and lexical modes of expression towards grammaticalization is motivated primarily by the learner's long term need 'to look for economy and
efficiency in language use and to stabilize the expressibility in the basic
communicative functions'; Dittmar, 1993, p. 216.)

At the same time, Perdue and Klein accord the source language some
influence in determining the rate of development and degree of eventual
success, beyond the basic variety. The extent of daily contact with the target
language is also found to be generally predictive of rate of progress though
a pessimistic view is taken of the role of instruction; however, these 'extrin-
sic' factors are discussed in fairly general terms. (*See* Chapter 8 for reference to the distinctive ethnographic work of some sub-groups within the
ESF team; Bremer *et al.*, 1993, 1996.)

5.5   'Time talk': developing the means to talk about past time

Some functionalist research concentrates in more detail on particular areas
of meaning and the ways language learners at different stages of development attempt to express them. We have already noted the interest of functionalist researchers in the means used by learners to talk about time
(temporality, e.g. Dietrich *et al.*, 1995). Others have also studied the means
used by learners to talk about place (spatial location, e.g. Becker and
Carroll, 1997), to maintain coherent reference in discourse (e.g. Broeder,
1995) and to to express modality (such as degrees of certainty or uncer-
tainty (e.g. Giacalone Ramat, 1995; Salsbury and Bardovi-Harlig, 2000).
To exemplify this research this section looks more closely at the development of 'time talk', as described in a recent review by Bardovi-Harlig
(2000).

Drawing on the European Science Foundation and other studies,
Bardovi-Harlig concludes that interlanguage users of any language will pass
through three successive stages when talking about time:

● Pragmatic stage – to express time, learners rely on: scaffolding by interlocutors; inference from the context; contrasting events; chronological
  order.

- Lexical stage – to express time, learners rely on: temporal and locative adverbials (e.g. *now, then, here, there*); connectives (e.g. *and, and then*); calendric references (e.g. *May, Saturday*); verb lexis (e.g. *start, finish*).
- Morphological stage – learners start to use verb morphology (tense and aspect) as indicators of temporality.

Examples of the use of pragmatic and/or lexical means to express temporality are plentiful in the European Science Foundation data quoted earlier in this chapter, as well as in the conversations of Sato with Thanh and Tai (*see* Section 5.3.3). The following example, a diary entry written by Hamad, a first-language Arabic learner of English as a second language, is particularly rich in adverbials (highlighted with italics):

> Deat [Date]: Jan 27
> It was Saturday is the wecknd I welk up *at 10:00 o'clock morning* I tulk my shoer and *after that* I go to my frind *when I pe there* they sead they well go to the mool [shopping mall] and I go with they we go around in the mool around 2 hours *than* we go to the movei in the Selima [cinema] in the mool to waching a good movei *after* the movei we go Back to our Dorms we seat to gather in our Friend room we talking to gather *and after that* every Budy go to he's room me too I go back to my room that all.
>
> (Bardovi-Harlig 2000, p. 58)

Indeed, some researchers have argued that the pragmatic or lexical stages are sufficient for most everyday communicative purposes, and many studies of uninstructed learners show that they may never progress beyond the lexical stage (Dietrich *et al.*, 1995).

Learners are considered by Bardovi-Harlig and others to have entered the morphological stage once examples of tense–aspect morphology are noted in their interlanguage utterances. This is called the 'emergence' of morphology, and does not necessarily mean that these forms are used accurately and consistently. Bardovi-Harlig (2000, pp. 111–13) lists four 'general principles' that have been found in studies of the emergence of verb morphology:

1. The acquisition of morphology is slow and gradual, and uninflected verb forms 'linger' in interlanguage.
2. Form often precedes function, that is, verb inflections may appear which to begin with do not seem to contrast in meaning or in function with other verb forms used at the same time.
3. Irregular morphology precedes regular morphology (e.g. irregular past forms such as English *went, came* appear ahead of forms such as *jumped, ended*).

4. Learners notice and use verbal suffixes to denote 'past' meanings, ahead of other means such as auxiliary verbs (e.g. use of a V-é form in place of the auxiliary plus past participle which make up the French passé composé).

Bardovi-Harlig also claims that tense and aspect morphology 'emerges' in interlanguage in regular sequences, which remain the same for particular target second languages, regardless of learners' first language background. Thus, for example, the order of emergence:

Past → past progressive → present perfect → pluperfect

was observed for second language English by Bardovi-Harlig (2000, pp. 169–) in a study including learners with Spanish, Korean and Japanese as first languages, and was also reported by Klein (1995) for first-language Italian learners of English. Finally, Bardovi-Harlig concludes that both observational and experimental studies show beneficial effects for instruction on the learning of second language tense and aspect morphology. However, her survey agrees with many others, in concluding that instruction is most effective when combined with positive motivation and 'input through L2 contact' (Bardovi-Harlig, 2000, p. 405); instructed learners still go through the same pragmatic and lexical stages as uninstructed learners, and acquire tense and aspect morphology in similar orders, though they may make faster progress and eventually reach a more advanced stage, with more extensive and accurate use of verb morphology.

5.6   The aspect hypothesis

One interesting developmental suggestion which links the learning of second language meaning and form is the so-called 'aspect hypothesis' (Andersen and Shirai, 1994). While grammatical aspect is commonly expressed through verb morphology (e.g. the English -*ing* form which marks progressive aspect), verbs can also be classified as possessing inherent lexical aspect, as part of their core meaning. In a well-known classification, Vendler (1967) proposed that verbs can be grouped into four types, according to their inherent aspect (examples after Salaberry, 1999):

- Statives (e.g. *to be, to have, to want*).
- Activities (e.g. *to run, to walk, to breathe*).
- Accomplishments (e.g. *to write a novel, to build a house*).
- Achievements (e.g. *to notice someone, to realize something, to reach the summit*).

The aspect hypothesis claims that 'first and second language learners will initially be influenced by the inherent semantic aspect of verbs or predicates in the acquisition of tense and aspect markers associated with or affixed to these verbs' (Anderson and Shirai, 1994, p. 133). Thus for example, Andersen (1991) has suggested that second language learners of Spanish will start to use the imperfect tense with verbs from the stative group, and will first of all use the preterite tense with achievement verbs.

The Aspect hypothesis has proved somewhat controversial, and Dietrich *et al.* (1995) say that the data from the naturalistic learners of the European Science Foundation project do not support it. However, numerous studies of classroom second language learners have produced results in line with the hypothesis. Thus, for example, Bayley (1994) found that Chinese first language learners of English as a second language were more likely to mark verbs for past tense if their meaning included an end point (e.g. transitive *sing a song*) than if it did not (e.g. intransitive *sing*). Salaberry (1999) found that post-beginner English first language learners of Spanish as a second language doing a narrative task were more likely to mark stative verbs as imperfect and accomplishment or achievement verbs as preterite, in line with Andersen's suggestions. Only the most advanced learners in Salaberry's study began to use verb tense more flexibly, to mark the speaker's viewpoint on the events making up the narrative.

5.7   Evaluation

What are the most important contributions of the functionalist tradition to our understanding of SLL?

5.7.1   The scope and achievements of the functionalist perspective

The functionalist tradition is well established in SLL theory. Its fundamental claim is that language development is driven by pragmatic communicative needs, and that the formal resources of language are elaborated in order to express more complex patterns of meaning. Functionalist research typically takes the form of naturalistic case studies of individuals or groups of learners; most often these have been adults in the early stages of second language learning, who are acquiring the language in informal environments rather than in the classroom. These studies have offered us numerous rich accounts of both the rate and route of naturalistic second language learning, at least in the early stages.

Functionalist reseachers vary, however, in the scope of their enquiries. Some have adopted a 'patch' approach, studying the use and evolution of selected second language forms, or the development of a second language within a semantic domain such as 'time' or 'space'. On the other hand, the European Science Foundation team has made quite strong claims for their proposed second language 'basic variety', which represents a proto-grammar stage that all learners should pass through. Below, we evaluate their contributions to understandings of the nature of interlanguage, the learning process and the language learner.

5.7.2 Functionalism and the nature of interlanguage

Rispoli (1999) argues that first language acquisition researchers have as yet made little systematic use of distinctively functionalist linguistic theory; instead, 'functionalist' first language acquisition researchers have simply given semantic and pragmatic considerations some role in the acquisition of (some parts of) formal linguistic systems. As we have seen, second language researchers have made some use of Givón's suggestions regarding information structure, in order to describe central underlying patterns in interlanguage utterances. Apart from this, Rispoli's comments arguably apply also to second language functionalist work such as the aspect hypothesis. The consensus among the European Science Foundation researchers, Bardovi-Harlig and others, that 'form precedes function', that is, that morphological forms appear in interlanguage ahead of any recognizable functional contrast in their use, reflects implicit acceptance of the at least partly autonomous nature of formal systems.

Descriptively, however, the functionalist tradition has added considerably to our understanding of interlanguage communication while the formal system is still in an underdeveloped state, and has made interesting suggestions about the interactions between formal and functional development. Functionalist researchers have demonstrated the wide range of devices (lexical and pragmatic as well as formal) which interlanguage users deploy in order to convey meaning. For example, the expanded treatment by functionalist researchers of the semantic notion of temporality has taken the study of how interlanguage users locate their utterances in time, well beyond a search for formal sequences in verb morphology development. The aspect hypothesis has suggested how learners may use overlaps in word meaning and morphological form as an entry point into various formal sub-systems of their target language.

Functionalist researchers have also drawn our attention to the issue of textual or discourse organization in learner language, and offered considerable evidence in support of the view that early learner varieties rely heavily on parataxis rather than on syntax in order to structure and express both individual propositions and inter-propositional relationships.

A continuing limitation on functionalists' characterization of interlanguage is that most attention has been paid to the earliest stages of development (the 'basic variety'). The interlanguage of more advanced learners has been explored thoroughly in some areas only (e.g. the development of reference to past time and the use of past-tense verb morphology surveyed by Bardovi-Harlig, 2000). The range of target languages investigated is also not very wide (most research has been done with Germanic or Romance languages) and the extent of influence of learners' first languages on post-basic varieties is not clear.

5.7.3   Functionalism on language learning and development

Functionalist researchers insist universally on the gradual nature of IL development and syntacticization, with learners working actively on only part of the system at any one time, but with possible reorganizational consequences that may spread widely through the system. At the same time, most functionalist researchers have so far adopted a 'patch' approach, working on overall utterance structure when studying the basic variety, or alternatively exploring development within a range of semantic and formal sub-systems (temporality, modality, space, pronouns, articles).

Linkages across these different sub-systems are not always clear, though functionalist researchers argue consistently for a multi-level approach to the analysis of IL data. Some valuable work has been done, for example demonstrating the role of intonation and prosody in demarcating utterances, or demonstrating how paratactic constructions mirror and prefigure their syntactic equivalents. The lexical level has also been studied, from the point of view of its relationship with the development of both morphology and syntax (e.g. Sato's speculations about the potential significance of items such as *think* and *know* for the development of subordination).

While their contribution at a descriptive level has been very strong and varied, however, the contribution of functionalist studies to the explanation of IL development has so far been limited. It has been clearly shown how effective a basic variety can be in meeting immediate communicative needs. But it is less clearly established that communicative need is the prime driver for syntacticization and development beyond the basic variety. As we have seen, even the European Science Foundation team wavers on this point, ultimately preferring 'social' explanations for morphological development. Sato articulates a number of reasons, grounded in close examination of the interactions in which her child learners were engaged, why communicative need might not be particularly effective in promoting syntactic development. Her suggestion, that the literacy demands of formal schooling might be more powerful, can be connected with Bardovi-Harlig's claims that instructed learners make more progress with the acquisition of tense and aspect morphology. But no distinctively functionalist explanation has been advanced, as to why instruction should be particularly beneficial for morphological development.

Functionalist research has also concentrated largely on the analysis of learners' interlanguage output, and has paid relatively less attention to input and even to interaction. There are some exceptions, mostly among those trying to provide functionalist explanations for the acquisition of tense and aspect morphology. Sato pays some attention to the formal features of input received by her subjects during data collection sessions, for example noting the rarity and lack of phonological saliency in interlocutor speech of regular past tense forms. Bardovi-Harlig notes the frequency in input of adverbial forms, and appeals to input processing theory (VanPatten, 2002; *see* Chapter 6) in suggesting that learners may therefore not need to notice or process verb morphology in the language that they hear. Conversely, Giacalone Ramat (1997) appeals to principles of frequency, salience and obligatoriness of morphology, in explaining different acquisitional patterns in cross-language studies. Andersen makes similar claims in respect to frequency patterns in input, when commenting on the acquisitional patterns associated with the aspect hypothesis.

As far as the European Science Foundation research is concerned, however, the main research team paid little attention to the details of input and interaction in which their subjects were engaged. An ethnographically oriented sub-group did provide very detailed commentaries on native speaker–non-native speaker interaction (Bremer *et al.*, 1993, 1996); however, their detailed commentaries on native speaker–non-native speaker interaction are concerned primarily with the immediate achievement of understanding, as we will see more fully below. They have not paid detailed or systematic attention to the emergence within interaction of new linguistic forms.

5.7.4   Functionalism on the language learner

Much functionalist research has concerned itself with naturalistic adult learners, acquiring a socially dominant TL in the workplace and other non-domestic settings. As we have seen, the driving forces promoting second language acquisition for such learners have been explained by the

European Science Foundation team as: (a) immediate communicative need and (b) a longer-term and more variable desire for social integration with the target language community. Functionalists have conducted extensive comparative cross-language research, but have been mainly interested in the discovery of universal rather than language-specific characteristics of the learning process, for example the emergence of the basic variety, or the development from pragmatic to lexical and morphosyntactic means of expression.

Functionalist research on the emergence of second language morphology has, however, concerned itself with instructed learners (e.g. the various studies reported in Bardovi-Harlig, 2000). These learners are seen as more successful in acquiring second language morphology, though functionalists generally agree that instruction works by increasing the rate of acquisition and pushing at least some learners further along the acquisitional route, rather than by altering the route of acquisition in any significant way. It is not however very obvious from a functionalist perspective why classroom learners should be more successful than uninstructed learners, as classroom communicative needs are often very reduced or indirect. It is possible that classroom discourse forces second language learners to attend to the communicative value of formal items such as tense and aspect morphology, which are non-salient or communicatively redundant in everyday discourse. But this idea has not been followed up systematically by any of the research groups whose work has been surveyed in this chapter. We will meet this proposal again in our survey of input and interaction theories in Chapter 6.

6

Input and interaction in second language learning

6.1 Introduction

In earlier chapters of this book, we have reviewed a range of current perspectives on second language learning (SLL) that are concerned primarily with understanding language learners as autonomous individuals, rather than making sense of learners' engagement with their social and linguistic environments.

In the next three chapters, we progressively turn our attention to theorists who view language learning in more social terms, and who are more centrally concerned to explain the role of language use in interlanguage development. In this chapter, we examine research that focuses directly on the role of environmental language in promoting SLL, in the shape of second language input received by the language learner, second language output produced by the learner and second language interaction between the learner and some other conversational partner. For the most part, this 'interactionist' perspective does not challenge the concept of an autonomous language module or cognitive mechanisms at work within the individual learner, which develop the interlanguage system by analysing and processing environmental language in a variety of ways. In Chapters 7 and 8 we examine research that views the learning process itself as social, and integrates to a significant degree the categories of language use and language development, which have been conceptually separate in the approaches reviewed earlier.

The work reviewed in this chapter takes its original inspiration from the **Input hypothesis** advanced by Stephen Krashen since the 1980s (Krashen, 1982, 1985, 1998). In Chapter 2, we examined the basic claim of the input hypothesis: that the availability of input which is comprehensible to the learner is the only necessary condition for language learning to take place – provided the learner is predisposed to pay attention to it (*see* the companion **Affective Filter** hypothesis). This claim sparked off a number of traditions of empirical research into the environmental conditions for learning, which are still highly active today.

In the early 1980s, the researcher Michael Long first advanced the argument that in order to understand more fully the nature and usefulness of input for SLL, greater attention should be paid to the interactions in which learners were engaged (Long, 1981, 1983a, 1983b). Long argued that these interactions should not be seen simply as a one-directional source of target language input, feeding into the learner's presumed internal acquisition device. Instead, when learners engaged with their interlocutors in negotiations around meaning, the nature of the input might be qualitatively changed. That is, the more the input was queried, recycled and paraphrased, to increase its comprehensibility, the greater its potential usefulness as input, because it should become increasingly well-targeted to the particular developmental needs of the individual learner. This view has become known as the **Interaction hypothesis** (Long 1981, 1983a, 1996).

A second challenge to Krashen was put forward by the researcher Merrill Swain, whose work with immersion students experiencing content-based second language French instruction in Canadian schools had led her to question the claim that comprehensible second language input was sufficient to ensure all-round interlanguage development. Swain advanced another set of claims about the relationship between language use and language learning, the so-called **Output hypothesis** (Swain, 1985, 1995). The immersion students studied by Swain and her colleagues were exposed to French-medium instruction for extended periods of time, and achieved comprehension abilities in French as a second language that were close to native speaker level. However their productive ability lagged behind, something which Swain attributed to the fact that their classroom involvement with French mostly involved reading and listening to second language input, without corresponding expectations that they themselves would speak or write in French at a high level. Swain argued that students could often succeed in comprehending second language texts, while only partly processing them, that is, concentrating on semantic processing. In her view, only second language production (i.e. output) really forces learners to undertake complete grammatical processing, and thus drives forward most effectively the development of second language syntax and morphology.

These theoretical claims have led to extensive empirical work, examining the detail of target language input, output and interaction involving second language learners, and seeking to explain its relationship with interlanguage development. In this chapter we review and evaluate this work, which has taught us a great deal about the kinds of interaction in which learners typically engage, and about a range of variables that seem to influence the quality of these interactions. (Other useful overviews can be found in Pica, 1994; R. Ellis, 1999a, 1999b; Nicholas *et al.*, 2001; Shehadeh, 2002; Gass, 2003.)

6.2   Input and interaction in first language acquisition

Before examining the second language interactionist tradition in more detail, however, it will be helpful to recap briefly on current understandings of the role of input and interaction in first language acquisition. It is well known that adults and other caretakers commonly use 'special' speech styles when talking with young children, and terms such as **baby talk** are commonly used to refer to this. The idea that 'baby talk' with its particular characteristics might actually be helpful to language acquisition, and the empirical study of caretakers' interactions with young children, date back to the 1960s. This empirical research tradition of investigating **child-directed speech (CDS)** has remained very active, although it has undergone criticism especially from Universal Grammar theorists. In 1986, for example, Noam Chomsky described as 'absurd' the notion that aspects of first language acquisition could be related to the input (quoted in Snow, 1994, p. 4). In turn, some child language specialists have criticized parameter-setting models of acquisition as overly deterministic (Valian, 1990) and ignoring substantial evidence of probabilistic learning from 'noisy' input (Sokolov and Snow, 1994, p. 52).

A collection edited by Gallaway and Richards (1994) provides a useful overview of the interactionist tradition within first language acquisition studies. The editors of this volume point out that child-directed speech might be expected to facilitate language acquisition in a wide variety of ways, including:

> managing attention
> promoting positive affect
> improving intelligibility
> facilitating segmentation
> providing feedback
> provision of correct models
> reducing processing load
> encouraging conversational participation
> explicit teaching of social routines.

(Richards and Gallaway, 1994, p. 264)

However, the contributors to the 1994 collection are cautious about the extent to which any of these possible child-directed speech contributions to language acquisition have been solidly demonstrated. Some of the clearest findings and conclusions from this tradition, which are also potentially relevant for SLL, are the following:

1. Child-directed speech has mostly been studied in English-speaking contexts in the developed world, and most usually in a middle-class family setting. In such contexts, child-directed speech is typically **semantically contingent**; that is, the caretaker talks with the child about objects and events to which the child is already paying attention. Richards and Gallaway (1994, p. 265) comment that 'there is much evidence that semantic contingency . . . is facilitative, [though] the final causal link is frequently lacking'. Also, in child-directed speech explicit formal corrections of the child's productions are unusual, but **recasts** are common; that is, utterances in which the caretaker produces an expanded and grammatically correct version of a prior child utterance:

CHILD: Fix Lily
MOTHER: Oh . . . Lily will fix it

(Sokolov and Snow, 1994, p. 47)

Sokolov and Snow (1994) argue that these recasts offer children potentially useful **negative evidence** about their own hypotheses on the workings of the target language, at least implicitly. There is also very substantial empirical evidence for positive correlations between the proportion of recasts used by a child's caretakers, and his or her overall rate of development.

2. As well as more general claims about the overall contribution of semantic contingency and of recasts, there is evidence for some more specific claims about the relationship of particular formal characteristics of child-directed speech and children's developing control of particular constructions. For example, there seems to be a relationship between the caretaker's use of inverted yes-no questions, for example *Have you been sleeping?*, and children's developing control of verbal auxiliaries in English as a first language, presumably because the fronted auxiliary is perceptually more salient than questions marked through intonation only (Pine, 1994, pp. 25–33). However, such relationships are complex and dependent on the precise developmental stage reached by the individual child. Again, we meet the notion of 'currently sensitive areas of development' already encountered in Chapter 5, or as some first language researchers have expressed it, ' "hot spots" of engagement and analysis that lead to a heavy concentration of available processing capacity on highly relevant

exemplars for stage-relevant acquisition' (Nelson *et al.*, 1989, quoted in Richards and Gallaway, 1994, p. 262).

3. Despite the potential usefulness of child-directed speech as input data, it is clear that caretakers are not typically motivated by any prime language-teaching goal, nor is their speech in general specially adapted so as to model the target grammar. Instead, its special characteristics derive primarily from the communicative goal of engaging in conversation with a linguistically and cognitively less competent partner, and sustaining and directing their attention (Pine, 1994, p. 19).

4. Cross-cultural studies of interaction with young children have made it clear that styles of child-directed speech found in middle class Anglophone societies are far from universal, and that societies can be found where infants are not seen as conversation partners (*see* review by Lieven 1994). For example, in Trackton, a poor rural community studied by Heath (1983), in the south-eastern USA, children are not usually addressed directly by adults, until they can themselves produce multi-word utterances. Similarly among the Kaluli of Papua New Guinea, infant babbling is seen as 'bird talk' and something to be discouraged rather than engaged with (Schieffelin, 1985). As children nonetheless learn to speak perfectly well under these widely differing conditions, this cross-cultural evidence seems to challenge strongly environmentalist explanations of language learning, by weakening any notion that finely tuned child-directed speech is actually necessary.

However, Lieven and others point out that even in cultures where child-directed speech of the Western type is rare or absent, children are constantly in group settings, and surrounded by contextualized talk routines. In such settings, their early utterances frequently include partial imitations and the production of 'unanalysed and rote-learned segments, picked up in routinised situations' (Lieven, 1994, p. 62). Indeed, in some cultures, such as that of the Kaluli, adults actively teach language by requiring children to imitate conversational routines directly. We also know that children will not normally learn a language to which they are merely exposed in a decontextualized way, for example on television (Snow *et al.*, 1976, quoted in Lieven, 1994, p. 59). As Lieven concludes:

> The study of child language development cross culturally supports the idea that children will only learn to talk in an environment of which they can make some sense and which has a structure of which the child is a part; on the other hand, children can clearly learn to talk in a much wider variety of environments than those largely studied to date. This is ... only partly because of the repertoire of skills that the child brings to the task of learning to talk. It is also because there are systematic ways in which the struc-

ture within which the child is growing up gives her/him access to ways of working out the language.

(Lieven, 1994, p. 73)

From a wide-ranging review of the whole area, Snow concludes that:

> The normally developing child is well buffered against variation in the input ... buffering implies either that only a relatively small amount of social support of the right sort might be necessary, or alternately that any of several different environmental events might be sufficient for some bit of learning to occur. Under these circumstances, variations at the margin in the quality of the linguistic environment a child is exposed to might not have any measurable effect on the speed or the ease of language acquisition.
>
> (Snow, 1994, p. 11)

This naturally makes the study of environmental effects very difficult! And researchers in this field seem generally to agree:

- that multi-dimensional (modular?) models of acquisition are necessary, which will in some way reconcile a range of components which will include parental input, learning mechanisms and procedures, and innate (linguistic) constraints built into the child (Sokolov and Snow, 1994, p. 51)
- that the way forward in clarifying just how it is that input and interaction may be facilitating language acquisition lies at present in close, detailed studies of relationships between particular features of the input, and of related features in the child's linguistic repertoire, as they evolve over time.

They remain hopeful that such studies will eventually demonstrate exactly how it is that environmental linguistic evidence interacts with and constrains the linguistic hypotheses under development by the child learner.

6.3 Input in second language acquisition: Krashen's 'Input hypothesis'

Just as 'baby talk' was noted in the early work on child language development, as a simplified register used to talk to children, so a number of sociolinguists in the 1960s and 1970s noticed and commented on what they called **foreigner talk**, a simplified and pidgin-like variety sometimes used to address strangers and foreigners (on *Me Tarzan, you Jane* lines; *see* review in Long, 1996, pp. 414–18). It has always been obvious that comprehensible and appropriately contextualized second language data is necessary for learning to take place. However, the precise developmental contribution of the language used to address second language learners first attracted serious attention from psycholinguists and second language researchers in the light of the **Input hypothesis** proposed by Stephen Krashen (1982, 1985; *see also* Chapter 2).

In its most developed form the Input hypothesis claims that exposure to **comprehensible input** is both necessary and sufficient for SLL to take place. The hypothesis states that:

> Humans acquire language in only one way – by understanding messages, or by receiving 'comprehensible input'. . . We move from i, our current level, to i + 1, the next level along the natural order, by understanding input containing i + 1 (Krashen, 1985, p. 2).

Linked to the hypothesis are two further ideas:

- Speaking is a result of acquisition and not its cause.
- If input is understood, and there is enough of it, the necessary grammar is automatically provided. (Krashen, 1985, p. 2)

According to this hypothesis then, how exactly does acquisition take place? At one point Krashen proposed three stages in turning input into **intake**: (a) understanding a second language i + 1 form (i.e. linking it to a meaning); (b) noticing a gap between the second language i + 1 form and the interlanguage rule which the learner currently controls; and (c) the reappearance of the i + 1 form with minimal frequency (Krashen, 1983, pp. 138–9). In other versions of the hypothesis, however, the concept of 'noticing a gap' is omitted, and it seems that acquisition takes place entirely incidentally or without awareness.

As numerous critics have pointed out, the Input hypothesis as originally formulated by Krashen is supported by rather little empirical evidence, and is not easily testable (e.g. McLaughlin, 1987, pp. 36–51). The concepts of 'understanding' and 'noticing a gap' are not clearly operationalized, or consistently proposed; it is not clear how the learner's present state of knowledge ('i') is to be characterized, or indeed whether the 'i + 1' formula is intended to apply to all aspects of language, including vocabulary and phonology as well as syntax. Above all, the processes whereby language in the social environment is analysed and new elements are identified and processed by the 'language acquisition device' so that they can influence and modify the learner's existing interlanguage system, are not spelled out.

In the following sections of this chapter, we begin by discussing those research traditions that ultimately take their inspiration from Krashen's proposals. First of all, we examine empirical research associated with the **Interaction hypothesis**, which has itself moved through two phases: an earlier, more descriptive phase, and a later phase which has been more strongly concerned with the processing of environmental language. Next, we examine the current state of the **Output hypothesis**. We then follow up researchers' growing interest in a particular aspect of interaction, that is, the provision of different types of **feedback** on learners' second language utterances, by teachers and other interlocutors, and its possible contributions to the acquisition process. Lastly, we examine briefly some alternative psycholinguistic theories and claims about the ways in which 'new' language elements in environmental discourse are identified, analysed and integrated into the developing second language system: the **'noticing' hypothesis**, the **'input processing' hypothesis** and the **'autonomous induction' hypothesis**.

6.4   Interaction in second language acquisition

As we have seen, Krashen's proposals encouraged other researchers to examine more closely the characteristics of the language input being made available to second language learners. A range of studies conducted in the 1970s and 1980s demonstrated that talk addressed to learners was rarely of the *Me Tarzan, you Jane* type. Instead, it was typically grammatically regular, but often somewhat simplified linguistically by comparison with talk between native speakers (e.g. using shorter utterances and a narrower range of vocabulary or less complex grammar; *see* review in Long, 1983a). However, as Long also showed, the degree of simplification reported in many descriptive studies was puzzlingly variable. Also, these studies typically stopped short at the description of distinctive features of Foreigner Talk Discourse, as it came to be known. They did not generally go on to demonstrate either that these special qualities made Foreigner Talk Discourse more comprehensible, or that it actually promoted second language acquisition.

Long proposed a more systematic approach to linking features of 'environmental' language, and learners' second language development. He argued that this could be done in the following way:

Step 1: Show that (a) linguistic/conversational adjustments promote (b) comprehension of input.
Step 2: Show that (b) comprehensible input promotes (c) acquisition.
Step 3: Deduce that (a) linguistic/conversational adjustments promote (c) acquisition.

(Long, 1985, p. 378)

In two studies reported in the same 1985 paper, he showed that 'lec-turettes' pre-scripted and delivered in a modified, Foreigner Talk Discourse style were more comprehensible to adult second language learners than were versions of the same talks delivered in an unmodified style, thus supporting the argument that linguistic modifications could promote comprehension of input. However, these lecturettes involved passive listening by the learners. In other work, Long shifted the attention of the second language acquisition field towards more interactive aspects of Foreigner Talk Discourse.

6.4.1   Long's 'Interaction hypothesis'

Long went on to propose his Interaction hypothesis as an extension of Krashen's original Input hypothesis. For his own doctoral research (Long, 1980, 1981, 1983a), Long conducted a study of 16 native speaker–native speaker and 16 native speaker–non-native speaker pairs, carrying out the same set of face-to-face oral tasks (informal conversation, giving instruc-tions for games, playing the games, etc.). He showed that there was little linguistic difference between the talk produced by native speaker–native speaker and native speaker–non-native speaker pairs, as shown on measures of grammatical complexity. However, there were important differences between the two sets of conversations when these were analysed from the point of view of conversational management and language functions per-formed. Specifically, in order to solve ongoing communication difficulties, the native speaker–non-native speaker pairs were much more likely to make use of conversational tactics such as **repetitions, confirmation checks, comprehension checks** or **clarification requests** (*see* Table 6.1 for examples).

As in child-directed speech, native speakers apparently resort to these tactics in order to solve communication problems when talking with less fluent non-native speakers, and not with any conscious motive to teach grammar (Long, 1983b). However, from the perspective of the Interaction hypothesis, such collaborative efforts should be very useful for language learning. As they struggle to maximize comprehension, and negotiate their way through trouble spots, the native speaker–non-native speaker partner-ships are incidentally fine-tuning the second language input so as to make it more relevant to the current state of learner development. That is, they are collaborating to ensure that the learner is receiving i + 1, in Krashen's terms, rather than i + 3, or indeed, i + 0. As Larsen-Freeman and Long put it:

> Modification of the interactional structure of conversation … is a better candidate for a necessary (not sufficient) condition for acquisition. The role it plays in negotiation for meaning helps to make input comprehensible while still containing unknown linguistic elements, and, hence, potential intake for acquisition.
>
> (Larsen-Freeman and Long, 1991, p. 144)

Following on Long's original studies, many others drew on the Interaction hypothesis and used a similar taxonomy of conversational moves to track meaning negotiations and conversational repair. These are usefully reviewed by Larsen-Freeman and Long (1991, pp. 120–8) and by Pica (1994). On the whole, these studies followed designs similar to that of Long (1980), tracking pairs of native and non-native speakers in various combinations, undertaking a variety of semi-controlled conversational tasks. They have taught us a good deal about the types of task that are likely to promote extensive negotiation of meaning, inside and outside the classroom. (For example, convergent, problem-solving tasks in which both partners control necessary information are more likely to promote negotiation than are more open-ended discussions.) They have also demonstrated that negotiation of meaning occurs between non-native speaker peers, as

Table 6.1   Examples of interactional modifications in NS conversations

NS	NNS
And right on the roof of the truck place the duck. The duck.	I to take it? *Dog?*[a]
Duck.	Duck.
It's yellow and it's a small animal. It has two feet.	*I put where it?*[b]
You take the duck and put it on top of the truck. *Do you see the duck?*[c]	*Duck?*[a]
Yeah. Quack, quack, quack. That one. The one that makes that sound.	
	Ah yes, I see in the–in the head of him.
OK. *See?*[c]	*Put what?*[b]
OK. Put him on top of the truck.	*Truck?*[a]
The bus. Where the boy is.	Ah yes.

[a] Confirmation checks: Moves by which one speaker seeks confirmation of the other's preceding utterance through repetition, with rising intonation, of what was perceived to be all or part of the preceding utterance.

[b] Clarification requests: Moves by which one speaker seeks assistance in understanding the other speaker's preceding utterance through questions (including *wh*-, polar, disjunctive, uninverted with rising intonation or tag), statements such as *I don't understand*, or imperatives such as *Please repeat*.

[c] Comprehension checks: Moves by which one speaker attempts to determine whether the other speaker has understood a preceding message.

(*Source*: Pica *et al.*, 1987, p. 74)

well as between more fluent and less fluent speakers, given the right task conditions.

However, as Long (1996) points out, these studies have mostly been undertaken in Western educational institutions, and we still know little about the kinds of negotiation and repair that may typify second language interactions in other contexts. Also, many early interaction studies did not go beyond the first descriptive steps of establishing the existence and general patterning of conversational repair.

6.4.2   Empirical studies linking interaction and comprehension

One of the first studies that attempted to establish a link between interactional modifications and increased comprehension, was conducted by Pica and colleagues (Pica *et al.*, 1987). Groups of second language learners listened to different versions of a script instructing them to place coloured cutouts on a landscape picture, and tried to complete the task. One group heard a linguistically modified version of the script (e.g. with increased redundancy and simplified grammar), but individuals were not allowed to ask any questions as they carried out the instructions. The second group heard a version of the script originally recorded with native speakers, but individuals were encouraged to ask for clarifications, etc., from the person reading the script. The main result of these requests was a great increase in repetitions of content words, rather than, for example, any particular simplification of grammar. Indeed, the authors note that 'interaction resulted in input that was more complex than input that was modified according to conventional criteria of linguistic simplification' (Pica *et al.*, 1987, p. 750).

Pica *et al.* (1987) were nonetheless able to show that the learners allowed to negotiate the meaning of an unmodified script were more successful on the task than those who simply heard the simplified script, and argue that this shows increased comprehension because of interactional modifications of the input. This study, and others like it, are relevant to Long's Step 1 quoted above (Long, 1985); they seem to show that interactional adjustments are more effective in promoting comprehension of input than are linguistic adjustments alone.

6.4.3   Empirical studies linking interaction and acquisition

In Long's Steps 2 and 3, he challenged researchers to link interactional modifications and learner comprehension to language acquisition. These links were pursued in several studies reported in the 1990s, though with somewhat mixed results. Three examples will be briefly considered here.

A study by Loschky (1994) involved the administration of listening comprehension tasks to learners of Japanese as a foreign language. The learners heard individual locative sentences (in Japanese) such as 'To the right of the pen is a ruler', 'A big black circle is above the big black square', and had to locate and number the correct items on a range of picture sheets. One group of learners heard these sentences without any further support; a second group heard linguistically modified versions (with some added redundancy) and a third group were allowed to ask for clarifications, etc., as the sentences were presented.

As in earlier studies, Loschky found that the third condition was most helpful to the learners in completing the task, that is, he offered further evidence that interaction around meaning aids second language comprehension. But Loschky also administered pre- and post-tests of language proficiency to his subjects, comprising a recognition test of relevant vocabulary, and a grammaticality judgement test on similar locative structures. Here, he found that all his subjects made significant gains in course of the study, but that no single group was advantaged over the others by the differing intervening treatment. Thus, while his study showed interactional modifications leading to increased comprehension (Long's Step 1), it failed to show any clear link between increased comprehension and acquisition (Long's Step 2).

In a not dissimilar study, Gass and Varonis (1994) asked native speaker–non-native speaker pairs to undertake a problem-solving communication game. As in the study by Pica *et al.* (1987) this involved placing figures in particular locations on a landscape scene. The 'game' was run twice, first of all with the native speaker participants issuing instructions to their non-native speaker interlocutors, and second, the other way around.

When the native speaker participants gave instructions on the first occasion, half were asked to follow a linguistically pre-modified script, and the other half followed an unmodified script. For each script, half the native speaker subjects were instructed to allow negotiation about meaning, and the other half were not. In this study, both the modified script *without* interaction, and either script *with* interaction, seemed to increase non-native speaker comprehension (as measured by success on the task), compared with those who heard the unmodified script and could not negotiate around it. This part of the study is obviously relevant once again to Long's Step 1.

In the second part of the experiment, however, when the non-native speaker participants took responsibility for giving instructions, they were not given any scripts to follow. Once more, half of them were allowed to negotiate meaning with their native speaker interlocutor, the other half were not. (The design of this experiment is shown in Figure 6.1.)

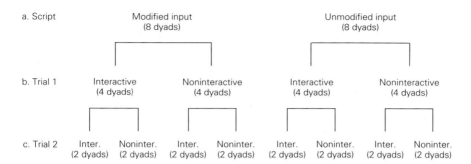

Fig. 6.1   The contributions of modified input and interaction to task success; diagram of experimental design (*Source*: Gass and Varonis, 1994, p. 290)

Interestingly, this time around, it did not make any difference to the success of the native speakers on the task, whether their non-native speaker instructors were allowed to interact with them or not. It seemed that the quality or intelligibility of non-native speaker directions could not be improved significantly by ongoing interaction.

A somewhat different kind of development did take place for the 'negotiation' group however. It turned out that those non-native speaker subjects who had been allowed to interact with their interlocutor during Trial 1, were significantly better at giving directions during Trial 2, than those who had not. Gass and Varonis consider the possibility that the non-native speakers might have learnt a larger number of useful vocabulary items during their interactive experience of Trial 1, only to reject it. Instead, they argue that the Trial 2 data shows evidence of non-native speakers having internalized various useful communicative strategies, as exemplified below:

First trial
JANE: All right now, above the sun place the squirrel. He's right on top of the sun.
HIROSHI: What is . . . the word?
JANE: OK. The sun.
HIROSHI: Yeah, sun, but . . .
JANE: Do you know what the sun is?
HIROSHI: Yeah, of course. Wh–what's the
JANE: Squirrel. Do you know what a squirrel is?
HIROSHI: No.
JANE: OK. You've seen them running around on campus. They're little furry animals. They're short and brown and they *eat nuts* like crazy.

Second trial
HIROSHI: The second will be . . . put here. This place is . . . small animal
            which *eat nuts*.
JANE: Oh, squirrel?
HIROSHI: Yeah (laughter).

(Gass and Varonis, 1994, p. 296)

Using the data from the example above, the researchers point out that the subject Hiroshi seems to have learnt, not the lexical item *squirrel*, but a strategy for defining it, using more basic vocabulary.

In a third study, Mackey (1999) set out to test whether opportunities to interact and negotiate for meaning would boost the knowledge of question forms among learners of English as a second language. Question forms were selected as the syntactic focus of the study for a number of reasons. They are readily elicited, and are present at all stages of learning; in addition, their acquisition has been well studied, and the normal six-stage acquisition sequence for English question forms is known (*see* Pienemann and Johnston, 1987). The participants in the study were lower-intermediate adult learners, who undertook a range of information-gap tasks that required them to ask and answer questions (e.g. story completion, spot the difference, picture sequencing). Some participants (the 'interactors') were allowed to negotiate meanings with their native speaker interlocutor, whereas others were not; all participants carried out further tasks as pretests and as post-tests.

Mackey's (1999) experimental study produced statistically significant results showing that the learners who had engaged in interaction progressed one (or more) stages in second language question formation, while the non-interactors failed to do so. The following extract illustrates this development, in the case of one 'interactor' participant:

Pretest   55 NNS: *The meal is not there?*
             56 NS: *No it's gone, what do you think happened?*
             57 NNS: *Happened? The cat?*
             58 NS: *Do you think the cat ate it?*
             59 NNS: *The meal is the is the cat's meal?*
             60 NS: *It's not supposed to be the cat's dinner. I don't think so.*
             61 NNS: *But although this, this cat have eaten it.*

Treatment   4 NNS: *What the animal do?*
              5 NS: *They aren't there, there are no bears.*
              6 NNS: *Your picture have this sad girl?*
              7 NS: *Yes, what do you have in your picture?*
              8 NNS: *What my picture have to make her crying? I don't
                       know your picture.*

	9	NS:	*Yeah ok, I mean what does your picture show? What's the sign?*
	10	NNS:	*No sign? . . . No, ok, what the mother say to the girl for her crying?*
	11	NS:	*It's the sign 'no bears' that's making her cry. What does your sign say?*
	12	NNS:	*The sign? Why the girl cry?*
Posttest	1	NNS:	*What do your picture have?*
Posttest	2	NNS:	*What has the robber done?*
		NNS:	*Where has she gone in your picture?*

(Mackey, 1999, p. 577)

In this example we see that the non-native speaker was using canonical word order with question intonation, in order to ask questions during the pre-test (Stage 2 of the developmental sequence proposed by Pienemann and Johnston, 1987). During the treatment the learner produced *wh*-fronting, but still with canonical word order (Stage 3). However, by the time of the second post-test (without any further English as a second language instruction), the learner was correctly placing an auxiliary verb in second position to *wh-* words (Stage 5). This kind of progress was not documented for the non-interactor group.

Mackey's study thus provides some of the clearest evidence available that 'taking part in interaction can facilitate second language development (1999, p. 565)', that is, in support of Long's Step 3. However, the somewhat contradictory findings of these three studies show a need for stronger theoretical models clarifying the claimed link between interaction and acquisition.

In fact, these research teams appeal to ideas of **noticing, consciousness-raising, attention,** etc., as elements to be added to the equation; *see* Section 6.8 below. Other researchers, such as Braidi (1995), also criticized the earlier interactionist research as being too one-sidedly preoccupied with functional aspects of second language interaction and of neglecting linguistic theory. Braidi went on to argue for a research agenda tracking the development of individual grammatical structures in second language interaction in much fuller detail (1995, pp. 164–5).

6.5   Rethinking the Interaction hypothesis

Over time, second language input or interaction researchers have shown themselves quite responsive to the ongoing development of both linguistic and information processing theory within second language acquisition studies. This is evident in Long's eventual reformulation of the Interaction hypothesis (1996), which places much more emphasis on linking features of put and the linguistic environment with 'learner-internal factors', and explaining how such linkages may facilitate subsequent language development (Long, 1996, p. 454).

Long's 1996 version of the Interaction hypothesis reads as follows:

> It is proposed that environmental contributions to acquisition are mediated by selective attention and the learner's developing L2 processing capacity, and that these resources are brought together most usefully, although not exclusively, during *negotiation for meaning*. Negative feedback obtained during negotiation work or elsewhere may be facilitative of L2 development, at least for vocabulary, morphology and language-specific syntax, and essential for learning certain specifiable L1–L2 contrasts.
>
> (Long, 1996, p. 414)

This new version of the hypothesis highlights the possible contribution to second language learning of **negative evidence** as to the structure of the target language, derivable from environmental language (i.e. from Foreigner Talk Discourse). It also highlights the attempt to clarify the processes by which input becomes intake, through introducing the notion of **selective attention**. These concepts are also repeatedly referred to, in current discussions of output and its contribution to language development. In the next section we review recent empirical investigations into Swain's Output hypothesis, before considering these concepts more fully in later sections.

6.6   Output in second language acquisition

Most language learning researchers agree that output is necessary to increase fluency, that is, learners must practise producing second language utterances if they are to learn to use their interlanguage system confidently and routinely. However, the **Output hypothesis** advanced by Swain (1985, 1995) makes a number of claims which go beyond this 'practice' function of output, and which have to do with the development of the interlanguage system, and not only increased efficiency in using it.

Swain (1995, p. 128) proposes three further functions for learner output:

- the 'noticing/triggering' function, or what might be referred to as the consciousness-raising role
- the hypothesis-testing function
- the metalinguistic function, or what might be referred to as its 'reflective' role.

That is to say, she believes that the activity of producing the target language may push learners to become aware of gaps and problems in their current second language system (first function); it provides them with opportunities to reflect on, discuss and analyse these problems explicitly (third function); and of course, it provides them with opportunities to experiment with new structures and forms (second function).

In her own ongoing research, Swain has concentrated largely on the 'reflective' role of output, and especially the possible contribution of meta-linguistic talk between peers to second language development (*see* Swain and Lapkin, 1995, 1998; the latter discussed more fully in Chapter 7). Other researchers have conducted research that tries to link learners' opportunities for output more directly to second language development. For example, R. Ellis and He (1999) and de la Fuente (2002) have researched the contribution of learner output to second language vocabulary acquisition.

In the first of these studies, R. Ellis and He (1999) worked with low-proficiency English second language learners, using a pool of unfamiliar furniture vocabulary (*lamp, cushion,* etc.). All the learners carried out a design task, placing small pictures of the furniture items around the plan of an apartment, but one group received pre-modified instructions that they could not negotiate. A second group received the same instructions but could negotiate if meanings were not clear, while the third group were required to give the instructions to an interlocutor. In this study, pre-tests and post-tests of the selected vocabulary showed that the third, 'output' group outperformed the others both receptively and productively. The de la Fuente study (2002) had a similar design, though with learners of Spanish as a second language rather than English. In this case, the 'output' group of learners also outperformed the rest of the students at post-tests, as far as productive vocabulary was concerned. However for receptive vocabulary, the 'negotiation' group achieved the same level as the 'output' group, while outperforming the 'no negotiation' group.

The studies just quoted seem to show clear benefits arising from 'pushing' students to produce second language output, at least as far as vocabulary is concerned. Regarding second language grammar, as Shehadeh (2002) points out, there is still relatively little evidence. Nobuyoshi and Ellis (1993) conducted a small-scale study of the role of output in the development of English past tense. They tried to encourage English second language learners to modify their output by means of clarification requests, as in the following example:

Learner:	last weekend, a man painting, painting 'Beware of the dog'
Teacher:	sorry?
Learner:	a man painted, painted, painted on the wall 'Beware of the dog'
	(Nobuyoshi and Ellis, 1993, p. 205)

Of the three students who had received this treatment, two maintained the resulting increased accuracy in using past tense forms, whereas no one in a comparison group improved.

Larger studies by Izumi *et al.* (1999) and Izumi and Bigelow (2000) explored the potential of pushed output to promote English second language students' learning of the counterfactual conditional in English (e.g. *If Ann had travelled to Spain in 1992, she would have seen the Olympics*). Experimental groups were given different kinds of texts including rich examples of the structure, and had to generate similar texts (in an essay writing task and a text reconstruction task). Control groups meanwhile received the same textual inputs, but did other activities based on them (e.g. answered comprehension questions). The writings of the experimental groups showed significant improvement during the experimental treatment, but on the eventual post-tests, focusing on the target grammar structure, the control groups performed just as well. Thus it seemed that rich input combined with a variety of 'noticing' activities, may have been enough in this case to lead to grammar learning, without any added benefit being derived from the output requirement.

Up to now therefore, it seems that the benefits of 'pushed output' remain somewhat elusive and hard to demonstrate, at least as far as second language grammar development is concerned. In an extensive review, Shehadeh (2002, p. 597) comments that 'there is still a severe lack of data showing that learner output or output modifications have any effect on second language learning'. Like Braidi (1995) he argues the need to trace learners' linguistic development much more closely, and also argues for a closer examination of the psycholinguistic and information-processing functions of learner output.

6.7   Feedback, recasts and negative evidence

In this section we look more closely at recent research on the role of feedback in second language interaction, and its possible contribution to interlanguage development. First, in Section 6.7.1, we return briefly to child first language acquisition and review the debate around the significance of adult recasts of child utterances for first language development. In sections 6.7.2 and 6.7.3 we then examine observational research into the naturalistic use of recasts and other related kinds of feedback with second language learners, in dyadic settings and in classrooms. Lastly, we consider experimental research where the occurrence of recasts was controlled and manipulated, and its impact on learner development was studied using pre-test and post-test designs.

6.7.1   Negative evidence in first language acquisition

We saw in Section 6.2 that the existence and usability of **negative evidence** in child-directed speech has become important in debates on first language acquisition. The argument sharpened as studies of child-directed revealed that caretakers' speech with young children was, in general, regular and well formed, that is, it seemed to provide essentially **positive** evidence on the nature of the language system to be learnt. Moreover, it seems that explicit negative evidence, in the form of parental correction of children's grammar mistakes, is rare.

Theorists arguing for a strongly innatist model of language learning have claimed that language is simply not learnable from the normal type of input, which provides mostly positive evidence of the structure of the target language, and lacks negative evidence in the form of, for example, grammar corrections (Wexler and Culicover, 1980; Pinker, 1989). In the absence of negative evidence, how are learners to discover the limits and boundaries of the language system they are learning? For nativists, the answer lies in the existence of some form of Universal Grammar, which is needed to eliminate many possible generalizations about language structure that are compatible with the input received, but are actually incorrect.

We saw in Section 6.2 that a number of child language researchers have responded to this view, by re-examining and reinterpreting child-directed speech data. Researchers such as Bohannon *et al.* (1990) and Farrar (1992) assert that negative evidence is much more prevalent in child-directed speech than was previously thought, in particular by asserting that caretakers' **recasts** of poorly formed child utterances offer implicit negative evidence about children's interim grammatical hypotheses. There is controversy among child language researchers on this issue, particularly concerning the standards to be applied to evidence supporting claims that recasts promote grammatical development (*see* Morgan *et al.*, 1995; Bohannon *et al.*, 1996). From his review, however, Long (1996) concludes that first language acquisition researchers have generally succeeded in demonstrating that (implicit) negative evidence: (a) is regularly available in child-directed speech; (b) exists in usable form; and (c) is picked up and used by child learners, at least in the short term. Whether negative evidence is **necessary** for the acquisition of core aspects of language (e.g. of the principles specified by Universal Grammar theory) still remains less clear, however.

6.7.2   Negative feedback and recasts in native speaker–non-native speaker and non-native speaker–non-native speaker discourse

In the light of this first language debate, related questions can be asked about the role of negative evidence in SLL. For example: To what extent is indirect negative evidence about the nature of second languages made available to second language learners, in the course of interaction? And to what extent do learners (a) notice and (b) make use of this evidence?

A number of studies have recently pursued these questions by analysing spoken interaction involving second language learners. These studies have looked for different kinds of **negative feedback** produced in response to learners' non-standard utterances, including negotiation moves such as clarification requests and confirmation checks, discussed in Section 6.4 above. However, particular attention has been paid to the occurrence of **recasts**, re-defined by second language researchers as 'responses to non-target non-native speaker utterances that provide a target-like way of expressing the original meaning' (Mackey *et al.*, 2003, p. 36). An example of a recast offered by Mackey *et al.* (2000, p. 11) reads:

Student:	Why does the aliens attacked earth?
Teacher:	Right. Why did the aliens attack earth?

Here, the teacher does not explicitly criticize the student's utterance, or provide any grammatical explanation, and this is typical of feedback in the form of recasts. However, such reformulations of faulty utterances are believed by many interactionist second language acquisition researchers to provide important indirect negative evidence for the learner about problems in their output. These researchers have also been very interested in uptake of the recasts, in immediately following utterances produced by the learner. The following example comes from Oliver:

Teacher	What did you do in the garden?
NNS student (child)	Mm, cut the tree
Teacher	You cut the trees. Were they big trees or were they little bushes?
NNS student (child)	Big trees

(Oliver, 2000, p. 140)

Here, the teacher recasts the child's first utterance 'cut the tree', expanding it by the addition of plural -*s*. The child's second utterance 'big trees' also includes plural -*s*, and can be interpreted as reflecting uptake of the foregoing recast.

In order to explore the extent to which negative feedback is actually available to second language learners, and how far they make use of it, Oliver (1995) recorded pairs of native speaker and non-native speaker children carrying out problem-solving tasks in English (picture completion). In this study, more than 60% of the errors made by the non-native speaker children received some form of negative feedback from their native speaker partner. Most frequent were negotiations of some kind (clarification requests, confirmation checks); these predominated where non-native speaker utterances included multiple errors or were semantically ambiguous. However, recasts also occurred, usually in response to utterances containing single errors, and also in association with particular types of grammar mistake (*see* the following example; *see also* Table 6.2 for the general relationships found in Oliver's data between error types and native speaker responses).

The following example illustrates the pattern in which a native speaker responded with negotiation when the NNS's meaning was ambiguous, such as that caused by poor word choice:

(4) NNS   NS
     It go just one line
                                      Just along the line?
     Yer.

In the next example, an error was recast as the meaning was transparent:

(5) NNS   NS
     And the . . . boy is holding the girl hand and . . .
                                      Yer.
                                      The boy is holding
                                      the girl's hand.
                                      (Oliver, 1995, p. 473)

Table 6.2 Child NS responses to different types of error

Error	Negotiate (%)	Recast (%)	Ignore (%)	*p*
Article (*n* = 69)	32	25	43	0.1645
Aux/copula (*n* = 132)	54	7	39	0.0001***
Sing/pl/conc (*n* = 17)	18	47	35	0.007**
Pronoun (*n* = 27)	63	7	30	0.0399*
Tense (*n* = 19)	37	16	47	0.7853
Word order/omission (*n* = 77)	53	14	33	0.0364*
Word choice (*n* = 78)	54	10	36	0.0102*
No subject (*n* = 39)	64	5	31	0.0032**
Pronunciation (obvious error) (*n* = 42)	48	26	26	0.1245

*$p<.05$; **$p<.01$; ***$p=0.001$

(*Source*: Oliver, 1995, p. 471)

As well as documenting extensive negative feedback produced by her native speaker subjects, Oliver also showed that her non-native speaker learners could make use of the information provided. In this particular study, the learners incorporated just under 10% of the recasts into their following utterances. This seems a low figure, but Oliver argues that on many occasions, it was not conversationally appropriate or possible to do so. She also points out that the learners were operating under developmental constraints:

> NNSs can only incorporate structures when it is within their morphosyntactic ability to do so (Meisel *et al.*, 1981; Pienemann, 1989). That is to say, input, and in this case, recasts can only be usable if they are within the learnability range of the NNS ... It is quite probable that a substantial proportion of the recasts that were not incorporated were beyond the current L2 processing abilities of the NNSs.
>
> (Oliver, 1995, p. 476)

Overall then, Oliver interprets her data optimistically as showing not only the availability of negative evidence in conversational Foreigner Talk Discourse involving children, but also its usability and take-up, within the limits of the learners' current processing ability.

Further studies of this type have been carried out with adult learners as well as children, and with non-native speaker interlocutors as well as native speaker interlocutors (Oliver, 2000; Mackey *et al.*, 2003). These later studies show that the amount of negative feedback made available is somewhat variable, depending on interlocutor and on setting. This is also true of the extent to which learners act upon it and make use of the recasts in following utterances. However, both these later studies confirm the basic finding of Oliver (1995): that negative feedback occurs regularly in most kinds of second language interaction, in response to non-target-like utterances, and that learners regularly avail themselves of the opportunities offered to produce more target-like utterances.

6.7.3 Negative feedback and recasts in the second language classroom

Further observational studies have examined the occurrence, and apparent effects, of negative feedback in the second language classroom. These classroom studies are variants on a quite longstanding tradition of research into classroom error correction, which had already suggested some benefits from active correction strategies (*see* detailed reviews in Chaudron, 1988, pp. 175–8; DeKeyser, 1993). They typically evaluate the usefulness of recasts as compared with other types of negative feedback, as reflected in student uptake in immediately following interaction sequences.

A number of studies by Lyster and colleagues illustrate this type of class-room investigation. For example, a study conducted in a Canadian immer-sion context (Lyster and Ranta, 1997) looked at different types of error feedback offered by teachers, during content lessons and 'thematic' French language arts lessons. They noted that recasts were much the most common type of feedback (60% compared with 34% for negotiation of form and 6% for explicit meta-linguistic corrections). However, recasts were much less likely to lead to immediate self-correction by the students, relatively speak-ing, than were other feedback types. A further analysis of the same recorded lessons (Lyster, 1998) showed that the kind of negative feedback provided by the teachers varied according to the type of error that had been made. The teachers were much more likely to respond to lexical errors with some kind of negotiation (e.g. clarification requests), while they typically responded to both grammatical and phonological errors with recasts. As far as the phonological errors were concerned, recasting seemed an effective teacher strategy, as the students later repaired more than 60% of these mis-takes. However, recasting was much less effective for repair of grammar mistakes; only 22% of all spoken grammar mistakes were corrected, and the majority of these grammar repairs happened when the teachers adopted the (less usual) strategy of negotiation. Similar evidence is offered by a study of a communicatively oriented adult English second language classroom, by Panova and Lyster (2002).

Lyster and his colleagues interpret their findings as showing that while recasts may offer valuable negative evidence, students are not necessarily under pressure to attend to them, at least in communicatively oriented classroom settings. They suggest that more interactive feedback modes may therefore be more effective in pushing classroom learners to amend their hypotheses about second language grammar, as well as vocabulary.

6.7.4   Experimental studies of negative feedback

How can we tell whether negative feedback provided during face-to-face interaction is promoting second language development? The studies that we have just described seem to make the assumption that improved perfor-mance in immediately succeeding utterances can be taken seriously as evi-dence of learning. However, the researchers responsible for these descriptive studies are generally aware that this is a somewhat speculative assumption. It is possible that the corrections which are produced by learn-ers immediately after negative feedback are quickly forgotten, and do not affect their underlying interlanguage system; it is also possible that recasts, etc., can function as effective input and lead to learning, without any explicit repair being produced.

For these reasons, a number of researchers have moved beyond descriptive accounts of negative feedback, and have tried to design more focused experimental studies of its effect on SLL. An example is the study by Mackey and Philp (1998) of the use of recasts, and their impact on the learning of English as second language question forms. In this study, 35 adult learners took part in a specially designed programme of information-gap tasks, which pushed them towards production of English as second language questions (story completion, picture sequencing, picture drawing). The students carried out the tasks with a native speaker interlocutor, and also completed a series of pre- and post-tests that identified their level on the Pienemann and Johnston (1987) developmental scale for English questions (*see* Section 6.4 above).

Some of the adults in the study received intensive recasting from the native speaker interlocutor whenever they made an error in question formation. Others did the same tasks, but without receiving the recasting 'treatment', whereas a control group did the pre- and post-tests only. During the actual study, the learners who received the recasts very seldom repaired or modified their utterances in response to them (only 5% of recasts were followed by learner repairs). However, the post-tests showed that most of the learners who began the study at Stage 4 on the developmental scale for questions, and who experienced recasting, progressed by at least one Stage (i.e. to Stage 5) in course of the study. No other group made similar progress; the researchers interpret these results as showing that recasting was beneficial for learners who were developmentally ready, in spite of the lack of overt uptake while interaction was actually in progress.

The Mackey and Philp (1998) study compared the effectiveness of interaction plus recasting, with interaction alone, and found that the inclusion of recasting seemed to promote interlanguage development as far as question formation was concerned (though only for the most advanced learners in the study). Similar results have been found in a small study of English as second language storytelling with and without interlocutor recasts (Han 2002); in this case, the recast condition led to greater consistency in use of English past tense inflections as measured on delayed post-tests. Other experimental studies have compared the provision of models (positive examples of selected second language structures) with the provision of reactive recasts (Long *et al.*, 1998; Ayoun, 2001). However, these studies have produced mixed findings. For example, the carefully designed study of Long *et al.* (1998) used communicative games played by learners with native speaker interlocutors, to explore the effect of recasts versus modelling on acquisition of four grammatical structures, two in Japanese as second language and two in Spanish as second language. In this case the 'recasting' condition produced significantly enhanced learning for only one of the four target structures.

As Nicholas *et al.* (2001) point out the findings to date for 'negative feedback' research are still somewhat inconclusive and difficult to interpret. One increasingly recognized problem is that we still know very little about how much attention learners pay to the feedback they receive, or how they interpret it. Some researchers are now trying to use a variety of introspection techniques, in order to tap into learners' thought processes during second language interaction. For example, Mackey *et al.* (2000) made video-recordings of dyadic interactions, and played them back to the learners concerned, asking them to recall their thinking during selected correction episodes, as these were replayed to them. The recall showed that learners had been aware of lexical and phonological correction episodes, which they could identify and comment on. However, they were less likely to have noticed grammatical episodes, or to identify them correctly if they did notice them, as the learner's comment on the following episode shows:

Morphosyntactic feedback without recall of content
NNS (on video):   It have mixed colours
NS: It has mixed colours
NNS: Mixed colours aha
NNS (subsequent recall):   Uh, I was thinking . . . nothing, she just repeat
                              what I said
(Mackey *et al.*, 2000, p. 486)

Here, the learner made a verb inflection mistake during the video interaction, which was recast by the native speaker interlocutor. However, her comments during the recall activity suggest she was aware only that her message was repeated, and had not noticed the grammatical correction in the recast.

6.8   Attention, consciousness-raising and 'focus on form'

We saw in Section 6.5 how recent versions of the Interaction hypothesis have given more importance to the internal processing capacities of the language learner. In particular, researchers have developed the idea that the amount of attention which the learner is paying to matters of form may influence the extent to which second language input and interaction actually produce second language **intake**, that is, new language which has been processed sufficiently for it to become incorporated into the learner's developing second language system. This argument is attractive, in view of the mixed results of studies of output, negative feedback, etc., and their effect on second language development.

One of the researchers who has been most influential in promoting this view is Richard Schmidt (1990, 1994, 2001). Schmidt is careful to distinguish among different types of attention that learners might pay to language form. He uses the term **noticing** to refer to the process of bringing some stimulus into focal attention, that is, registering its simple occurrence, whether voluntarily or involuntarily ('for example when one notices the odd spelling of a new vocabulary word', Schmidt, 1994, p. 17). He reserves the terms **understanding** and **awareness** for explicit knowledge: 'awareness of a rule or generalisation' (Schmidt, 1994, p. 18).

Schmidt is generally optimistic about the contribution of both kinds of attention to language learning. His main evidence in support of the significance of **noticing** comes from his own personal diary, kept while learning Portuguese (with accompanying tapes of his own conversational development; Schmidt and Frota, 1986). An extract from the diary, recording evidence of noticing for certain Portuguese question forms is presented below:

> Journal entry, Week 21 . . . I'm suddenly hearing things I never heard before, including things mentioned in class. Way back in the beginning, when we learned question words, we were told that there are alternative long and short forms like *o que* and *o que é que*, *quem* or *quem é que*. I have never heard the long forms, ever, and concluded that they were just another classroom fiction. But today, just before we left Cabo Frio, M said something to me that I didn't catch right away. It sounded like French *que'est-ce que c'est*, only much abbreviated, approximately [kekse], which must be *(o) que (é) que (vo) cê . . .*
>
> Journal entry, Week 22. I just said to N *o que é que você quer*, but quickly: [kekseker]. Previously, I would have said just *o que*. N didn't blink, so I guess I got it right.
>
> (Schmidt, 1990, p. 140)

Schmidt comments on this data extract as follows:

> In this particular case, it is very clear that these forms had been present in comprehensible input all along. *É que* variants of question words were used by my interlocutor on all the conversational tapes; 43 per cent of all question words on the first tape are of this type. I heard them and processed them for meaning from the beginning, but did not notice the form for five months. When I finally did notice the form, I began to use it.
>
> (Schmidt, 1990, p. 141)

On the basis of this kind of evidence, Schmidt (1994, p. 17) has argued that 'noticing is the necessary and sufficient condition for the conversion of input to intake for learning', though he later modified this view to the weaker claim that 'more noticing leads to more learning' (Schmidt, 1994, p. 18).

The possible significance of attention for second language uptake is highlighted by Long in the revised version of his Interaction hypothesis, as pointed out above in Section 6.5, and has been commented on by a range of interactionist researchers (Pica, 1994; Nicholas *et al.*, 2001). In particular, Nicholas *et al.* (2001) try to explain the mixed results of research into the effectiveness of negative feedback, by stressing the linked issues of saliency and attention, quoting Doughty (1999) to the effect that:

> recasts in L2 classrooms are effective if they are accompanied by some additional cue, telling learners that it is the *form* and not only the meaning of their utterance that is in focus.
>
> (Nicholas *et al.*, 2001, p. 748)

Some interactionist researchers have recently undertaken empirical investigations to clarify how selective attention, or 'noticing', may be influencing the processing of utterances during second language interaction. In a laboratory study, Philp (2003) gave English second language learners a story completion and a picture learning task, similar to those used in previous studies of question formation by Mackey and colleagues. The learners had to ask questions to complete the tasks, and their errors received active recasts from their native speaker interlocutors. However, at intervals the learners were prompted by a signal to repeat what the interlocutor had just said, and their ability to do this was taken as evidence that they had been 'noticing' the recasts, at least enough to be holding them in working memory.

It turned out that the participants in Philps' study could reproduce a high proportion of the recasts that they heard. However, the accuracy of these repetitions depended on: (a) the learner's language level; (b) the length of the recast; and (c) the number of corrections it contained. In particular, learners had great difficulty in repeating question forms that were not currently part of their interlanguage grammar, unless the utterances containing them were very short. Philp concludes that:

> In terms of understanding the processes of SLA, these findings support the claim for an interface between interaction, noticing, and SLA (Long 1996). However, the relationship between interactional modifications, noticing, and intake is highly complex, balancing the learner's IL knowledge and attentional resources against linguistic forms in the input.
>
> (Philp, 2003, p. 120)

Introducing another recent experimental study, Leeman (2003) discusses further the ambiguous status of recasts. She argues that they are best interpreted as offering both positive and negative evidence about second language form (the positive evidence being contained in the recasting utterance itself, the negative evidence in the contrast between the recast and the foregoing erroneous utterance). Like Nicholas *et al.* (2001), she claims that the most important feature of recasts may not be the negative evidence they provide. Instead, it may be the increased prominence or **saliency** of the new form within the recast, which is most helpful in catching the attention of the learner, and thus making the second language form available for processing and internalization.

In Leeman's laboratory study with adult learners of second language Spanish, noun–adjective agreement was the language focus. The learners completed picture comparison tasks working in pairs with native speakers in which objects (such as chairs and tables) were only distinguished by features (such as colour). Leeman (2003) tried to trace the effects of the different aspects of recasts, by providing and comparing the following treatments:

- Negative evidence alone: learners are told that they have made an error but not given any positive model.
- Enhanced salience alone: learners are given exaggerated models of the target form (normally unstressed endings are stressed).
- Recasts (interpreted as negative evidence plus enhanced salience): learners receive conventional recasts.
- Control: learners receive ordinary models of the target form.

The results of this laboratory study showed that the recasts group and the enhanced salience group both significantly outperformed the control group on almost all measures of noun-adjective agreement, while the negative evidence group did not. This leads Leeman to conclude that:

> The findings reported here are highly suggestive regarding the role of attention and salience in SLA . . . A logical interpretation is that enhancing the salience of certain forms led learners to attend to those forms . . . It seems that some interactional features, recasts among them, can lead to greater development by highlighting specific forms in the input.
>
> (Leeman, 2003, p. 57)

6.9   Theorizing input and interaction research

Our survey of input, output and interaction research has shown that a good deal of the research carried out has been descriptive in nature, and attempts to link different types of second language use with SLL have so far produced only mixed results. Commentators such as Braidi (1995) and Shehadeh (2002) have argued for greater clarity about the linguistic models which underpin this research, and numerous commentators have argued for more detailed attention to the internal processing which makes externally encountered language stimuli interpretable and usable for restructuring the interlanguage system. That is, it seems that stronger theorizing is required, for interaction studies to progress.

Clearly, interactionist researchers themselves are increasingly interested in modelling internal linguistic and psycholinguistic factors, as their concern, for example with selective attention, shows. However, no very full or detailed models of language processing have been proposed by any of the interactionist researchers discussed so far in this chapter.

In this section we comment briefly on two models that have been advanced with the intention of solving this problem: these are known as **input processing** theory and **autonomous induction** theory.

6.9.1   Input processing

Input processing theory has been developed over the last decade by Bill VanPatten and associates (VanPatten, 1996, 2002). This particular theory has become well known largely because of an associated research programme on language pedagogy, known as **processing instruction** (*see* VanPatten and Cadierno, 1993). The theory is concerned to explain how environmental second language input becomes converted into intake:

> Intake is defined as the linguistic data actually processed from the input and held in working memory for further processing. As such, IP attempts to explain how learners get form from input and how they parse sentences during the act of comprehension while their primary attention is on meaning.
>
> (VanPatten, 2002, p. 757)

Input processing theory does not offer a complete model of these processes. Instead, it offers a set of 'principles' that seem designed primarily to explain the apparent failure of second language learners to process completely the linguistic forms encountered in second language input, and hence to explain their impoverished intake which in turn restricts the development of grammatical form. The input processing principles assume that learners have preferences for semantic processing over morphological processing, so that, for example, they process content words in the input before anything else, prefer to extract semantic information from lexical items rather than grammatical items (such as inflections), and prefer to process 'meaningful' morphology rather than 'non-meaningful' morphology. Take, for example, an English sentence such as, *We travelled to London by train yesterday*. In this sentence, past time is signalled twice, by the *-ed* verb inflection, and by the adverb '*yesterday*'. According to input processing theory, learners are likely to parse a sentence like this only incompletely, extracting temporal information from the adverb and ignoring the 'redundant' verb inflection. (We have come across similar suggestions associated with other theories, e.g. the Output hypothesis.)

Input processing theory also imputes to learners a number of other operating strategies, such as the 'first-noun' strategy which assigns the role of Subject to the first noun encountered in an utterance, and a preference for processing the beginnings and ends of sentences, over analysing medial elements. (This preference would also favour the processing of sentence-final '*yesterday*' in the earlier example.)

This approach has led to a series of pedagogical experiments that have tried to force second language classroom learners to parse input morphology more fully. In these experiments, learners are typically provided with input data in which morphology provides the main clues as to meaning. For example, they may be exposed to input in which verb inflections are the only available clues that provide temporal information, or in which prepositional phrases are the only available clues for location; *see* various studies reviewed in VanPatten (2002).

However, input processing theory is primarily focused on explaining the shortcuts and restricted processing strategies which learners seem to use. Thus it clearly does not offer a complete model of normal or successful processing of input, which presumably involves full parsing of input on a number of levels, plus procedures for the linking of form to meaning. Input processing theory also does not offer any extended explanation of how intake (defined here as analysed input, held in working memory) is processed further and becomes integrated more permanently in some way into the developing interlanguage system.

6.9.2   Autonomous induction theory

A much more complete and ambitious model of these processes is offered by Suzanne Carroll's Autonomous Induction theory (Carroll, 2000).

Carroll reminds us that the understanding of second language acquisition processes requires:

- an adequate theory of the representation of language in the mind (i.e. a property theory)
- an adequate theory of how language is processed, both receptively and productively
- a theory of how our mental representations of language can be changed, when we discover that our (interlanguage) representations are not adequate to process the environmental language we encounter (i.e. a transition theory).

Carroll accepts that our mental representations of language involve a number of distinct modules, as suggested by Universal Grammar, with limited interconnections. However, she rejects parameter (re)setting as a totally inadequate metaphor for the ways in which SLL takes place, that is, it is inadequate as a transition theory. Instead, she proposes a version of inductive learning (i-learning), which is initiated when we fail to parse incoming language stimuli adequately using our existing mental representations and analysis procedures. 'Inductive learning' is the term applied to learning by generalization from examples. It has been commonly criticized as inadequate with reference to language learning, because it fails to explain why learners processing the environmental language around them are so successful at working out the complexities of natural language, and in particular, why they never produce so-called 'wild grammars'. Carroll argues that the i-learning of Autonomous Induction theory differs from other inductive language learning theories such as the Competition Model (MacWhinney, 1999; 2001) because it is constrained by the pre-existing mental representations of language, which are strongly resistant to change.

Carroll's model is complex, and the full details are beyond the scope of this book. However, it is relevant to this chapter because she also presents a well-developed critique of interactionist research, for its theoretical limitations; for example, for its neglect of the detail of language processing which converts language stimuli into interpretable input. For example, she challenges a commonplace among interactionist researchers, who claim that increased comprehension (of second language meaning) can lead to identification and acquisition of language form, in a sequential manner (Steps 2 and 3 in Long's original Interaction hypothesis). Carroll points out that this is logically impossible. For one thing, unless enough formal analysis is done so that elements such as phonemes, syllables and words are identified in the speech stimulus as it flows by the learner, there is no way of generating any interpretation of its meaning.

6.10   Evaluation: the scope of interactionist research

The Input, Output and Interaction hypotheses have led to very active strands of empirical research. A first phase of research leaned heavily towards documenting the phenomenon of meaning negotiation. If it could be shown that negotiation increased comprehensibility of target language input, it was assumed that this would also enhance second language acquisition.

Later phases of interactionist research have developed in at least two ways. First, researchers have shown rather more concern to relate environmental factors in language learning to linguistic theory, and in particular to the assumptions of Universal Grammar. One obvious manifestation of this concern has been the recent interest in the possible significance of the negative evidence made available in second language interaction, for language acquisition. On the other hand, interactionist researchers have still not fully clarified their views regarding the most appropriate property theory that could be used to conceptualize the target of interaction-based learning. Some researchers have suggested that interaction may be most helpful in learning those aspects of the target language that fall outside the Universal Grammar core (e.g. peripheral, language-specific features of syntax). But it is still rare to find extensive discussions of these issues in the interactionist literature (with clear exceptions such as Carroll, 2000).

Second, interactionist research has paid increased attention to information processing issues, and the complications that are involved in the conversion of environmental language firstly into input, and subseqently into intake. Again however, interactionists have fixed on particular aspects of this problem, such as the possible role of selective attention, the usefulness of heightened saliency for promoting language processing, or the possible influence of a variety of processing constraints on intake. Attempts such as those of VanPatten and of Carroll to build fuller and more detailed models of the complete parsing process, and of what happens when parsing fails, remain relatively unusual and have not been fully integrated with the empirical traditions of interactionist research. However, calls for a more principled approach to theory building continue to be made (Nicholas *et al.*, 2001; Shehadeh, 2002).

6.10.1   Achievements of interactionist research

The achievements to date of research in the Input or Interaction tradition may be summarized as follows:

- It has been shown that native speaker and non-native speaker interlocutors (child and adult) can and will work actively to achieve mutual understanding, at least when undertaking a fairly wide range of problem-solving tasks.
- It has been shown that these negotiations involve both linguistic and interactional modifications, which together offer repeated opportunities to 'notice' aspects of target language form, whether from positive or negative evidence.
- It has been shown that non-native speaker participants in 'negotiations for meaning' can attend to, take up and use language items made available to them by their native speaker interlocutors.
- It has been shown that learners receiving negative feedback, relating to particular target language structures, can in some circumstances be significantly advantaged when later tested on those structures.

6.10.2   Limitations of interactionist research

However, the achievements of this tradition are still constrained by a number of important limitations:

- Work on interaction has been carried out almost entirely within a Western or Anglophone educational setting; more cross-cultural studies of second language interaction will be needed, before any claims can be made that 'negotiation for meaning' is a universal phenomenon.
- All researchers in the Input or Interactionist tradition seem to accept in general terms that second language acquisition must be the result of interaction between environmental stimuli, a learner-internal language system, and some language-specific learning capabilities. Attempts at modelling this interaction are mostly still very fragmentary and incomplete however, and the best-developed theoretical models (Carroll, 2000) have as yet not been widely adopted to guide empirical research. This means that we are still far from identifying what may be the most productive research questions to ask, about the role of interaction, etc., in learning.

- Much research on interaction, etc., has been of a broad-brush kind, for example producing global characterizations of interactional modifications, or demonstrating the existence of recasts or learners' re-use of negotiated items. There are still not very many studies that focus on particular language structures, tracking them through processes of instruction, negotiation, output or recasting, and documenting learners' subsequent use and control of these particular items. Such focused studies as exist have differing theoretical motivations, and do not (yet) add up to a coherent and developmentally oriented treatment of different aspects of target language grammar.
- It is clear that negotiation, recasts, etc., can vary in their usefulness for acquisition, and it seems that this variation is related to the developmental stage of the learner, as well as to different areas of the target language system (lexis, phonology, syntax, etc.). There is now some interactionist research that tries to take account of developmental readiness (Mackey and Philp, 1998; Mackey, 1999) and to differentiate among linguistic sub-systems (Lyster, 1998). But we are still not in a position to generalize or to make any very powerful predictions about the likely usefulness of interaction in either of these domains of variability.

One thing is clear, however, while Input or Interaction research remains highly active, it cannot solve these difficulties alone. Its future is intertwined with the development of more comprehensive models of the learner-internal second language acquisition process itself. (As we shall see, however, many of these comments apply not only to this particular research perspective but also to other primarily 'environmentalist' traditions to be explored in following chapters.)

7
Socio-cultural perspectives on second language learning

The co-construction of linguistic knowledge in dialogue is language learning in progress.

(Swain and Lapkin, 1998, p. 321)

7.1 Introduction

In this chapter and the next (Chapter 8), we turn our attention to theorists who view language learning in essentially social terms. In both these chapters, we examine the work of those who claim that target language interaction cannot be viewed simply as a source of 'input' for autonomous and internal learning mechanisms, but that it has a much more central role to play in learning. Indeed, for some researchers, interaction itself constitutes the learning process, which is quintessentially social rather than individual in nature. This is not a new view (*see* Hatch, 1978), but it was given extra impetus in the 1990s by an increasing interest in applying learning theory associated with the name of the Soviet developmental psychologist, Lev S. Vygotsky, to the domain of second language learning (SLL). In this chapter, we review and evaluate this strand of thinking and research, here called 'socio-cultural' theory following most current writers in this field.

Since the 1980s, the foremost figure advocating the relevance of socio-cultural theory to SLL has been James Lantolf. In the mid-1990s Lantolf edited two collections of papers that illustrate the application of different facets of Vygotskyan thinking to SLL (Lantolf, 1994; Lantolf and Appel, 1994). These have been followed by a further collection, which illustrates ongoing work in this tradition (Lantolf, 2000b), plus surveys by Lantolf and others which provide useful updates about theoretical developments as well as summarizing a wider range of empirical socio-cultural research (Dunn and Lantolf, 1998; Lantolf, 2000; Swain *et al.*, 2002).

7.2   Socio-cultural theory

Lev Semeonovich Vygotksy was born in 1896, the same year as the Swiss developmental psychologist, Jean Piaget, whose views on language development were briefly mentioned in Chapter 1. Born in the Russian provinces, Vygotsky was active in Moscow between 1925 and his early death in 1934. Like Piaget, he was a researcher and theorist of child development; however, his work fell into disfavour within Soviet psychology, and the first of his many writings to be translated into English, *Thought and Language*, appeared only in 1962. Since that time his views on child development have become increasingly influential, having been taken up and promoted by psychologists and child development theorists such as Jerome Bruner (1985), James Wertsch (1985, 1998) and Barbara Rogoff (1990, 1995), and applied in classroom studies by many educational researchers (Mercer, 1995, 2000; Wells, 1999). Parts of his wide-ranging writings remain untranslated, and contemporary interpretations and modifications to Vygotsky's original ideas mean that current socio-cultural theory is best described as 'neo-Vygotskyan'. Here, we will outline a number of key ideas current in contemporary interpretations or discussions of Vygotsky, which as we shall see, have recently been taken up by SLL theorists.

7.2.1   Mediation and mediated learning

In a recent formulation, Lantolf explains that:

> The central and distinguishing concept of sociocultural theory is that higher forms of human mental activity are *mediated*. Vygotsky (1987) argued that just as humans do not act directly on the physical world but rely, instead, on tools and labour activity, we also use symbolic tools, or signs, to mediate and regulate our relationships with others and with ourselves. Physical and symbolic tools are artifacts created by human culture(s) over time and are made available to succeeding generations, which often modify these artifacts before passing them on to future generations. Included among symbolic tools are numbers and arithmetic systems, music, art, and above all, language. As with physical tools, humans use symbolic artifacts to establish an indirect, or mediated, relationship between ourselves and the world. The task for psychology, in Vygotsky's view, is to understand how human social and mental activity is organised through culturally constructed artifacts and social relationships.
>
> (Lantolf, 2000a, p. 80)

This quotation shows clearly the socio-cultural belief in the centrality of language as a 'tool for thought', or a means of mediation, in mental activity. Through language, for example, we can direct our own attention (or that of others) to significant features in the environment, rehearse information to be learnt, formulate a plan or articulate the steps to be taken in solving a problem. In turn, it is claimed that the nature of our available mental tools can itself shape our thinking to some extent. For example, David Olson (1995) has argued that once writing systems were invented, these 'mental tools' changed our understanding of the nature of language itself, because they provided humanity with concepts and categories for thinking about language, such as the 'word' the 'sentence', or the 'phoneme', which did not exist before the development of literacy. Similarly, Lantolf (2000a) quotes studies by Warschauer (1997) and Thorne (2000), which show how new forms of computer-mediated communication, such as the use of chat rooms or text messaging, have new and distinctive characteristics different from those of traditional written communication, and shaped by the technology itself.

From the socio-cultural point of view, learning is also a mediated process. It is mediated partly through learners' developing use and control of mental tools (and once again, language is the central tool for learning, though other semiotic modes of representation play a role: Wells, 1999, pp. 319–20). Importantly, learning is also seen as socially mediated, that is to say, it is dependent on face-to-face interaction and shared processes, such as joint problem solving and discussion. How these learning processes are claimed to work is explored further in the next section.

7.2.2   Regulation, scaffolding and the Zone of Proximal Development

The mature, skilled individual is capable of autonomous functioning, that is of **self-regulation**. However, the child or the unskilled individual learns by carrying out tasks and activities under the guidance of other more skilled individuals (such as caregivers or teachers), initially through a process of **other-regulation**, typically mediated through language. That is, the child or the learner is inducted into a shared understanding of how to do things through collaborative talk, until eventually they take over (or **appropriate**) new knowledge or skills into their own individual consciousness. So, successful learning involves a shift from collaborative inter-mental activity to autonomous intra-mental activity. The process of supportive dialogue which directs the attention of the learner to key features of the environment, and which prompts them through successive steps of a problem, has come to be known as **scaffolding** (Wood *et al.*, 1976).

The domain where learning can most productively take place is christened the **Zone of Proximal Development**, that is, the domain of knowledge or skill where the learner is not yet capable of independent functioning, but can achieve the desired outcome given relevant scaffolded help. The Zone of Proximal Development was defined by Vygotsky, as:

> the difference between the child's developmental level as determined by independent problem solving and the higher level of potential development as determined through problem solving under adult guidance or in collaboration with more capable peers.

(Vygotsky, 1978, p. 85)

These ideas are illustrated in an example taken from the general educational literature (Mercer, 1996):

> *You have a square sheet of card measuring 15 cm by 15 cm and you want to use it to make an open cuboid container by cutting out the corners. What is the maximum capacity the container can have?*

EMILY:	This box is bigger than what it should be 'cos if you get 15 by 15 you get 225, but if you times um 9 by 9 times 3 you still get 243 and I haven't got that much space in my box.
A:	You have.
EMILY:	But the 15 by . . .
B:	If can be, it can work, I think.
EMILY:	But surely . . .
B:	You cut off corners.
EMILY:	Yeh but that surely should make it *smaller*.
B:	I think that is right.
EMILY:	(*counting squares marked on the paper*) Hang on, 1, 2, 3, 4, 5 . . .
C:	You're not going to get 243.
EMILY:	I shouldn't get 243 'cos if the piece of paper had 225 then, um . . .
C:	Hang on, look . . . 9 times 9 times how many was it up?
A:	But, don't you remember Emily it's got all this space in the middle.
EMILY:	Yeh, but . . .
A:	It's got all that space in the middle.
EMILY:	(*sounding exasperated*) No, it hasn't got anything to do with it. If my piece of paper had only 225 squares on it, I can't get more out of the same piece of paper.
A:	You can because you're forgetting, things go *up* as well, not just the flat piece of paper like that.
EMILY:	Oh, yeh.
A:	It's going up.
A:	It's going up.
C:	It's because, look, down here you've got 3 and it's going up.
A:	You're going 3 up, it's getting more on it. Do you see it will be 243?
EMILY:	Yeh.
C:	It's right, it should be.

(Mercer, 1996, pp. 34–5)

Here, Emily is a secondary school student who is struggling to make sense of a mathematical problem (which involves the relationship between area and volume). She is already proficient in the necessary arithmetical skills, so that the problem is in principle accessible to her (in Vygotskyan terms, it lies within her personal Zone of Proximal Development). Her peers direct her attention to different aspects of the problem, and their activities illustrate the concepts of other-regulation and scaffolding. Eventually the successive attempts of Emily's friends to direct her attention to the three-dimensional nature of the problem seem to be successful, as evidenced in her non-verbal reaction in Line 24, and her subsequent contributions. The claim is that a qualitative change in Emily's understanding has occurred, so that she could in future solve similar problems without help. In Vygotskyan terms, Emily has **appropriated** the necessary concepts, and should be more capable of regulating her own performance on another similar occasion.

The metaphor of **scaffolding** has been developed in neo-Vygotskyan discussions to capture the qualities of the type of other-regulation within the Zone of Proximal Development which is supposedly most helpful for the learning or appropriation of new concepts. According to Wood *et al.* (1976), scaffolded help has the following functions:

- recruiting interest in the task
- simplifying the task
- maintaining pursuit of the goal
- marking critical features and discrepancies between what has been produced, and the ideal solution
- controlling frustration during problem solving
- demonstrating an idealized version of the act to be performed.

As Donato (1994, p. 41) puts it, 'scaffolded performance is a dialogically constituted interpsychological mechanism that promotes the novice's internalisation of knowledge co-constructed in shared activity'.

7.2.3   Microgenesis

The example just quoted illustrates in miniature the general principles of socio-cultural learning theory. For Vygotsky, these principles apply on a range of different timescales. They apply to the learning that the human race has passed through over successive generations (**phylogenesis**), as well as to the learning that the individual human infant passes through in the course of its early development (**ontogenesis**). For the entire human race, as well as for the individual infant, learning is seen as first social, then individual. Consciousness and conceptual development are seen firstly as inter-mental phenomena, shared between individuals; later, individuals develop their own consciousness, which becomes an intra-mental phenomenon. For the human race, and also for the individual infant, language is the prime symbolic mediating tool for the development of consciousness.

Throughout their life, of course, human beings remain capable of learning; and the local learning process for more mature individuals acquiring new knowledge or skills is viewed as essentially the same. That is, new concepts continue to be acquired through social or interactional means, a process that can sometimes be traced visibly in the course of talk between expert and novice. This local, contextualized learning process is labelled **microgenesis**; it is central to socio-cultural accounts of SLL, as will be clear below.

7.2.4   Private and inner speech

Young children are well known to engage in **private speech**, talk apparently to and for themselves rather than for any external conversational partners. From the point of view of classic Piagetian theory of child development, this talk has been interpreted as evidence of children's **egocentrism**, or inability to view the world from another's point of view. However, private speech is interpreted very differently in socio-cultural theory. Here, it is seen as evidence of children's growing ability to regulate their own behaviour – when, for example, a child talks to himself while painting a picture, or solving a puzzle. For Vygotsky, private speech eventually becomes **inner speech**, a use of language to regulate internal thought, without any external articulation. Thus, private speech reflects an advance on the earliest uses of language, which are social and interpersonal. The fully autonomous individual has developed inner speech as a tool of thought, and normally feels no further need to articulate external private speech. However, when tackling a new task, even skilled adults may accompany and regulate their efforts with a private monologue.

7.2.5   Activity theory

The last important idea that we need to consider is that of **activity theory**, primarily developed by one of Vygotsky's successors, A. N. Leontiev (Leontiev, 1981; Lantolf and Appel, 1994; Zinchenko, 1995). Socio-cultural theorists are keen to study and make sense of both individual and collaborative behaviour and motivation within its socio-cultural setting (*see* papers in Wertsch *et al.*, 1995). Activity theory thus comprises a series of proposals for conceptualizing the social context within which individual learning takes place. A helpful account is offered by Donato and McCormick:

> Activity is defined in terms of sociocultural settings in which collaborative interaction, intersubjectivity, and assisted performance occur . . . In his analysis, Leontiev conceived activity as containing a subject, an object, actions, and operations. To illustrate these constituents of activity we use the classroom as an example. A student (a subject) is engaged in an activity, for example, learning a new language. An object, in the sense of a goal, is held by the student and motivates his or her activity, giving is a specific direction. In the case of our language learner, the object could range from full participation in a new culture to receiving a passing grade required for graduation.
>
> To achieve the objective, actions are taken by the student, and these actions are always goal-directed . . . Different actions or strategies may be taken to achieve the same goal, such as guessing meaning from context, reading foreign language newspapers, or using a bilingual dictionary to improve reading comprehension . . .
>
> Finally, the operational level of activity is the way an action is carried out and depends on the conditions under which actions are executed. For example, how one attends to driving a car depends in large part on the context of the activity (e.g. weather conditions, purpose of trip, type of vehicle, etc.). These operational aspects of actions can become routinized and automatic once the conscious goal is no longer attended to. Returning to our example of the language learner, if the goal of the learner was to become proficient in deriving meaning from context rather than from the bilingual dictionary, contextual guessing during reading becomes automatized once the learner becomes adept at this strategy . . . The model of human activity depicted in activity theory is not static, however. Routinized operations (automatic strategies) can become conscious goal-directed actions if the conditions under which they are carried out change. In the case of our second language reader who has operationalized at the unconscious level the strategy of contextual guessing, it is quite conceivable that this strategy will be reactivated at the conscious level if the learner is confronted with a difficult passage beyond his or her strategic ability, i.e. if the conditions of strategy use change.
>
> (Donato and McCormick, 1994, p. 455)

What we see in such formulations are proposals for a research methodology that sees all human actions (and 'mediated action' in particular) as configurations of influences, both social and individual, within a dynamic system (Wertsch, 1995, p. 63). It is these dynamic systems that must be investigated holistically, rather than their discrete parts. We will see this commitment to a holistic methodology at work in empirical socio-cultural investigations of SLL.

7.3   Applications of socio-cultural theory to second language learning

From a socio-cultural perspective, children's early language learning arises from processes of meaning-making in collaborative activity with other members of a given culture. From this collaborative activity, language itself develops as a 'tool' for making meaning (Newman and Holzman, 1993, in Dunn and Lantolf, 1998, p. 420). Similarly, the second language learner has an opportunity to create yet more tools and new ways of meaning, through collaborative activity with other users of the target second language. This point of view is radically different from the dominant discourses of SLL discussed elsewhere in this book, from a number of points of view. The unitary concept of activity theory challenges the compartmentalization of social and psychological aspects of language learning; the concept of microgenesis of new language forms in social interaction disputes distinctions between surface performance and underlying competence; and the concept of the Zone of Proximal Development links processes of instruction, organized learning and 'naturalistic' development or acquisition in a single site. Thus, for example, the similarity perceived by some commentators between Krashen's Input hypothesis and the Zone of Proximal Development, is disputed by socio-cultural theorists (Dunn and Lantolf, 1998; Kinginger, 2001). The Input hypothesis prioritizes psycholinguistic processes, with linguistic input just ahead of the learner's current developmental stage systematically affecting the learner's underlying second language system (i + 1; *see* Chapter 6). Application of the Zone of Proximal Development to SLL assumes that new language knowledge is jointly constructed through collaborative activity, which may or may not involve formal instruction and meta-talk, and is then appropriated by the learner, seen as an active agent in their own development.

What are the particular lines of enquiry into SLL that have been sparked off by the current climate of interest in socio-cultural theory? In turn, we will consider a selection of second language research studies that have appealed to a number of key Vygotskyan ideas: private speech, activity theory, and the role of scaffolding and the Zone of Proximal Development in language learning.

7.3.1   Private speech and self-regulation in second language discourse

Instances of **private speech** have regularly been noted in naturalistic studies of child second language acquisition, as in other studies of child language. However, their significance has been variously interpreted. The following example is quoted by Hatch (1978), from a study by Itoh (1973) of a Japanese first language child learning English as a second language:

H:	House.
Takahiro:	This house?
H:	House.
T:	House.
	To make the house.
	To make the house.
	To make the house.
	This?
	House.
	Garage.
	Garage house
	house
	big house
	Oh-no!
	broken.
H:	Too bad.
T:	Too bad.
H:	Try again.
T:	I get try.
	I get try.
H:	Good.

For Hatch (1978, p. 411), Takahiro's extended speech turn, accompanying a construction activity of some kind, is viewed somewhat negatively as 'not social speech at all but [only] language play'. She goes on to argue defensively that the fact that it is merely 'language play', need not necessarily mean it is useless for language acquisition; but she does not analyse its positive functions any further. From a Vygotskyan perspective, however, this extended spoken accompaniment to action provides evidence about the role of language in problem-solving and self-regulation. (It also provides evidence for the **appropriation** by the child of the new lexical item *house*, initially supplied by the supportive adult, but then quickly re-used by Takahiro in a range of syntactic frames.)

The first phase of studies that explicitly brought Vygotskyan conceptions of private speech to bear on language learner data mostly worked with data elicited from older learners, in semi-controlled settings (*see* review by McCafferty, 1994). In one of the first attempts to apply any aspect of Vygotskyan theory to SLL, Frawley and Lantolf (1985) reported an empirical study of English second language learners undertaking a narrative task, based on a picture sequence. They were critical of **schema theories** of narrative, which propose that stories are narrated in a deterministic manner, according to a previously internalized template (situation, actors, events, problems, resolutions, etc.); they also argued that **information processing models** of communication, which view communication primarily as the encoding and transmission of a predetermined message, could not account adequately for their data. (This is a common theme in sociocultural critiques of second language acquisition research; *see also* Platt and Brooks, 1994, pp. 498–9.)

The picture sequence used by Frawley and Lantolf (1985) comprised the following frames:

- Frame 1:   A boy walks along a road.
- Frame 2:   He sees an ice cream seller.
- Frame 3:   He buys a 50-cent ice cream cone.
- Frame 4:   He gives the cone to a small boy.
- Frame 5:   A man approaches the small boy.
- Frame 6:   The man takes the cone from the small boy. The small boy cries.

In re-telling this story, the English second language learners produced accounts that were, as narratives, disjointed and incoherent. However, they incorporated into their accounts many utterances which involved direct reactions or descriptions of individual pictures (*I see a boy on the road*), or externalizations of the task itself (*You want me to say what they are doing? This is the problem now*, etc.). These meta-comments were entirely absent from the fluent performances of a group of native speakers (*A little boy is walking down the street . . .* etc.).

Frawley and Lantolf (1985, p. 26) interpreted the data as demonstrating the learners' need to 'impose order on the task by speaking and identifying the task'. In Vygotskyan terms, they argued that the learners were struggling to move beyond **object-regulation** (in this case, evidenced in direct reactions to the pictures, or descriptions of them) towards **self-regulation** and control over the task. Because they could not take self-regulation for granted, their efforts to gain control were explicitly articulated throughout their performance.

Figure 7.1 shows a pair of narratives taken from a different study (McCafferty 1992), which used a similar methodology.

McCafferty argued that many utterances incorporated within the narrative of the second language subject were examples of private speech, which reflected object-regulation (*I see a man on . . . in the picture*), other-regulation (here defined as any utterances which are dialogic in form, e.g.

The task in this study required subjects to narrate a series of six pictures concerning a hat seller who falls asleep under a tree only to wake up and find that a group of monkeys has taken his hats and is up in the tree above him. He eventually discerns that the monkeys imitate his actions and is able to retrieve the hats by throwing his own to the ground.

Low-intermediate L2 subject:

1) I see a man on . . . in the picture. He's looking at some monkeys – the monkeys are in the tree. Monkeys are playing in the tree. There is a house next to the tree. There are some hats in baskets . . . two baskets. Maybe the man is thinking about how happy are the monkeys? Maybe he's looking at the sky.

2) What do I see? There is another basket of hats. Now, the monkeys look at the man. The man is sleeping. Now, because the man is sleeping the monkeys are playing with the hats.

3) Suddenly, the man wakes up and looked at the monkeys. He surprised about the monkeys because the monkeys put on, on their, on their heads the hats.

4) The man is angry. He wants to take his hats. The monkeys are happy, they are doing a sign, a sign of victory to the man . . . 'we have the hats!' They have the hats.

5) Oh no! It's different! The monkeys are copying the signs of the man, and in this picture the man is thinking – I don't know about what. Maybe he's thinking about what he can – he do, and the monkeys, they take out, take off the hats and look at the man, and they are copying the same signs of the man.

6) Ah. Ok. Suddenly, the man had a . . . has one idea – he, he thought, 'I'm going to fell down, fell down my hat so the monkeys are going to fell down, fall down they . . . my hats too.' Ok. And the man fell down the hats and the monkeys copy to the man and do that too.

Adult native speaker

1) The man's watching the monkeys playing . . . and the monkeys want to get all his hats – I guess.

2) And when he falls asleep the monkeys come down, get his hats, and put them on back in the tree.

3) When he wakes up, he realizes that the monkeys are wearing all of the hats that he wants to sell . . . and he's pretty surprised.

4) He tries to get the monkeys to give him back his hats and gets mad at them, and the monkeys just imitate him.

5) Then, he starts thinking about the situation and the monkeys act like they're thinking about something too – imitating him.

6) In the end, he figures out that the monkeys will do what he does and so, ah, he throws down his hat and the monkeys imitate him . . . so he gets his hats back and he's happy.

Fig. 7.1 Private speech in first language narrative (*Source*: McCafferty, 1994, p. 426)

self-directed questions like *What do I see?*), and self-regulation (here defined as meta-comments indicating that a subject has suddenly understood or mastered a source of difficulty, as here in Frame 6).

In this and other studies, McCafferty systematically contrasted the extent of private speech to be found in the narratives produced by learners at different levels of proficiency as well as by native speakers, demonstrating that there is a systematic relationship between the use of private speech to regulate task performance and the degree of task difficulty. He argued that in producing second language discourse, learners may expend just as much effort to self-regulate as to communicate; 'a Vygotskian view of private speech affords a valuable window onto the intra-personal processes in which adult L2 learners engage in their efforts to self-regulate in the face of the very complex process of learning a second language' (McCafferty, 1994, p. 434).

More recently there has been a growth in naturalistic studies of private speech within second language learners. For example, Anton and DiCamilla (1999) have studied the uses of first language English by adult students who were audio-recorded while working collaboratively to complete a second language Spanish classroom writing task. Alongside collaborative uses of English, these researchers recognized the use of English in private speech with regulatory and task management functions.

Lastly, growing numbers of researchers have used individual microphones to record learners' private second language speech in ordinary classroom settings, and have investigated possible links between this type of private speech and the appropriation or internalization of new language forms. A striking example is the work of Amy Snyder Ohta (2001), who conducted longitudinal case studies of seven adult learners of Japanese as a second language, in two different classroom settings. The learners regularly wore personal microphones, so that their private speech was recorded alongside other types of language use. In the Ohta study, the learners were judged to be using second language private speech when they whispered or spoke with reduced volume, compared with their usual speech, or when they spoke but were not attended to by others (e.g. by the teacher). Most of the learners in this study used second language private speech regularly during whole-class interaction.

Ohta identifies three main types of second language private speech. The most common form was **repetition**, where the learners privately repeated the utterances of the teacher or of other students. This was common practice with newly introduced lexical items or with sentences that were the focus of class attention. The example below shows learner, Rob, repeating a new Japanese word privately (the symbols °, °° and °°° are indicators of lowered speech volume):

1	T:	Ja shinshifuku uriba ni nani ga arimasu ka?
		So, what is there in the men's department?
2	S9:	Kutsushita ga arimasu.
		There are socks.
3	T:	Kutsushita ga arimasu.
		There are socks.
4	S10:	Jaketto.
		Jackets.
5	S11:	Nekutai.
		Ties.
6	T:	Jaketto ga arima:su. Un S12-san? Nekutai ga arimasu. S12-san?
		There are jackets. Uh S12? There are ties. S12?
7	S12:	Uh [kutsushita ga arimasu.
		Uh there are socks.
→ 8	R:	[°°Nekutai nekutai°° (.) °nekutai nekutai
		°°*Tie tie*°° *(.)* °*tie tie*°.

(Ohta, 2001, pp. 57–8)

Learners also produced **vicarious responses**, when they responded privately to a question from the teacher, or repaired or completed someone else's utterance. An example is shown below, where learner Kuo-ming produces an incorrect vicarious response first of all, and then self-corrects privately after hearing the teacher's utterance:

1	T:	Eto jaa kanji no kuizu arimashita ne::. (.) arimashi<u>ta</u>. (.) ne
		arimashita ne, muzukashikatta desu ka?
		Um well there was a kanji quiz wasn't there. (.) there was (.)
		right? There was, was it difficult?
→ 2	Km:	°Um°
3	Ss:	Iie
		No
→ 4	Km:	°E::h yasashi desu°
		°*E::h it is easy*° *((error: should be in the past tense))*
5	T:	Yasa[shikatta desu um
		It was easy um
→ 6	Km:	[°°Yasashikatta desu°°
		°°*It was easy*°°
7	T:	Ii desu ne::. Jaa kanji ii desu ka?
		That's good. Is everyone okay with the kanji?

(Ohta, 2001, p. 51)

Finally, learners engaged in **manipulation**, when they privately constructed their own second language utterances, manipulating sentence structure, building up and breaking down words, and engaging in sound play.

Ohta claims that her case study learners typically engaged in second language private speech when confronted with 'new or problematic' language. This private speech reflected their active engagement with classroom discourse in a variety of ways. It allowed them to develop phonological and articulatory control of new material (through repetition). It provided opportunities for hypothesis testing about sentence construction, for example through comparison of privately produced candidate forms with the utterances of others, or through working on segmentation problems. Private speech during whole-class talk also allowed for simulation of social interaction and conversational exchanges, ahead of, for example, involvement in pair or group work. Altogether, Ohta argues that:

> Analysis reveals the extent to which covert learner activity is a centerpiece of learning processes, deepening our understanding of how learners appropriate language through interactive processes ... results suggest the power of engagement as a factor in L2 acquisition, as the data reveal instances in which linguistic affordances acted on by the learner in private speech are incorporated into the learner's developing linguistic system.
>
> (Ohta, 2001, pp. 30–1)

7.3.2   Activity theory and small group interaction

As we have seen earlier, Vygotskyan theorists of SLL are generally critical of 'transmission' models of communication, in which ready-made messages are passed from speaker to hearer (Donato, 1994; Lantolf, 1996). Similarly, they are critical of input and interactional models of language learning in which 'negotiation of meaning' is central, and where researchers are preoccupied with how learners' utterances influence each other in terms of form and function (*see* Chapter 6). Platt and Brooks view this perspective as failing to capture the prime characteristics of language use:

> What we are suggesting is a more robust view that incorporates an understanding of talk or, more specifically, speech activity as cognitive activity that humans press into service in order to solve problems, regardless of its communicative intent.
>
> (Platt and Brooks, 1994, p. 499)

Moreover, the tenets of activity theory (*see above*) lead researchers in this tradition to argue strongly for the distinctive nature of individual interactions as experienced by the participants, even where preset communicative tasks appear to be 'the same'. According to activity theory, the personal goals with which an individual approaches a particular task or problem may vary; thus, for example, a language learner may approach a conversational task under test conditions with a prime personal goal of achieving an accurate performance, even if the task designers intended it as a test of fluency, or vice versa. The entry levels of knowledge and skill which individuals bring to particular tasks will of course also vary, as well as being subject to change in the course of the task itself. (In Vygotskyan terms, the less expert participant can **appropriate** and internalize knowledge or skill which is collaboratively developed in the course of the interaction.)

In support of these claims, Coughlan and Duff (1994) examined data gathered through an 'identical' picture description task in a variety of language learning settings, and argue that such features as subjects' willingness to stray off the point were highly context dependent (depending on how well they knew their interlocutor, how much time they believed was allocated to the task, the interlocutor's ongoing reactions, the sequence of tasks in which the picture description activity was embedded, etc.). Similarly, Roebuck (2000) studied learner activity when adult learners of Spanish as a second language were asked to listen to varied texts in both first and second languages, and to write down as much as they could recall. The learners responded in different ways to this difficult task, some recalling and narrating content in the order they had heard it, others producing lists and plans, or even translating. Roebuck also detects evidence of changing learner subjectivity and orientation towards the task, reflected in meta-statements and marginal comments. For example she quotes a student who completed the task, and then wrote: 'A cruel thing to make students read' (Roebuck, 2000, p. 93)! Roebuck interprets this evaluation as a claim by the student to equal status with the 'authority figure' that had devised the task in the first place. For her as for others who use activity theory to interpret second language interaction, student subjectivity is an inalienable component of tasks in progress.

Platt and Brooks (1994) recorded pairs and groups of students undertaking a variety of communicative problem-solving tasks in second language classroom settings, and used activity theory to interpret the resulting discourse. The tasks included map-reading and jigsaw puzzle completion, that is, the sorts of activities which interaction theorists view as useful, because they supposedly promote the negotiation of meaning and the availability of comprehensible input, and hence provide rich opportunities for second language acquisition. However, Platt and Brooks argue that these tasks did not provide a uniform learning environment for participating learners, because different learners experienced them differently. They claim that students' own immediate task-related goals are critical in influencing the nature of the activity as actually experienced. Their examples include:

- Students 'going through the motions' of English second language task performance, rehearsing a problem which they appear already to understand (role playing the demonstration of an oscilloscope).
- A student who engages in long stretches of private speech to regulate his own performance as he addresses the 'same' oscilloscope demonstration task, apparently incapable of attending to his peers who try to redirect him.
- Students learning Swahili at beginner level who successfully carry out a map-based information exchange task, using a combination of paralinguistic means and single word paratactic constructions.
- High school students making extensive use of first language to define and redefine the ground rules for an second language Spanish jigsaw puzzle completion task, and to comment on task performance.

Platt and Brooks claim that the learners in these cases were working towards task completion by diverse routes, which were highly variable in the language learning opportunities available.

In a later paper (Platt and Brooks, 2002), reflecting in detail on ongoing changes in learner activity when undertaking the same map-based and jigsaw puzzle tasks, Platt and Brooks argue that 'task engagement' must take place, if learners are to move from 'mere compliance' to take control of given classroom tasks, make maximum use of the second language, and create the most favourable conditions for language learning. They document in detail how two different pairs of learners shift from desultory pre-engagement, to high levels of task engagement and success. With the map-based task, the turning point comes where one student asks his partner for assistance, and receives scaffolded help, which makes the task seem manageable; with the grid completion task, one student discovers a more systematic approach to working through the grid, and communicates her excitement about her new strategy to her partner. In such cases, claim Platt and Brooks:

> Achieving this transformation establishes a platform from which the individual changes from one who stumbles and searches for words to one who is motivated to solve a difficult problem using his or her emergent yet still imperfect linguistic system and other mediational tools.
>
> (Platt and Brooks, 2002, p. 393)

Platt and Brooks are concerned with clarifying how learners set about completing tasks and solving problems, and how they may transform their motivation and available strategies during this process. They only indirectly infer related changes in language learning opportunities. However, McCafferty *et al.* (2001) apply activity theory more directly to a language learning issue – the acquisition of second language vocabulary. These researchers ran a small-scale comparative study with two groups of learners of second language Spanish. One group was given a list of previously unknown words about animals, and asked to include them in an essay about zoos. The second group was asked to devise and run an interview with fellow students about their early language learning experiences, and were told they could ask for any vocabulary items they needed to fill gaps. It was found that the vocabulary items requested by individual members of the second group, and then actively used by them during the interview process, were retained much more than the animal words made generally available to the first group. It was also found that individual members of the interview group were much better at remembering words that were central to their own individual interview agenda, than they were at remembering new words used by other members of their group. McCafferty *et al.* (2001) interpret these results as showing that the learner's chances of learning a given new item derives from the role of the item within an ongoing activity, and in particular, its relation to 'goal-directed action'.

7.3.3   Scaffolding and second language learning in the Zone of Proximal Development

In this section we examine more clearly how new **language** knowledge is supposed to arise in the course of social interaction, according to socio-cultural theory, and how it is internalized by the learner.

Many naturalistic studies conducted by researchers working outside the Vygotskyan tradition offer evidence which can be interpreted as showing the sharing and transfer of new second language lexical and grammatical knowledge between speakers. We have already seen the child learner, Takahiro, appropriating and using the word *house*, offered to him by an adult carer (Hatch, 1978, p. 410). Another of Hatch's examples, taken from Brunak *et al.* (1976), shows an adult learner eliciting and using an expression she needs (*last year*) from a co-operative interlocutor:

NS:	O that's a beautiful plant!
	I like that.
	Did you buy that?
Rafaela:	Excuse me . . .
	This is the . . .
	October 24.
	The how you say . . .
	The . . . (writes '1974')
	year, ah?

NS: 1974. Last year.
R: Ah! Last years.
NS: One. (Correction of plural form)
R: Last year.
       Last year a friend gave me it.

From an input or interaction perspective, such passages would be interpreted as instances of negotiation of meaning, conversational repair, etc., and would be seen as maximizing the relevance of the available input for the learner's acquisitional stage. From a Vygotskyan perspective, it would be argued that we are witnessing **microgenesis** in the learner's second language system, through the appropriation of a new lexical item from the scaffolding talk of the native speaker.

However, most of the research into dialogue and its role in SLL that has been conducted from an explicitly socio-cultural point of view has taken place in classrooms rather than in informal settings. Following the classic Vygotskyan view of the Zone of Proximal Development as involving interaction between an 'expert' and a 'novice', one group of socio-cultural studies has examined the second language development which appears to take place during scaffolded teacher–student talk.

Aljaafreh and Lantolf (1994) conducted a pioneering study of this type. The participants in this longitudinal study were adult English as second language learners receiving one-to-one feedback from a language tutor on weekly writing assignments. At each weekly tutorial, the students first of all re-read their own writing, and checked for any errors they could identify without help; the tutor and student then worked through the assignment together sentence by sentence. When an error was identified, the tutor aimed to scaffold the learner to correct it in a contingent manner: 'the idea is to offer just enough assistance to encourage and guide the learner to participate in the activity and to assume increased responsibility for arriving at the appropriate performance' (Aljaafreh and Lantolf, 1994, p. 469).

The learners were tracked and audio-recorded for eight weeks; the study focused on their developing capability (or microgenetic growth) on four grammatical points in written English (articles, tense marking, use of prepositions, and modal verbs). First, the researchers looked for an increase in accuracy in the use of these forms over time, as well as for any generalization of learning beyond the specific items that had received attention in tutorial discussion. Second, even where these errors continued to appear in students' writing, they looked for evidence of students' developing capacity to self-correct, and reducing dependency on other-regulation by the tutor.

Aljaafreh and Lantolf developed a 'Regulatory Scale' to illustrate how the tutor's interventions could be ranged on a continuum from implicit to explicit correction; this scale is shown as Table 7.1.

When the feedback needed by individual students moved closer to the Implicit end of the scale, they were considered to be moving towards more independent and self-regulated performance, and this was consequently taken as positive evidence of learning.

The protocols presented in Figure 7.2 illustrate the type of data collected and discussed by these researchers.

In Protocol L, we see the tutor and student F attempting to work out the correct tense markings for modal + main verb constructions. The tutor provides progressively more explicit feedback on the student's written error (cited in lines 2/3), actually modelling the correct past tense form for modal auxiliary *can* in Line 23. Later in the same tutorial, the same problem is encountered again (Protocol M, lines 1/2). Initially, the learner focuses on a different problem: she has written *do* for *to*, an error that she notices and corrects. However, once the tutor draws her attention to the incorrect verb pattern, she supplies firstly the correct auxiliary past tense form *could*, and then the untensed form of the main verb, *go*.

Table 7.1   Ranking error feedback on an implicit/explicit scale

Regulatory scale – Implicit (strategic) to Explicit

0	Tutor asks the learner to read, find the errors, and correct them independently, prior to the tutorial
1	Construction of a 'collaborative frame' prompted by the presence of the tutor as a potential dialogic partner
2	Prompted or focused reading of the sentence that contains the error by the learner or the tutor
3	Tutor indicates that something may be wrong in a segment (e.g. sentence, clause, line) – 'Is there anything wrong in this sentence?'
4	Tutor rejects unsuccessful attempts at recognizing the error
5	Tutor narrows down the location of the error (e.g. tutor repeats or points to the specific segment which contains the error)
6	Tutor indicates the nature of the error, but does not identify the error (e.g. 'There is something wrong with the tense marking here')
7	Tutor identifies the error ('You can't use an auxiliary here')
8	Tutor rejects learner's unsuccessful attempts at correcting the error
9	Tutor provides clues to help the learner arrive at the correct form (e.g. 'It is not really past but something that is still going on')
10	Tutor provides the correct form
11	Tutor provides some explanation for use of the correct form
12	Tutor provides examples of the correct pattern when other forms of help fail to produce an appropriate responsive action

(*Source*: Aljaafreh and Lantolf, 1994, p. 471)

(L) *F1*

1. T: Okay, 'to the . . . [yeah] to the US. [Okay] In that moment I can't
2. . . . lived in the house because I didn't have any furniture.'
3. Is that . . . what what is wrong with that sentence, too?
4. What is wrong with the sentence we just read? . . . 'In that
5. moment I can't lived in the house because I didn't have any
6. furniture' . . . Do you see?
7. F: No
8. T: Okay . . . ah there is something wrong with the verb with the
9. verb tense in this this sentence and the modal . . . Do you know
10. modals?
11. F: Ah yes, I know
12. T: Okay, so what's what's wrong what's wrong here?
13. F: The tense of this live
14. T: Okay, what about the the . . . is it just in this or in this, the
15. whole thing?
16. F: The whole this
17. T: Okay, how do you correct it? . . . Okay, 'In that moment, . . . What?
18. . . . What is the past tense of can? what was
19. happening . . . what . . . the past, right? what was happening
20. . . . what . . . the event happened in the past right? so what
21. is the past tense of this verb can? . . . Do you know?
22. F: No
23. T: Okay, ah could
24. F: Ah yes
25. T: Okay, 'I could not . . .'
26. F: Live
27. T: Ah exactly, okay. So when you use this in the past then the second verb is the simple . . .
28. F: Yes
29. T: Form, okay . . . aah 'in that moment I could not . . .'
30. F: Live in the house

(M) *F1*

1. T: Okay, 'I called other friends who can't went do the party.' Okay,
2. what is wrong here?
3. F: To
4. T: 'Who can't went do the party because that night they worked at
5. the hospital.' Okay, from here 'I called other friends who
6. can't went do the party.' What's wrong in this?
7. F: To?
8. T: Okay, what else? . . . what about the verb and the tense? The
9. verb and the tense? . . .
10. F: Could
11. T: Okay, here
12. F: Past tense
13. T: All right, okay, 'who [alright] could not.' Alright? And? . . .
14. F: To
15. T: Here [points to the verb phrase], what's the right form?
16. F: I . . . go
17. T: Go. Okay, 'could not go to [that's right] to the party . . .'

(N) *F2*

1. T: Is there anything wrong here in this sentence? 'I took only Ani
2. because I couldn't took both' . . . Do you see anything
3. wrong? . . . Particularly here 'because I couldn't took both'
4. F: Or Maki?
5. T: What the verb verb . . . something wrong with the verb . . .
6. F: Ah, yes . . .
7. T: That you used. Okay, where? Do you see it?
8. F: (Points to the verb)
9. T: Took? Okay
10. F: Take
11. T: Alright, take
12. F: (Laughs)

Fig. 7.2 Microgenesis in the language system (*Source*: Aljaafreh and Lantolf, 1994, pp. 478–9)

The researchers argue that this reduced need for other-regulation itself constitutes evidence for microgenetic development within the learner's Zone of Proximal Development.

Protocol N provides further performance data, this time from the tutorial that took place around the student's next assignment, one week later. The researchers claim that here again 'we see evidence of microgenesis both in production of the Modal + Verb construction and the extent of responsibility assumed by the learner for its production' (Aljaafreh and Lantolf, 1994, p. 479). The learner has independently produced the correct past tense form *could* in her written text. She has still marked the main verb incorrectly for tense, but interrupts the tutor to identify the error (Line 6), and offers the correct form *take* with very little hesitation (though her laughter and embarrassment show that self-regulation is still not automatized or complete). In later essays, this student's performance on this particular construction is error-free, and there is some evidence of generalization to other modals.

In a later study, Nassaji and Swain (2000) set out to test more formally the claim of Aljaafreh and Lantolf that effective scaffolding is contingent on the state of the learner's Zone of Proximal Development. These researchers worked with two case study learners, both Korean first language adult learners of English as a second language. As in the earlier study, the learners each met a tutor weekly to review and correct written English assignments; however, this study concentrated on just one feature of English grammar, the use of definite and indefinite articles. When working with one of the learners, the tutor followed the principles of the Aljaafreh and Lantolf regulatory scale. That is, when an error was identified the tutor provided the most implicit feedback to begin with, but if the learner did not respond, progressively more explicit feedback was provided until the learner could correct her error. Thus, it is claimed, scaffolding appropriate to the learner's current Zone of Proximal Development was provided. (It turned out that of the two, the more explicit feedback was more helpful.) With the other learner, however, the tutor did not 'scale' the feedback, but provided randomly chosen feedback, which might be explicit or implicit.

The two learners' progress in English article usage was tracked over several weeks' assignments, and at the end of the study, specially developed tests based on the learners' own compositions were also administered. By the end of the study, the first learner had substantially improved her article usage, while the second learner had not. Most of the time, it seemed, the randomly selected feedback had not been helpful, while the negotiated Zone of Proximal Development-related scaffolding had led to microgenesis. The researchers interpret these findings as:

Consistent with the Vygotskian sociocultural perspective in which knowledge is defined as social in nature and is constructed through a process of collaboration, interaction and communication among learners in social settings and as the result of interaction within the ZPD.

(Nassaji and Swain, 2000, p. 49)

While Vygotsky's original formulation of the Zone of Proximal Development was concerned with interaction between 'novice' and 'expert', current socio-cultural theorists have expanded the concept to include other forms of collaborative activity, including pair and group work among peers:

To learn in the ZPD does not require that there be a designated teacher; whenever people collaborate in an activity, each can assist the others, and each can learn from the contributions of the others.

(Wells, 1999, p. 333)

One of the most active strands of socio-cultural research on SLL now involves the study of peer interaction in the language classroom; there are useful reviews of this work by Lantolf (2000) and by Swain *et al.* (2002). Different types of peer interaction have been studied, including how learners support each other during oral second language production, how they work together during 'focus on form' activities, and how they collaborate around second language writing activities. Here, we briefly examine examples of each type.

The longitudinal study by Ohta (2000, 2001) of seven adult learners of Japanese as a second language has already been mentioned. Ohta's naturalistic classroom recordings provide abundant examples of effective peer scaffolding, during oral pair work. Table 7.2 lists the array of strategies used by peers in Ohta's study to support their partner. Like Aljaafreh and Lantolf, she ranks these strategies in order of explicitness, though the resulting scale is shorter. The extract below illustrates both repair and co-construction, in an episode where learners Bryce and Matt are describing what people in magazine pictures are wearing:

	1	B:	Un. Hai um kuroi ti-shatsu o kiru, to: um
			Yeah. Yes um he wears a black t-shirt, a:nd um
→	2	M:	Kiteimasu?
			He's wearing?
	3	B:	Kiteimasu? (.) um (.) ahh
			He's wearing? (.) um (.) ahh
→	4	M:	Han::=
			Ha::lf=
	5	B:	=Han- han- han- han-zubon (.) han zubon o um haiteimasu?
			=Half- half- half- half-slacks (.) he's um wearing half-slacks?
			(literally, "half-slacks" means "shorts")

6   M: Um hm:
7   B: Ah kutsu o:: (.) a:::h haiteimasu, (.) s- (.) um socks he//he
            Ah he's a:::h wearing (.) shoes, (.) s- (.) and socks hehe
→ 8   M: Kutsushita
            Socks (literally, "under-shoes")
9   B: Sha uh?
10   M: Kutsushita.
            Under-shoes.
11   B: Kutsushita o:, [o::
            Socks ACC:, (.) ACC::
→ 12   M: [Haite?
                      Wear-?
13   B: Haiteimasu un haiteimasu, (.) Ah tokai o um hai um
           hameteimasu?
           *Wearing yeah wearing, (.) ah he's um wearing a watch
           ((mispronounced))?*

(Ohta, 2001, p. 84)

The data provided by Ohta includes some evidence of learners prompting
and scaffolding others with language material which they are not capable of
producing reliably themselves, during their own oral production. Ohta

Table 7.2 Methods of assistance occurring during classroom peer
interaction

Methods (when interlocutor is struggling)	Degree of explicitness*	Description
Waiting	1	One partner gives the other, even when struggling, time to complete a L2 utterance without making any contribution
Prompting	2	Partner repeats the syllable or word just uttered, helping the interlocutor to continue
Co-construction	2–3	Partner contributes an item (syllable, word, phrase, etc.) that works towards completion of the utterance
Explaining	4	Partner explains in L1 (English)

Additional methods (when interlocutor makes an error)	Degree of explicitness*	Description
Initiating repair	1–2	Partner indicates that the preceding utterance is somehow problematic, for example saying 'huh?' This provides an opportunity for the interlocutor to consider the utterance and self-correct
Providing repair	3	Partner initiates and carries out repair
Asking the teacher	4	Partner notices the interlocutor's error and asks the teacher about it

*(1 = least explicit, 4 = most explicit)

(*Source* after Ohta, 2001, p. 89)

explains this by drawing on concepts from cognitive theory: selective attention, and the limited capacity of working memory. She argues that for beginning learners, formulating and producing a second language utterance takes up enormous attentional resources, for the solution of a whole variety of phonological, lexical and syntactic problems, and they may simply lack the capacity to solve them all in real time. However the listening partner, who is not burdened with the attentional demands of actual production, has capacity available to both analyse what is being said, and also to project what might come next. They thus have sufficient attentional resources available to collaborate with the speaker, to handle discrepancies and provide assistance even for language points where their own productive ability is not yet automatized (Ohta, 2001, pp. 77–9).

Other researchers have looked at peer interaction during the performance of classroom activities with a focus on form. For example, Donato (1994) cites a number of examples of adult English first language learners of French working on English-to-French translation problems. These examples are taken from small group planning sessions that were the prelude to oral presentations, to take place in a later lesson. Figure 7.6 shows three learners collaborating to construct the past compound tense of the reflexive verb *se souvenir*, 'to remember':

Protocol

A1	Speaker 1	. . . and then I'll say . . . *tu as souvenu notre anniversaire de mariage* . . . or should I say *mon anniversaire?*
A2	Speaker 2	*Tu as . . .*
A3	Speaker 3	*Tu as . . .*
A4	Speaker 1	*Tu as souvenu* . . . 'you remembered'
A5	Speaker 3	Yea, but isn't that reflexive? *Tu t'as . . .*
A6	Speaker 1	Ah, *tu t'as souvenu*
A7	Speaker 2	Oh, it's *tu es*
A8	Speaker 1	*Tu es*
A9	Speaker 3	*tu es, tu es, tu . . .*
A10	Speaker 1	*T'es, tu t'es*
A11	Speaker 3	*tu t'es*
A12	Speaker 1	*Tu t'es souvenu*

(Donato, 1994, p. 44)

As Donato points out, no single member of the group possesses the ability to produce this complex form without help, yet through their successive individual contributions the verb form is collectively reshaped. Speaker 3 provides the reminder that the verb is reflexive, that is, a supplementary pronoun must be inserted (line A5); Speaker 2 corrects the choice of auxiliary (line A7, *es* not *as*); and finally, the first speaker can integrate these separate items of information so as to produce the correct form (line A12). Again, it is tempting to explain these partial contributions by different members of the group in terms of limited attentional resources and working memory capacity.

In support of the claim that linguistic development indeed follows from this type of collaborative interaction, Donato analysed the oral presentations which took place next day, and logged the extent to which forms worked on during the planning session were available for use. Thirty-two cases of scaffolded help had been identified during the planning sessions; 24 of the forms worked on collaboratively in this way were successfully re-used during the learners' individual oral presentations. Donato (1994, p. 52) concludes that 'in this way, independent evidence is given that peer scaffolding results in linguistic development within the individual'.

In a more recent study, Swain and Lapkin (1998) recorded pairs of immersion students undertaking a jigsaw task in second language French. Each student was given half of a set of pictures, which together told a story; the task for the pair was to reconstruct the complete story and to produce a written version. In their report, Swain and Lapkin concentrate on what they call 'language related episodes' recorded during the activity, that is, episodes where the learners were discussing points of form such as whether or not a verb was reflexive, or sorting out vocabulary problems. They focus on one pair of students (Kim and Rick), who produced the best quality written story, having also invested most time in the task, and having produced the largest number of language related episodes. The researchers report in detail on the strategies used by Kim and Rick to co-construct their written story, generating and assessing alternatives, correcting each other's second language productions, and also using the first language as a tool to regulate their behaviour. Swain and Lapkin claim that this cognitive activity led to microgenesis taking place for both vocabulary and for grammar. This is argued from the evidence of the oral protocols themselves, and from the written story which resulted, but also from the evidence of specially devised post-tests, which checked the students' recall of some of the words and grammar points discussed during the observed language related episodes.

The students Kim and Rick discussed by Swain and Lapkin (1998) were both strong students who worked effectively together; these researchers note that there was great variation in the use of language related episodes and other aspects of collaboration, by other pairs who took part in their study. Other researchers have noted that students undertaking pair work may act competitively rather than collaboratively, and the work of Storch

(2002), for example, has provided evidence that in such cases, supportive scaffolding and the transfer of second language knowledge is considerably reduced.

Socio-cultural theory, and activity theory in particular, can clearly explain and accommodate these complications. But what can be done to maximize the effectiveness of peer scaffolding and collaboration? In the general education literature, Mercer (2000) describes his primary school 'Talk Project', which aimed 'to raise children's awareness of how they talk together and how language can be used in joint activity for reasoning and problem-solving . . . coupled with group-based tasks in which children have the opportunity to practise ways of talking and collaborating' (Mercer, 2000, p. 149). Similar training with second language learners has achieved positive results (Klingner and Vaughn, 2000), and Swain (2000) reports a small scale experiment which trained adult learners to verbalize their meta-cognitive strategies co-operatively while undertaking problem-solving pair tasks, again with positive outcomes.

7.4   Evaluation

In comparison with most other theoretical perspectives on SLL reviewed in this book, socio-cultural theory is still a relative newcomer to the field. What are its most original features, and how far have its claims been established empirically?

7.4.1   The scope of socio-cultural research

Second language researchers working in a socio-cultural framework are making an ambitious attempt to apply a general theory of cognition and of development that has been influential in other domains of social and educational research, to the language-learning problem. Dunn and Lantolf (1998) remind us of some of the most distinctive features of this general theoretical position. First, the conventional separation between social and psychological aspects of cognition and development is rejected. Similarly, the classic Saussurean view of language as a formal abstract system that has an existence distinct from language use, is also in principle rejected. Learning is seen as a social and inter-mental activity, taking place in the Zone of Proximal Development, which precedes individual development (viewed as the internalization or appropriation of socially constructed knowledge). These are challenging ideas for a second language research community accustomed to the Chomskian distinction between language competence and language performance, and to psycho-linguistic assumptions about the primacy of individual development, whether through the 'triggering' associated with Universal Grammar theory, or the 'restructuring' associated with cognitive perspectives. They may, however, be more appealing to language educators, who can find that socio-cultural theory offers an exhilarating agenda for the renewal of second language classroom practice.

The empirical research that we have sampled in this chapter has used a varied range of socio-cultural constructs (private speech, activity theory, scaffolding, the Zone of Proximal Development) to address a variety of aspects of SLL (from the acquisition of lexis and grammar, to meta-cognition and the development of learning strategies, via the development of skills such as second language writing). Studies to date have typically been small scale, and have generally employed qualitative and interpretive research procedures, concentrating on the recording and analysis of classroom activity. This commitment to ethnographic research techniques is in line with the tenets of activity theory about the unique and holistic character of interaction within the individual Zone of Proximal Development. The 'close up' accounts of learner activity, including private speech during whole-class talk (as recorded by Ohta), or the growing numbers of detailed accounts of peer interaction during problem-solving, writing and form-focused tasks, greatly enrich our insights into classroom processes.

However, these research approaches are affected by some of the usual difficulties in developing causal explanations and generalizations through naturalistic research. In particular, providing compelling evidence regarding cause and effect is hard. For example, the learners Kim and Rick studied by Swain and Lapkin (1998) are described as high achieving students, with a positive working relationship. In their collaborative story-writing task, they discussed language form extensively – but did this discussion contribute to the high quality of their second language writing, or was it a by-product of it? The students studied by Aljaafreh and Lantolf (1994) also improved the accuracy of their written English – but with what confidence can this improvement be attributed to the tutor's effective scaffolding, rather than, for example, to the passage of time and ongoing exposure to English input? Researchers working in this tradition are conscious of these problems, and we have seen examples of recent studies which have tried to address them (Storch, 2002, who compares the developmental outcomes achieved by pairs of learners using different interactive patterns; Nassaji and Swain, 2000, who varied the nature of the scaffolding provided by an 'expert' tutor, and again traced the learning consequences). But up to now the strongest socio-cultural claims about the relationship between interaction and learning have been made on a local scale, with reference to discrete elements of language. Their potential as a general account of language learning has not yet been demonstrated.

7.4.2   Socio-cultural interpretations of language and communication

Socio-cultural theory views language as a 'tool for thought'. It is therefore critical of 'transmission' theories of communication, which present language primarily as an instrument for the passage back and forth of predetermined messages and meanings. Dialogic communication is seen as central to the joint construction of knowledge (including knowledge of language forms), which is first developed inter-mentally, and then appropriated and internalized by individuals. Similarly, private speech, meta-statement, etc., are valued positively as instruments for self-regulation, that is, the development of autonomous control over new knowledge.

In addition to these general claims regarding the functions for which language may be used, we have already noted the rejection by socio-cultural theorists of the classic Saussurean idea of language as an autonomous abstract system, and hence implicitly of Chomsky's distinction between competence and performance (Dunn and Lantolf, 1998). However, socio-cultural theorists of SLL do not offer in its place any very thorough or detailed view of the nature of language as a system – a 'property theory' is lacking. What is the relative importance within the language system of words, of pragmatic functions, or of grammar? Is language a creative, rule-governed system, or a patchwork of prefabricated chunks and routines, available in varying degrees for recombination? With some exceptions (e.g. Ohta, 2001, who argues for a significant role for prefabrication and the appropriation of readymade interactional routines, at least in early language development), socio-cultural researchers have had little to say in detail on these issues. Indeed, most socio-cultural studies of language development within the Zone of Proximal Development have focused on individual lexical items or morphosyntactic features as defined in traditional descriptive grammars, as we have seen in some of the transcripts quoted earlier (Donato, 1994). This limitation is recognized by researchers in the field (Aljaafreh and Lantolf, 1994, p. 480); if this tradition is to realize its ambitions to transform SLL research, it will need to locate itself more explicitly with respect to linguistic theory.

7.4.3   The socio-cultural view of (language) learning

Like the cognitive perspectives reviewed in Chapter 4, socio-cultural theorists assume that the same general learning mechanisms will apply to language, as apply to other forms of knowledge and skill. However, all learning is seen as first social, then individual; first inter-mental, then intra-mental. Also, learners are seen as active constructors of their own learning environment, which they shape through their choice of goals and operations. So, this tradition has a good deal to say about the **processes** of learning, and has invested considerable empirical effort in describing these in action

Ohta in particular has developed a very full account of language learning that integrates a range of socio-cultural concepts with cognitive ideas about learning processes (Ohta, 2001). She sees private speech as giving rich opportunities for repetition and rehearsal of new language items, hypothesis testing, the manipulation of target structures during language play, and the private rehearsal of interactional routines prior to use. All this can be related to ideas of automatization and proceduralization of new knowledge. Similarly, she sees peer interaction and co-construction as providing learners with increased opportunities for noticing, selective attention to different aspects of target language production and increasing the capacity of working memory. Her classroom data provides rich exemplification in support of these detailed claims.

What counts as evidence of 'learning' in this tradition, however, is not uncontroversial. In much socio-cultural discussion, the co-construction of new language and its immediate use in discourse, is equated with learning:

> Unlike the claim that comprehensible input leads to learning, we wish to suggest that what occurs in collaborative dialogues *is* learning. That is, learning does not happen outside performance; it occurs in performance. Furthermore, learning is cumulative, emergent and ongoing . . .
>
> (Swain and Lapkin, 1998, p. 321)

However, some researchers have aimed to show explicitly that new language has not only been successfully co-constructed, but has been internalized and subsequently re-used. For example, Donato (1994) studied the co-construction of French morphosyntax during the planning of an upcoming oral presentation. He claims that the new material had been 'learnt', because it was re-used next day, by individuals carrying out the presentations. Aljaafreh and Lantolf (1994), and Nassaji and Swain (2000), argue similarly that learning has taken place during one-to-one second language tutoring, on the grounds of increased accuracy in students' later second language written productions.

In general, however, the learning documented in socio-cultural research is local, individual and short term. Ohta's attempt to track over a full year her case study students' developing control of 'good listener' formulae in their Japanese second language classroom talk (such as *aa soo desu ka*) remains unusual in the field. Compared with other traditions that have addressed the issues of **rates** and **routes** of learning very centrally (*see* Chapter 3), the Vygotskyan tradition has almost nothing to say. There are some suggestions in recent studies (Nassaji and Swain, 2000; Storch, 2002) that people who receive timely and effective scaffolding or means of mediation learn faster than those who are denied this help. But while socio-cultural theorists are ready to claim that Zone of Proximal Development-supported intentional learning can precede development (Dunn and Lantolf, 1998), they have not seriously addressed the empirical question as to whether intervention in the Zone of Proximal Development simply scaffolds people more rapidly along common routes of interlanguage development, or whether it can bypass or alter these routes, by skilled co-construction. For example, Ohta's longitudinal study makes an isolated claim to have detected a common developmental route for the acquisition of formulaic 'listener response expressions' (Ohta, 2001, p. 228), but does not make any similar claims regarding morphosyntax, which is discussed in a much more short term, item-focused way. By comparison with other theoretical traditions, this is a major gap.

Finally, the preoccupation of socio-cultural SLL theorists with classroom learning should be noted. This reflects current enthusiasm among educators more generally for Vygotsky's ideas (Wells, 1999; Mercer, 2000). Concepts such as the Zone of Proximal Development, scaffolding and activity theory provide appealing alternative interpretations of the SLL and developmental opportunities afforded by classroom basics such as teacher–student interaction, problem-solving and communicative tasks, learner strategy training, focus on form and corrective feedback. This ensures that socio-cultural theory will receive continuing attention, despite its apparent 'incommensurability' with the vision of language as an autonomous and abstract system acquired through specialized mechanisms, which predominates in SLL research and has inspired most of the empirical work reviewed in this book.

8

Sociolinguistic perspectives

At present, SLA could probably benefit from an enhanced sense of the empirical world's complex socio-cultural diversity.

(Rampton, 1995a, p. 294)

8.1 Introduction

In this chapter we review aspects of the relationship between sociolinguistics and second language learning (SLL) theory. As we have seen in earlier chapters, theorizing about SLL has largely concentrated on modelling the development of language within the individual learner, in response to an environment defined fairly narrowly as a source of linguistic information. In much of this work sociolinguistic issues were addressed only as afterthoughts, if at all. However, it is clear that some sustained programmes of empirical research are now developing, in which sociolinguistic ideas are viewed as much more central to the understanding of SLL.

Sociolinguistics, or the **study of language in use**, is itself a diverse field, with multiple theoretical perspectives. This is clear from any of the current survey volumes (Coupland and Jaworski, 1997; Holmes, 2001; Mesthrie *et al.*, 2000; Wardhaugh, 2002). Here, we will necessarily be selective, identifying the theoretical strands within contemporary sociolinguistics and anthropological linguistics that are having the clearest impact on the field of SLL. Successive main sections of the chapter will therefore deal with:

- variability in second language use
- second language socialization
- communities of practice and situated SLL
- SLL and the (re)construction of identity
- affect and emotion in SLL.

8.2   Variability in second language use

8.2.1   Introduction

Socially patterned variation in language use has been seen by socio-linguistics as one of its major themes: '[Sociolinguists] are interested in explaining why we speak differently in different social contexts' (Holmes, 2001, p. 1). Variability is also an obvious feature of both child language and of learners' second language interlanguage, which has been noted and discussed in many studies, and was briefly introduced in Section 1.4.4; Towell and Hawkins (1994) argued that it is one of the basic characteristics of interlanguage which SLL theorists have to explain. In this opening section we review a wide range of factors that have been invoked to explain patterns of interlanguage variability, and highlight the extent to which these originate in sociolinguistic theory. We show how quantitative research methods developed by sociolinguists have been used to study these patterns, and finally, we assess how far interlanguage variability can be attributed to socially motivated choices by second language learners.

By variability, we refer to the fact that second language learners commonly produce different versions of particular constructions, more or less close to the target language form, within a short time span (even, perhaps, within succeeding utterances). In Chapter 2 we have already referred briefly to Schumann's (1978a) case study of Alberto, an adult learner of English as a second language. Schumann reports an example of variability in Alberto's English interlanguage, where two alternative forms were in use to express negation. Alberto seemed to be a slow, almost fossilized learner, who:

> showed considerably less development than any other subjects. He used both *no V* and *don't V* constructions throughout; however *no V* was clearly the most dominant of the two and consistently achieved a higher frequency of use until the very last sample.
>
> (Schumann, 1978a, p. 20)

The point to note here is that although one pattern was more common, two patterns were clearly in use simultaneously, by a single learner, over an extended period of time (the Alberto study ran over a period of 40 weeks). In Section 1.4.4 above, we have already cited other similar examples of variability for child second language learners.

The phenomenon of variability has led to considerable debate in the second language acquisition literature, not least over the problems it creates for the notion of 'acquisition' itself. Is a target language form to be counted as 'acquired', on the first occasion when a learner is observed to use it without immediate prompting or suppliance by an interlocutor? Or, must we wait to accept that it has been fully 'acquired', until the learner is producing the form in 90% or more of expected contexts? At different points in this book, we have encountered second language acquisition theorists and researchers who have adopted different positions on this key issue.

But apart from the need to take account of variability in trying to establish definitions of 'acquisition', we also need to explain why it is such a striking and distinctive feature of second language use. In a recent review, Romaine (2003) comments that second language variability is usually 'conditioned by multiple causes'. She lists a series of possible explanations for second language variability, which she sub-divides into 'internal' and 'external' groups. Romaine's typology is summarized below under these two headings. The reader will notice that her 'internal' list is a mixed grouping of linguistic and sociolinguistic elements, while the 'external' list is entirely sociolinguistic in origin.

8.2.2 Explanations for internal variability

Linguistic markedness: Romaine's first suggestion is narrowly linguistic; it is claimed that second language learners will tend to produce more target-like performance for structures which are 'unmarked' in linguistic terms, and will produce less target-like performance for 'marked' structures. As an example, Romaine cites the study of Gass and Ard (1984), which found that 'acquisition of English relative clauses by learners of various L1 backgrounds proceeded from left to right in the … accessibility hierarchy postulated by Keenan and Comrie (1977): Subject > Direct Object > Indirect object > Oblique > Genitive > Object of comparison' (Romaine, 2003, p. 414). Keenan and Comrie had proposed that languages in general are most likely to form relative clauses applying to Subject position (the unmarked end of the hierarchy), and least likely to form them at Object of comparison position (the marked end). English allows relative clauses to be created at all points on the hierarchy, but second language learners of English begin by producing Subject relative clauses and move systematically towards the marked end of the hierarchy as they develop the ability to produce other types of relative clause. This gradual acquisitional process will give rise to variability in relative clause production at any given moment in time.

Language change: sociolinguists have long been interested in the idea that current variation in a given language may reflect ongoing processes of language change. The suggestion is that a new language rule may be implemented initially only in a particular linguistic environment, and can then spread step by step to other environments. A linguistic snapshot at a given moment will show the rule being applied in some environments but not others. Such a 'wave' model of language change has been used by some researchers to explain variability in learner interlanguage. Romaine cites a study by Gatbonton (1978) of the acquisition of English interdental fricatives [θ] and [ð] by French Canadian learners; her results show that 'new pronunciations move through learner interlanguage systems in a similar way to forms undergoing change in native-speaker varieties' (Gatbonton 1978, cited in Romaine, 2003, p. 416).

Universal developmental constraints: since the 1980s, scholars have been interested in the possibility that second language interlanguages share characteristics with other 'simple' and rapidly evolving linguistic systems, in particular contact languages such as *pidgins* (Andersen, 1983; Romaine, 1988). Pidgin languages are contact varieties without native speakers, which arise in settings of military or trade contact, slavery or plantation labour (Sebba, 1997; Mesthrie *et al.*, 2000, Chapter 9). By comparison with other natural languages, pidgins appear simplified in characteristic ways, having the following cluster of grammatical features:

- no definite or indefinite article
- no copula *to be* (at least in present tense)
- tense, aspect, modality and negation marked externally to the verb – often by a content word like an adverb
- no complex sentences (therefore e.g. no relative clauses)
- no passive forms
- very few or no inflections for number, case, tense, etc.
- analytic constructions used to mark possessive, for example X of Y rather than Y's X (Sebba, 1997, p. 39).

Some researchers have suggested that pidgins themselves developed as a result of SLL in circumstances of very limited and/or multilingual input (Bickerton, 1977; deGraff, 1999). This encouraged investigations that showed 'how the early stages of SLA shared features with pidgins' (Romaine, 2003, p. 418). For example, in the case of the learner Alberto, mentioned at the start of this section, negation was expressed variably by use of pre-verbal *no* and *don't*. The reader will notice other overlaps between the grammatical characteristics of pidgins, with the 'Basic Variety' stage of interlanguage development described by Perdue and Klein (*see* Chapter 5). Such resemblances led Schumann (1978a, p. 110) to make the more general claim that 'pidginisation may be a universal first stage in second language acquisition', a view maintained by, for example, deGraff (1999, p. 493) at least with reference to adult SLL.

L1 transfer: finally, Romaine (2003) suggests that first language transfer is also a source of linguistic variability in second language interlanguage. She cites a number of studies of the acquisition of the definite article in a range of European languages, by learners from different first language backgrounds (some with article systems, some without). Generally, these studies show that learners whose first language has an article system make faster progress than those without (e.g. Italian first language vs Turkish first language learners of second language German: Gilbert, 1983, cited in Romaine, 2003, pp. 419–20). However, these findings co-exist alongside evidence of pidginization (even learners from first language backgrounds with article systems do not use second language articles consistently, and also do not use the full range of forms). Romaine comments that the Gilbert study 'supports the idea that there are universal principles of pidginisation, as well as positive and negative transfer effects. These manifest themselves in variable frequencies of occurrence of different features in L2' (Romaine, 2003, p. 420).

8.2.3   Explanations for external variability

Style and task-based variation: it is well established by sociolinguists that first language speakers vary their language use in regular ways, dependent on style, task, interlocutor, etc. Similarly, Tarone (1988) has suggested that second language learners control a number of varieties of second language, ranging from a more pidgin-like style used in informal and unmonitored speech, to a more target-like 'careful style' used in tasks with a focus on form. For example, Tarone's own work showed that both Japanese first language and Arabic first language learners of English as a second language supplied the third-person singular verb inflection *-s* more reliably in formal contexts. However, Romaine (2003) concludes from her survey that stylistic variation is relatively weak among second language learners, and also points out the problems involved in trying to conflate attention or degree of monitoring (both psycholinguistic concepts) and the sociolinguistic concept of style. In Section 8.2.5 below, we report similar conclusions by researchers working with learners of immersion French.

Gender-based variation: many sociolinguistic studies of native varieties have suggested that women have a preference for more conservative or high prestige speech styles, as compared with men. Romaine (2003, p. 428) suggests that there is little evidence for this type of social variability in second language speech. We follow this issue further in Section 8.2.5, where we discuss studies of immersion French students in Canada that provide some evidence of gender-based variability.

Widening beyond Romaine's gender focus, some studies have shown that change of interlocutor may also have an effect on second language speech style. For example, Young (1991) studied the extent to which Chinese first language learners of English marked plural -*s* on English nouns. His main finding was that linguistic factors such as the position of the noun within the Noun Phrase, its syntactic function and its phonological context, all affected the likelihood that these learners would produce the plural ending. However, he found that the identity of the interlocutor – Chinese or English – also influenced the likelihood that learners would mark or fail to mark English nouns as plural.

R. Ellis has proposed an alternative typology for interlanguage variability, shown here as Figure 8.1. This typology differs from Romaine's list in two main ways, both of which tend to weaken the idea that sociolinguistic influences are central to second language variability. First, Ellis divides his explanations of systematic variation into three, including the 'psycholinguistic context' as a possible source of variation, alongside the linguistic context and external or situational context considered by Romaine. This fills a rather obvious gap in Romaine's list; as we have seen, for example, in

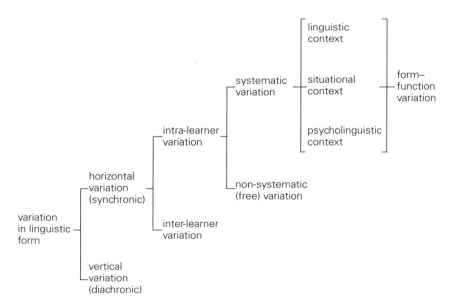

Fig. 8.1   A typology of variation in interlanguage (*Source*: R. Ellis, 1994, p. 134)

Chapter 4, it is now commonplace to explain variation in learner performance in terms of psycholinguistic factors such as processing constraints,
short term memory load, planning time available, etc. For example, in a
study of task based learning, Foster and Skehan (1996) found considerable
variation in accuracy of performance depending on the extent of pre-task
planning.

A second noticeable difference between this typology and Romaine's is
the inclusion of the category of **non-systematic variation**. Ellis has
argued consistently that some variation in second language performance is
simply free or random (for a recent overview, *see* R. Ellis 1999a). Others
have argued that variation which appears to be 'unsystematic' may merely
be variation for which the underlying system has not yet been discovered
(Schachter, 1986; Preston, 1996a, 1996b). However, Ellis (1999) claims
that there is a positive psychological reason for the existence of non-
systematic or free variation. He argues that learners experience an expres-
sive need for greater variety in their interlanguage, which leads them to
learn new forms piecemeal and to use them as alternative expressions for
existing form–meaning combinations. Once these items are being used in
free variation, they are then available for subsequent integration into the
interlanguage system, and will also eventually acquire differentiated social
or pragmatic functions. Ellis interprets the changing patterns of English
second language article *da* usage by the Hmong first language learner Ge,
already discussed in Section 5.3.2, as reflecting this progression. At an early
stage, once the *da* form was available, Ge used it with most NPs, without
any identifiable functional constraints. For Ellis, this is an example of an
item only loosely connected to the interlanguage system, that is, in free variation. Subsequently, Ge progressively systematized his usage of *da*, as he
sorted out the functional constraints which apply to definite article usage in
native speaker English.

In this introductory section we have briefly surveyed a wide range of factors that have been linked with interlanguage variability, and shown that
they may be linguistic, psycholinguistic or sociolinguistic. However, from
this brief survey, the overall significance of sociolinguistic factors is not
clear. In Section 8.2.4 we examine in more detail the extent to which there
is quantitative evidence for the existence of sociolinguistically inspired
second language variability.

8.2.4 Quantifying second language variability

In trying to make sense of the variability phenomenon, one group of second
language acquisition researchers has turned to a quantitative approach to

the description of variation in interlanguage use which was originally developed within mainstream sociolinguistics to study first language variation (*see* Bayley and Preston, 1996; Preston 1996b).

In the 1970s the sociolinguist William Labov pioneered this approach to studying variability in everyday speech. He concentrated on features in spoken language, often pronunciation features, where choices are possible that are endowed with positive or negative value by a given speech community. An example from contemporary spoken British English would be variation between the alveolar plosive [t] or glottal stop [ʔ] to realize the /t/ phoneme in words such as *better, Britain,* etc. The glottal stop variant is very common in many forms of spoken English; yet it is typically described as 'lazy', 'sloppy' speech, etc., that is, it has negative social value or prestige. Labov has proposed the term sociolinguistic **marker** for such items, whose use involves some value-laden choice.

Labov and his followers systematically recorded first language speech samples from people representing different social groups, in a variety of situations. In many studies they have shown that the relative frequencies of use for more positively or negatively esteemed variants can be correlated with factors such as the immediate linguistic context, the speaker's social class, age and gender, and the formality or informality of the speech setting (for an overview, *see* Labov 1972).

Table 8.1 shows an example drawn from 1970s quantitative research in the Labov tradition, discussed by Preston (1996b). This study investigated the simplification of word-final consonant clusters in English among African American speakers from Detroit city (i.e. the deletion of final [t] or [d] in these phonetic environments). The researchers recorded extended

Table 8.1   t/d deletion in Detroit African-American speech

Environments	Social classes			
	Upper middle	Lower middle	Upper working	Lower working
Following vowel:				
t/d is past morpheme				
(e.g. 'missed in')	0.07	0.13	0.24	0.34
t/d is not past morpheme				
(e.g. 'mist in')	0.28	0.43	0.65	0.72
Following consonant:				
t/d is past morpheme				
(e.g. 'missed by')	0.49	0.62	0.73	0.76
t/d is not past morpheme				
(e.g. 'mist by')	0.79	0.87	0.94	0.97

(*Source*: Wolfram and Fasold, 1974, cited in Preston, 1996b, p. 4)

speech samples from their subjects, and analysed the percentage of final consonant clusters within which [t] or [d] deletion was found.

As Table 8.1 shows, in this study the percentage of observed occasions of deletion of final [t] and [d] could be linked both to the immediate linguistic context and to speakers' social class.

Researchers in this tradition moved to a greater level of statistical sophistication, with the development of a computer program known as VARBRUL. (For a guide to using current versions of the program in second language research, see Young and Bayley, 1996.) This program is based on the statistical procedure known as logistic regression. VARBRUL draws on data such as presented in Table 8.1 and calculates the statistical probability that speakers will produce one variant rather than another, in a range of given contexts. Probabilities are expressed in terms of weightings ranging from 1.00 to 0.00; a weighting of 0.50 or more means that a form is systematically more likely to be produced in a given environment, a weighting of less than 0.50 means that this is less likely. One important feature of VARBRUL-type programs is that they can handle simultaneously a number of different contextual factors that may influence learner production, and can also handle interactions between them.

Preston (1996b) has run the VARBRUL program on hypothetical raw data based on the table presented earlier as Table 8.1. This VARBRUL analysis produced the pattern of probabilities for the different linguistic and social contextual factors, shown in Table 8.2.

(The term 'input probability' used in this table refers to the overall likelihood that the deletion rule will operate – note the specialized use of

Table 8.2   VARBRUL results for t/d deletion by African-American speakers from Detroit: hypothetical data inferred from Table 8.1

Result	Probability
Following vowel (V)	0.25
Following consonant (C)	0.75
Morpheme (M)	0.31
Non-morpheme (N)	0.69
Upper middle class (UMC)	0.29
Lower middle class (LMC)	0.42
Upper working class (UWC)	0.60
Lower working class (LWC)	0.69
Input probability	0.60

(*Source*: Preston, 1996b, p. 10)

the term 'input' here!) In this hypothetical example we see that two linguistic factors, 'Following Consonant' and 'Nonmorpheme' have probabilities higher than 0.50, and are therefore predictive of consonant deletion; the same applies for working class membership (whether 'Upper' or 'Lower'). Thus we see that the likelihood of consonant deletion depends in this case on a combination of both linguistic and social factors.

Preston and others have applied different versions of the VARBRUL tool to the study of variation in second language use, and its relationship with a range of contextual factors. For example, a study by Bayley (1996) investigated variability in word-final [t] or [d] deletion by Chinese learners of English. This study analysed more than 3000 final consonant clusters produced during lengthy second language-medium sociolinguistic interviews by a group of 20 learners, and compared patterns of [t] or [d] deletion with those reported for native speakers of English. Using the VARBRUL procedure, the extent to which the final consonant was deleted was related to a wide range of factors, including the immediate phonetic environment, the grammatical category of the word to which the consonant cluster belonged, different speech styles (reading aloud, narrative, and informal conversation) and the learners' reported social networks (first language mono-cultural, or mixed American and Chinese).

Table 8.3 shows part of the resulting analysis. It shows VARBRUL values for [t] or [d] deletion for the first language Chinese learners in the study, for the different grammatical categories studied, and compares them with values found in various other studies of North American English. The table shows that [t] or [d] deletion occurred to some extent for all grammatical categories, but was the most usual choice of the second language speakers

Table 8.3 t or d absence by grammatical category in Chinese–English interlanguage and in native English dialects

Variety	Single-morpheme word (e.g. *just*)	Semi-weak verb (e.g. *he lef + t*)	Regular past participle (e.g. *he had walk#ed*)	Regular preterite (e.g. *he walk#ed*)
Chinese–English interlanguage	0.46	0.39	0.47	0.66
African-American English vernacular %	0.68	0.46	–	0.35
Philadelphia and NYC white English	1.00	0.91	0.49	0.52

(*Source*: Bayley, 1996, p. 109)

only for regular past tense inflections. This contrasted, for example, with the African American speakers, who deleted final [t] or [d] most for single morpheme words, but least where the final [t] or [d] was a grammar morpheme (past tense inflection).

Bayley explains this finding by arguing that not one, but two variable rules are operating for the second language speakers. Unlike the native speakers, they are not consistently inflecting verbs for past tense. So, their use of, for example, *he walk* in past tense contexts results on some occasions from the use of a non-inflected verb form (as in the Basic Variety described in Chapter 5), and on other occasions from 'true' [t] or [d] deletion. (The researchers claimed they could distinguish the two patterns, by making comparisons with the same learners' use of base forms versus inflected past tense forms for irregular verbs, e.g. use of *come* vs. *came* in past tense contexts.)

8.2.5 Acquiring sociolinguistic variation in interlanguage

The Bayley (1996) study of [t] or [d] deletion illustrates Romaine's view that variability between second language learners has mixed origins, and that sociolinguistic factors play a relatively restricted role. However, there is another recent group of studies concerned with the learning of second language French that shows that second language learners may become sensitive to sociolinguistic variation in the target language, and may vary their usage patterns over time to accommodate increasingly to the norms of the target community. Much of this work has been conducted with English first language learners in Canada, who are learning French as a second language in an immersion setting (i.e. receiving French-medium education but alongside other English first language students rather than French first language students; *see* Rehner *et al.*, 2003 for a review). Work has also been carried out in Europe with advanced learners studying French in an academic setting (Regan, 1996; Dewaele and Regan, 2002).

Rather than studying individual sociolinguistic markers in isolation, as in the studies we have looked at earlier, Rehner *et al.* (2003, p. 129) are aiming to study the acquisition by second language French learners of a 'complete repertoire of variants and of their linguistic and extra-linguistic constraints'. According to their description, contemporary spoken French has three types of variant:

- Vernacular: non-conforming to the rules of standard French, associated with lower class speakers and stigmatized.

- Mildly marked: non-conforming to the rules of standard French, but not socially stratified or stigmatized.
- Formal: typical of careful speech and written standard French, associated with speakers from upper social strata.

Their studies show that immersion students rarely or never use vernacular variants (such as the non-standard Canadian French lexical items *ouvrage* = job, *rester* = to reside). However, they do make use of mildly marked variants, though at lower frequency than native speakers. For example, in formal written French, the first person plural pronoun *nous* predominates. In spoken Canadian French, this form is almost entirely replaced by the mildly marked variant *on* (studies regularly report over 95% use of *on*). In a global analysis of interview data collected from 41 immersion students, Rehner *et al.* (2003) report that the *on* variant was used 56% of the time, and *nous* was used 44% of the time. However, factor analysis using a version of VARBRUL showed that girls were more likely to use *nous* than *on*, whereas boys showed the reverse pattern. The same was also true of middle class students compared with working class students. On the other hand, the more contact the students reported with French-speaking people and environments, the greater the predominance of *on* in their speech. This study suggests that even students who encounter the second language mainly in school are acquiring a repertoire of variants, including some awareness of their social meaning. These findings are generally confirmed in studies of other French sociolinguistic variants. For example the advanced learners studied by Regan (1996), who were interviewed before and after an extended stay in metropolitan France, became much more native-like in respect of deletion of the negative particle *ne*, as shown when a VARBRUL-type program was used to compare Time 1 and Time 2. However, the research of Rehner *et al.* (2003) has shown much the clearest relationships between the acquisition and use of sociolinguistic variants, and factors such as gender, social class and extent of contact with first language speakers. The evidence that second language learners acquire and use stylistic constraints on variation is much less clear (Rehner *et al.*, 2003, p. 134).

This brief survey of research into second language variability confirms its complex nature. For our present purposes, it is clear that sociolinguistic factors play a role, although probably outweighed in importance by linguistic factors. There is little hard evidence that beginning second language learners control stylistic variation. On the other hand, it is clear that more advanced learners who engage actively with first language users move rapidly towards community norms of (mildly) informal usage. Their motivations for doing so are explored in following sections of this chapter.

8.3   Second language socialization

8.3.1   Introduction

In this section we turn to a strand of sociolinguistic research that is centrally concerned with language learning and development: the study of **language socialization**. This work has its roots in anthropological linguistics (Foley, 1997), and centres on ethnographic studies of children learning to talk (and to read and write) their first language, in non-Western, non-urban societies. The work by Elinor Ochs in Western Samoa (Ochs, 1988), and that of Bambi Schieffelin among the Kaluli people of Papua New Guinea (Schieffelin, 1990), are influential examples. The work of Shirley Brice Heath on children's first language development among rural working class communities in south-eastern USA can also be linked to this tradition (Heath, 1983, 1986).

8.3.2   Developmental links between first language and culture

Researchers in the language socialization tradition believe that language and culture are not separable, but are acquired together, with each providing support for the development of the other:

> It is evident that acquisition of linguistic knowledge and acquisition of socio-cultural knowledge are interdependent. A basic task of the language acquirer is to acquire tacit knowledge of principles relating linguistic forms not only to each other but also to referential and nonreferential meanings and functions . . . Given that meanings and functions are to a large extent socioculturally organised, linguistic knowledge is embedded in sociocultural knowledge. On the other hand, understandings of the social organization of everyday life, cultural ideologies, moral values, beliefs, and structures of knowledge and interpretation are to a large extent acquired through the medium of language . . . Children develop concepts of a socioculturally structured universe through their participation in language activities.
>
> (Ochs, 1988, p. 14)

In a 1995 review, Ochs and Schieffelin stress the relevance of language socialization even to grammatical development:

> This approach rests on the assumption that, in every community, grammatical forms are inextricably tied to, and hence index, culturally organised situations of use and that the indexical meanings of grammatical forms influence children's production and understanding of these forms.
>
> (Ochs and Schieffelin 1995, p. 74)

They point out that a language socialization perspective differs from functionalist approaches to grammar development, which concentrate on studying the local, moment-to-moment performance of speech acts, or creation of information structure, and their influence on the selection and learning of isolated elements of the language system. A language socialization perspective, in contrast, aims to take systematic account of the wider frameworks and socially recognized situations within which speech acts are performed. In summary, a language socialization perspective predicts that there will be a structured strategic relationship between language development and 'culturally organized situations of use'.

First, Ochs and Schieffelin (1984, 1995) examine talk to children and by children in a variety of different societies, and show that these practices are themselves culturally organized. In the well studied white middle class communities of North America, infants are viewed as conversational partners almost from birth, with caretakers interacting with them extensively one-to-one, and compensating for their conversational limitations by imputing meaning to their utterances, and engaging in clarification routines (e.g. by use of comprehension checks and recasts). In Samoa, by contrast, infants are not viewed as conversational partners at all for the first few months (though they are constantly in adult company, as 'overhearers' of all kinds of social interactions). After this time, they are encouraged to get involved in different types of interaction, for example being taught explicitly to call out the names of passers-by on the village road. Among the Kaluli, there is much direct teaching of interactional routines (*elema*); however, in both communities, children's unintelligible utterances are seldom clarified or recast. These features are explained by reference to wider social structures that characterize the Pacific communities. For example, in the Samoan community described by Ochs, individuals are strictly ranked, and higher-ranked persons do not have any particular responsibility to figure out the intended meanings of lower-ranked persons (such as small children); thus, extended comprehension checks and recasts of children's utterances would be inappropriate.

In all these cultural settings, of course, children learn successfully to talk, leading Ochs and Schieffelin (1995, p. 84) to conclude that: 'grammatical development per se can not be accounted for in terms of any single set of speech practices involving children'. But do children's different cultural experiences influence the course of language acquisition, and if so in what way? Ochs (1988) examines children's early utterances, and provides examples of links between linguistic development and socialization into particular roles and routines. For example, the first word produced by Samoan infants is generally claimed to be *tae* ('shit'), symbolic of the naughtiness and wildness expected of little children, and Ochs documented instances of infants' early vocalizations being interpreted in this way.

Ochs and Schieffelin (1995) provide further instances of young children's language productions, which show that their grammar choices are also linked to their social and gender roles. In Samoan, for example, the language offers a choice of first-person pronouns, including the neutral form *a'u* ('I', 'me') and the form *ta ita* which is marked for affect ('poor me'). In the early productions of the children studied by Ochs, the affect-marked form appeared several months before the neutral form (Ochs, 1988, p. 186), linked to a speech act of 'begging' (usually for food); children generally 'are concerned with the rhetorical force of their utterances, and . . . rhetorical strategies may account for certain acquisition patterns' (Ochs, 1988, p. 188). In Kaluli, the imperative verb form, *elema* 'say like that', is regularly used by female caregivers prompting a very young child to copy and produce an utterance. This form is quickly learnt and used by girls from age two onwards, both in play and to direct even younger children to 'say like that'. However, boys never produce this imperative verb form, though they know and use other forms of the verb (Schieffelin, 1990). It seems in this case that the children's language choice is influenced by their socialization into gender-appropriate behaviour, rather than, for example, by the frequency with which forms are encountered in input.

8.3.3   Second language socialization

The language socialization perspective has proved appealing to second language acquisition researchers who are concerned to develop a more integrated perspective on language learning, viewed as 'both a cognitive and a social process' (Watson-Gegeo and Nielsen, 2003, p. 156). One of the first second language researchers to use this perspective was Poole (1992), who conducted an ethnographic study of adult English second language classrooms, claiming that 'a teacher's language behaviour is culturally motivated to an extent not generally acknowledged in most L2 literature' (Poole, 1992, p. 593). For example, Poole shows that the teachers in her study scaffolded their learners extensively, and led and directed whole class tasks as group activities. However, in the closing stages of these same tasks, the teachers praised the students as if they alone had accomplished them. This was reflected in the teachers' pronoun usage; thus one teacher introduced a task with 'Describe the picture and see if *we* can make a story out of it'. However, at the end of that same task, the teacher praised the class: 'Good work you guys! That's hard! *you – you* did a good job. I'm impressed'

(Poole, 1992, p. 605). Poole argues that the same pattern is found in other novice-expert settings in white middle class American culture (such as child-rearing), and that this reflects a deep-seated cultural norm concerned with the attribution of success to individuals rather than groups. She did not, however, trace in detail the impact of these teachers' socialization activities on their learners.

Poole's study has been followed by other classroom-based work using a language socialization perspective, which provides rather more evidence about learner development. Much of this has focused on young children who are learning a new language in a primary school context. For example, Pallotti (2001) traced how a five-year-old Moroccan girl, Fatma, developed as a conversational participant over a period of eight months in an Italian nursery school. To be accepted in this setting, full of fluid, multi-party talk, Fatma had to learn to take conversational turns, which were both relevant to the ongoing conversational topic and interesting to other partcipants. Pallotti shows that Fatma's main early strategy was to repeat the utterances of others, or parts of them. In the beginning she simply joined in choral performances of activities like greeting or requesting. She began to make individual conversational contributions by appropriating words and phrases already produced by others, but adding minimal new elements, such as a negative expression. The example below comes from a mealtime interaction involving another child, Idina, and a teacher, when Fatma has been in nursery school for a few weeks only:

Idina:	Ho fre:ddo
	I'm cold
Teacher 2:	Hai freddo? In effeti è un po' freddo
	You're cold? It's a bit cold actually
Teacher 2:	Mangia Fatma. Tieni (placing a bowl of custard before her)
	Eat Fatma. Take it.
Teacher 2:	È buona (giving custard to Idina)
	It's good
Fatma:	(turns to T2 and touches her)
Teacher 2:	(doesn't turn, as she is turned to Idina)
Fatma:	Maestra (still touching her)
	Teacher
Fatma:	Maestra (still touching her)
	Teacher
Teacher 2:	(keeps looking at Idina, then turns to Fatma)
Fatma:	No no io freddo, [ke] questa (pointing to sleeve of pullover), questa no freddo
	No no I cold, [ke] this, this no cold
Teacher 2:	Non hai freddo? (looks at Fatma)
	You're not cold?

Fatma: Questo (pointing to arm) questo no freddo
             This, this no cold
Teacher 2:   (Throws a grape in front of Fatma)
Fatma: (Picks up grape and eats it)

(after Pallotti, 2001, p. 307)

This example shows Fatma trying to add her own contribution to an existing conversational topic ('being cold'), though a little late – the teacher has already moved on to the topic of 'food'. Her turns include a mix of borrowed and new language, plus vigorous gestures, to make her point (that she is kept warm by her pullover). The topic is a here-and-now one, which can be supported by reference to the immediate context, and Fatma makes up to some extent for linguistic gaps by determined repetition. The small group setting and regular routines of the nursery school provide Fatma with guidance on how to become an accepted participant, though conversation still presents her with many challenges, and it is only after several months that she can engage in more 'open' talk about non-present topics.

Routines and repetition are prominent in numerous other second language socialization studies of young children, for example the study of English first language children in Japanese immersion kindergarten reported by Kanagy (1999). Over 12 months, Kanagy traced the children's participation in three structured classroom routines: morning greetings or *aisatsu*; checking attendance (*shusseki*); and personal introductions (*jiko-shookai*). The children learnt both the verbal and non-verbal behaviour appropriate to Japanese classroom culture, by imitating the teacher's 'carefully staged demonstrations of Japanese societal and educational norms' (Kanagy, 1999, p. 1489). Especially through the 'personal introductions' routine, they appropriated an increasing variety of formulaic expressions (questions and answers about name, age, eye colour, etc., etc.), and could eventually use them in new combinations and with new people. However, their creative use of Japanese progressed at a much slower pace than for children such as Fatma, or others in 'mainstream' second language education, like the first grade children of diverse language backgrounds studied by Willett (1995). While mainstreamed young second language learners seem to use the predictable routines and socialization of primary education as a sheltered context for rapid grammar development, the creative utterances of the early immersion children studied by Kanagy developed slowly and had not progressed beyond the one-word level by the end of the first immersion year.

As the examples just quoted show, most second language research from a language socialization perspective uses ethnographic methods of inquiry and is relatively small scale. Watson-Gegeo and Nielsen (2003) see some weaknesses in this developing field, which they believe must be addressed if it is to make a more significant contribution to our understanding of 'social-isation through language and socialisation to use language' (Ochs, 1988, p.14). In particular, they argue that language socialization researchers have concentrated too one-sidedly on language use, and need to pay more systematic attention to the cognitive dimensions of linguistic and cultural development. A researcher who is clearly trying to develop an integrated approach of this kind is Ohta (1999, 2001). As we have seen in Chapter 7, Ohta's classroom study of adult Japanese second language learners makes links between neo-Vygotskyan theory and language processing theory to explain learner development. However, Ohta (1999) also shows that the second language socialization perspective is relevant to adult classroom learning. Her example is the achievement of Japanese-style conversational 'alignment' among interlocutors, that is, the culturally appropriate use of a range of expressions to show interlocutor interest and collaboration. In the classrooms studied by Ohta (1999), teacher-led classroom interactional routines are shown to play a part in socializing her case study learners into appropriate use of Japanese-style follow-up expressions, and thus into the achievement of this alignment.

8.4   Communities of practice and situated second language learning

8.4.1   Introduction

Sociolinguists have traditionally studied the social roles of language in structuring the identities of individuals and the culture of entire communities and societies. In particular, ethnographers of communication have studied the characteristics of *speech events* that have patterning and significance for members of a particular *speech community* (*see* Hymes, 1972; Saville-Troike, 1989). Examples of speech events with their own distinctive structures and routines in current urban society might be telephone conversations, service encounters (in shops, banks, etc.), classroom lessons or job interviews. The ability to participate appropriately in relevant speech events has been seen as an important part of communicative competence, generally accepted since the 1970s as the broad eventual target of SLL, as well as of first language development.

Ethnographers of second language communication aim similarly to study contexts and events where participants are struggling to achieve communicative goals through the means of a second or other language. However, while the traditional ethnography of communication has typically studied relatively well-established and stable speech events and communities, those studied by ethnographers of second language communication have frequently been more fluid and transitory, and involve participants whose roles and identities as well as their linguistic abilities may be much more problematic and subject to change.

The need to explain processes of interaction and development among changeable and dynamic groups and situations has led a number of sociolinguists and second language researchers to turn to an alternative concept of greater flexibility, the *community of practice*, proposed by Lave and Wenger (1991). The sociolinguists Eckhert and McConnell-Ginet suggest the following definition for a community of practice:

> An aggregate of people who come together around mutual engagement in an endeavour. Ways of doing things, ways of talking, beliefs, values, power relations – in short, practices – emerge in the course of this mutual endeavour. As a social construct, a community of practice is different from the traditional community, primarily because it is defined simultaneously by its membership and by the practice in which that membership engages.
>
> (Eckhert and McConnell-Ginet, 1992, p. 464)

Different individuals may be *peripheral members* or *core members* of a given community of practice. All may be engaged to different degrees in the joint enterprise, but they may have differential access to the 'repertoire of negotiable resources' accumulated by the community (Wenger, 1998, p. 76). For Lave and Wenger (1991, p. 49), learning itself is socially situated, and involves 'increasing participation in communities of practice', alongside experienced community members who already possess the necessary resources. The social structure of communities and the power relations obtaining within them define the learning possibilities available to members.

8.4.2 Empirical studies of second language learning as a situated social practice

The ideas of socially situated learning which takes place through participation in the activities of one or more communities of practice, has been used to study second language development among both children and adults. One obvious application is to view the classroom as a community of practice, as Toohey (2000, 2001) has done in an ethnographic study of a group of six young English as second language learners. Over a three-year period, the study tracked the children's developing identities and patterns of participation as they progressed from kindergarten through to second grade of elementary school. Toohey shows that some children were more successful than others in establishing themselves as legitimate peripheral participants in the classroom community, and that this affected the extent to which they gained conversational and other language learning opportunities, including access to resources. For example a Polish first language child, named Julie, who had come to school speaking little English, successfully graduated over time from her English as second language status and established herself as an 'average' mainstream student. Another Punjabi first language child, named Surjeet, was positioned differently as a 'struggling' student who would need continuing English as second language support. Disputes were common among the children in the class, and Toohey (2001) analyses these in some detail, showing how Julie's relatively aggressive and skilful responses to threats of subordination allowed her to develop a more powerful place in the classroom community, and consequently to win access to resources and conversational opportunities. Surjeet, on the other hand, was regularly subordinated by peers and excluded from conversation. The following example drawn from a dispute about the recognition to be given to work completed, illustrates Surjeet's non-powerful position:

Surjeet:	Look! Two more pages. [She shows her notebook to Jean Paul.]
Earl:	So what?
Jean Paul:	I don't care.
Earl:	Yeah, we don't care.
Jean Paul:	We've got two pages too. Look!
Surjeet:	No, three.
Jean Paul:	[aggressive tone] Oh! There's not three.
Earl:	I've got one page.
Jean Paul:	Let's see.
Surjeet:	[to Earl] You're m:::

[She watches as Jean Paul inspects Earl's book.]

(Toohey, 2001, pp 266–7)

A similar incident shows Julie's greater ability to switch topic and achieve acceptance as a conversationally interesting participant:

Julie: I'm almost finished Martin! Look Martin, I'm almost finished.
[Martin does not look, and for a few turns, other children take over the conversation.]
Julie: See, I'm just colouring this part.
[Martin does not look, and he and Julie keep on colouring.]

Julie:	Who has the Lion King video? I have the Lion King.
Martin:	I have the Lion King.
Earl:	I have the Lion King.
Daisy:	Clark doesn't.

[Children laugh.]

(Toohey, 2001, p. 267)

Another ethnographic study that adopts the same overall view of language learning as a social practice, located in communities of practice, is that of Norton (Pierce, 1995; Norton, 2000). This study was conducted with five adult women from diverse language backgrounds, all of them recent immigrants to Canada, who were attending English as second language classes but also using English to different degrees at home and in a variety of workplaces. The women participants completed questionnaires and diaries, and were also interviewed at intervals, over a space of two years.

One participant in the study was a Polish girl called Eva, who was living with a Polish partner, and hoped eventually to study at university. In the meantime, however, she was working at a restaurant called Munchies, where at first she could not approach her co-workers or engage them in conversation:

> When I see that I have to do everything and nobody cares about me because
> – then how can I talk to them? I hear they doesn't care about me and I don't
> feel to go and smile at them.
>
> (Norton, 2000, p. 128)

As time passed, however, she gained enough confidence to find conversational openings, joining in conversations about holidays with her own experiences of holidays in Europe, for example, getting her boyfriend to offer lifts to fellow workers on social outings, or teaching a little Italian to a colleague. In these ways she gained acceptance as a 'legitimate speaker' (Bourdieu, 1977), and correspondingly developed her opportunities for using English. At the beginning, also, Eva was allocated tasks in the restaurant that did not involve interacting with customers. However, she paid close attention to how her fellow workers did this, appropriated their utterances during routines such as ordering meals, and took the initiative to start serving customers directly. In this way Eva widened her participation in the linguistic practices of the restaurant, and further increased her own language learning opportunities as a result.

In a joint review of their two studies, Toohey and Norton (2001) argue that the qualities that make the adult Eva and the child Julie relatively successful second language learners have to do only partly with their own actions and interventions. Critical to their success was the fact that they both gained more and more access to the social and verbal activities of the target language community of practice. In both cases, they experienced attempts to subordinate or isolate them; however, they could and did draw on both social and intellectual resources to overcome these difficulties. Eva's attractive boyfriend, and Julie's big cousin, Agatha, were both seen as socially desirable by the very different groups of Munchies workers and elementary school children, and this seemed to reflect positively on the learners themselves. We have seen how Eva used her knowledge of Italian to build relationships, and Julie similarly used cultural knowledge such as 'secrets' to position herself as a desirable playmate. In both cases the learners' success in being accepted was central to access to language learning opportunity; and this success derived partly from their own actions, partly from their respective communities' willingness to adapt and to accept them as legitimate participants.

8.4.3   Power relations and opportunities for second language learning

Norton (2000, p. 7) is also concerned to investigate how 'relations of power impact on language learning and teaching'. For example, another relatively successful participant in Norton's study of English as second language immigrants in Canada was a girl named Mai, of Vietnamese origin. On arrival in Canada, Mai lived in an extended multilingual family in which she was subject to the patriarchal authority of her brother, the head of the household, who wished to marry her off quickly to another immigrant. However, Mai resisted the proposed marriage and found a job, so that she could contribute economically to the family. She also developed her relationship with her brother's (English-speaking) children, despite his initial suspicion, and made herself useful in looking after them. Thus in two ways she negotiated greater independence of her brother's patriarchal authority, and at the same time created increased opportunities for using and learning English.

Norton's study relies primarily on interviews and reports by immigrant English as second language learners about their second language encounters, positive and negative. More direct evidence of the nature of such encounters, and the power relationships which prevail within them, is provided by the European Science Foundation study of adult migrants learning a range of second languages informally in European settings, previously discussed in Chapter 5. As we have seen, the main concern of the European Science Foundation team was to clarify the linguistic course of development of the Basic Variety. A sub-group within the European Science Foundation team also undertook more sociolinguistically oriented work, and concentrated in particular on examining adult migrants' encounters with a wide variety of *gatekeepers* (Bremer *et al.*, 1993, 1996). These European Science Foundation sociolinguists focused on speech events such as job interviews, counselling or advice sessions, or service encounters (in shops, travel agencies, etc.), where the migrant workers were seeking some instrumental goal (to find a job, to send a parcel, etc.). Sometimes the events studied were real, sometimes simulated, but in all cases they involved interaction with 'genuine' officials or service personnel, who controlled the desired outcomes. Thus these speech events involved a clear mismatch of power, with the TL speaker as the more powerful gatekeeper, the second language speaker as the less powerful (potential) beneficiary of the encounter.

In their detailed analysis of specific encounters, Bremer and colleagues concentrate on how the participants succeeded (or failed) in developing and maintaining mutual understanding from moment to moment. For them, understanding is an interactive process, 'mutually constructed in the course of inferencing by all participants in an encounter' (Gumperz, 1982, in Bremer *et al.*, 1996, pp. 15–16). It is clearly a prerequisite for ongoing and sustained language learning opportunity.

An example of the data collected and analysed by the European Science Foundation researchers in their work on gatekeeping encounters is taken from a meeting between a Moroccan informant (Abdelmalek), a learner of French as a second language, and a French travel agent. This extract shows, first of all, how misunderstanding can arise from a mishearing of a single lexical element. (Abdelmalek mishears *par quoi* 'how', as *pourquoi* 'why', and proceeds to explain his reasons for needing to travel.) But, second, it illustrates the additional communication problems arising from a mismatch in power relations, at least as perceived by Abdelmalek. It is not normally appropriate for a travel agent to enquire about a client's reasons for a trip, so why did Abdelmalek think that *pourquoi* 'why' was a reasonable interpretation of what he had heard? Bremer *et al.* (1996) suggest that Abdelmalek had already experienced many official encounters during his short stay in France, when he had been interrogated about his motives and his personal life; he assumed that a travel agent, too, had the right to ask such questions. But on this occasion the travel agent is merely puzzled, and indicates that Abdelmalek's response was not appropriate – though on this occasion he remains sufficiently co-operative to rephrase his original query:

(1) A: je partir à casablanca, maroc
           i am leaving for casablanca, morocco
      N: par quoi vous voulez partir ↑
           how do you wish to go ↑
      A: [se] beaucoup problèmes là-bas papa malade
           je partir tout de suite
           a lot of problems there father is ill
           i'm leaving right away

(5) N: je comprends pas là qu'est-ce que vous voulez
où vous voulez aller ↑
i don't understand that what do you want
where do you want to go ↑
(Deulofeu and Taranger, 1984, in Bremer *et al.*, 1996, pp. 12–13)

A final, classroom-based example of the ways in which unequal power relations can affect learners' participation in a second language community of
practice, and hence their learning opportunity, is offered by Losey (1995).
In this classroom study, Losey moves beyond a concern with teacher–
student relations, to examine the classroom roles of different ethnic and
gender groups. The study again involves adult minority informants, but the
research setting is a North American adult literacy classroom. The students
were a mix of monolingual (English as first language) Anglo Americans and
bilingual (Spanish as first language) Mexican Americans. A first analysis
showed that in teacher-led, English-medium whole-class discussions, the
Anglo students dominated overwhelmingly. Closer study also showed a
striking gender difference within the Mexican American group; the few
Mexican American males participated at a similar rate to the Anglo
students, while Mexican American women scarcely contributed at all to
whole-class discussions, though they comprised almost half the class. In
small group settings, however, whether with peers or with a tutor, these
women talked freely, asking many work-related questions, and jointly
solving problems. Losey (1995, p. 655) attributes the women's silence in
class – and hence, their restricted learning opportunity – to their powerless
position as a 'double minority', in terms of both ethnicity and gender.

8.5   Second language learning and the (re)construction of identity

8.5.1   Introduction

The concept of **social identity** has been borrowed into SLL studies and
applied linguistics from social psychology. A notable theorist of social identity has defined it as 'That part of an individual's self-concept which derives
from his knowledge of his membership of a social group (or groups)
together with the emotional significance attached to that membership'
(Tajfel, 1974, p. 69, quoted in Hansen and Liu, 1997, pp. 567–8). Social
identity, therefore, is the sense of 'belonging' to a particular social group,
whether defined by ethnicity, by language, or any other means.

As originally proposed by Tajfel and others, the concept of social identity
has been criticized for being too static, and being too focused on the

individual (though Tajfel himself is defended by McNamara, 1997). In her research with adult immigrant language learners, Norton aimed to develop a more dynamic view of identity:

> I use the term identity to reference how a person understands his or her relationship to the world, how that relationship is constructed across time and space, and how the person understands possibilities for the future.
>
> (Norton, 2000, p. 5)

For Norton, language, identity, and context interact mutually:

> I foreground the role of language as constitutive of and constituted by a language learner's social identity ... It is through language that a person negotiates a sense of self within and across different sites at different points in time, and it is through language that a person gains access to – or is denied access to – powerful social networks that give learners the opportunity to speak.
>
> (Norton, 2000, p. 5)

8.5.2   Adult transformations of identity

Norton's longitudinal study explored changes in the participants' social identity over time, and in particular, their struggles to achieve the right to speak in second language settings. Thus, the young worker Eva transformed her self-concept over time from that of unskilled immigrant with no right to speak, to that of multicultural citizen possessing 'the power to impose reception' (Bourdieu, 1977, in Norton, 2000, p. 128). Another participant in Norton's study was Martina, a Czech-speaking immigrant in her 30s and a mother, who relied at first on her own children's support in undertaking a range of both public and domestic English-medium negotiations. But Martina viewed herself as the primary caregiver in the family, and struggled to resume these responsibilities herself (e.g. challenging the landlord by phone, in a disagreement over rental payments). Similarly, in the fast food restaurant where she worked, she was bossed around initially by her teenage fellow workers; but soon she reasserted her status as an adult with authority over children, and claimed the 'right to speak' in this role:

> In restaurant was working a lot of children, but the children always thought that I am – I don't know – maybe some broom or something. They always said 'Go and clean the living room', and I was washing the dishes and they didn't do nothing. They talked to each other and they thought that I had to do everything. And I said 'no'. The girl is only 12 years old. She is younger than my son. I said 'No, you are doing nothing. You can go and clean the tables or something'.
>
> (Norton, 2000, p. 99)

Pierce argues that as Martina's identity changed, from submissive immigrant to caregiver, so did her opportunities to speak and to learn English.

While Norton relies largely on self-report, the European Science Foundation researchers again provide analyses of ongoing second language interactions that illustrate the local negotiation of aspects of learner identity. In particular they pay attention to learner *face* and *self-esteem*, and how they may be threatened or consolidated by attempts to negotiate understanding. Thus, threats to second language speakers' self-esteem can arise, when misunderstandings are too frequent in interactional data. For example, a Spanish first language speaker, Berta, living in a French-speaking environment, attempted to get some shelves made to order in a woodworking shop (Bremer *et al.*, 1996, p. 91). She failed to cope with the shop assistant's more technical enquiries, and eventually lost his attention to another customer. The European Science Foundation data show that first language speakers in service encounters are often not very co-operative with second language learners, so that the major burden of achieving understanding rests with the latter. In face-threatening situations, second language speakers may use a range of strategies. At one extreme, the European Science Foundation team found examples of **resistance**, that is, more or less complete withdrawal from second language interaction, and a re-assertion of the speaker's first language identity (e.g. by switching to monolingual first language use); the minority speakers resorting to this strategy were most usually women. At the other extreme, they found speakers who worked hard during second language interactions to assert a positive, native-speaker-like identity, by, for example, indicating explicitly that they had understood, or using excuse formulae when they had to interrupt to clarify meaning (Bremer *et al.*, 1996, p.100). These speakers were mostly men, though Berta was one of the women learners who eventually discovered ways of asserting herself and taking more conversational control.

8.5.3   Adolescents and second language identities

Other ethnographic studies of adolescent second language learners produce similarly complex and dynamic portraits. McKay and Wong (1996) studied a group of Chinese first language immigrant adolescents attending high school in the USA, many of whom were 'caught in the [conflicting] demands made by multiple discourses in their environment' (McKay and Wong, 1996, p. 598). These included colonialist or racialized discourses which positioned immigrants as deficient and backward; 'model minority' discourses which celebrated the economic success of Asian Americans (by contrast e.g. with African Americans); Chinese cultural-nationalist discourses which defined 'being Chinese'; social and academic school discourses, and gender discourses. The individual students 'managed' their identities differently in this complex environment, with differential consequences for their ambitions and success in learning English oral and literacy skills.

Further illustrating the relationship between identity construction and second language development, Lam (2000) conducted a case study of a single adolescent English as second language learner, Almon, whose English literacy was poor even after five years of schooling in the USA. However, Almon became interested in computer-mediated communication and developed a new identity and 'nurturing' relationships, with teenage peers, through chat-room friendships. Almon described the change this way in an email message:

> I believe most people has two different 'I', one is in the realistic world, one is in the imaginational world. There is no definition to define which 'I' is the original 'I', though they might have difference. Because they both are connect together. The reality 'I' is develop by the environment changing. The imaginative 'I' is develop by the heart growing. But, sometime they will influence each other. For example me, 'I' am very silent, shy, straight, dummy, serious, outdate, etc. in the realistic world. But, 'I' in the imaginational world is talkative, playful, prankish, naughty, open, sentimental, clever, sometime easy to get angry, etc. . . . .I don't like the 'I' of reality. I'm trying to change myself.
>
> (Lam, 2000, p. 475)

Almon's development of this alternative identity, and his engagement with a global community of practice through computer-mediated communication, produced a qualitatively different relationship to English:

> even if it's still not very good, I can express myself much more easily now . . . it's not a matter of typing skill, it's the English . . . now I've improved, it's because of [instant messaging] or email or other reasons . . . Now it's somewhat different, before I was the type who hated English, really, I didn't like English. Maybe it was a kind of escapism, knowing I wasn't doing well at it, and so I used hating it as a way to deal with the problem. But I think it's easier for me to write out something now . . . to express better.
>
> (Lam, 2000, p. 468)

8.5.4   Autobiographical narrative

Finally, Pavlenko (1998) has analysed yet another kind of data in order to explore relationships between SLL and identity formation on a more strategic level. She has studied autobiographical narratives produced by literary figures who successfully learnt a second language after puberty, and became writers in that language. Using a range of these writings, Pavlenko argues that 'language learning in immigration' involves a first stage of continuous losses (rather than immediate acquisition), and only later a stage of gains and (re) construction. These stages can be subdivided as follows:

The stage of losses	*The stage of gains and (re)construction*
• Careless baptism: loss of one's linguistic identity	• Appropriation of other's voices;
• Loss of all subjectivities	• Emergence of one's own voice, often first in writing;
• Loss of the frame of reference and the link between the signifier and the signified	• Translation therapy: reconstruction of one's past
• Loss of the inner voice	• Continuous growth 'into' new positions and subjectivities
• First language attrition	

Pavlenko (2001) further explores the transformation among women second language English learners of their gendered identities and subject positions, as documented in a larger corpus of autobiographical narratives. She identifies a range of spaces as central to the (re)negotiation of gendered identities: educational sites, intimate relationships, friendships, parent–child relationships and workplaces. She claims that many women second language users in this corpus chose or accepted second language English as 'the language that gives them enough freedom to be the kind of women they would like to be' (Pavlenko, 2001, p. 147), perhaps because of positive associations between American English and feminist discourses. Conversely, other studies have documented the ambivalence with which English first language learners of Japanese as a second language regard Japanese 'feminine' identity, and show how they resist features of spoken Japanese, such as a raised pitch level, which are associated with being 'polite, cute, gentle, weak, and modest' (Ohara, 2001).

8.6   Affect and investment in second language learning

Many researchers in SLL have tried to explain differing degrees of learner success by appealing to factors, such as instrumental or integrative motivation, which are assumed to be relatively fixed and stable (*see* Section 1.5.2). The research reviewed in previous sections of this chapter already suggests that learners' attitudes and feelings about SLL may be much more dynamic and negotiable. In this section we look more closely at sociolinguistic discussions of the role of affect and language attitudes in promoting or inhibiting learning success, and introduce the sociolinguistic concept of 'investment' as an alternative to the traditional social psychological concept of motivation.

Krashen's **affective filter** is perhaps the best-known hypothesis in SLL theory, which tries to deal with the impact of attitudes and emotion on learning effectiveness (*see* Chapter 2). However, like the social psychological construct of motivation, the affective filter hypothesis can be criticized as insufficiently flexible and asocial.

For adult migrant learners such as Berta, the second language is the only available communicative option, in many difficult encounters with the powerful (Bremer *et al.*, 1996). Her emotional response to the second language is inextricably entwined with the social context in which she has to use it. For example, the European Science Foundation team recorded a conversation with Berta in which she retells her experience in hospital, where she had gone to enquire after her child, hurt in an accident, late in the evening. She had located the relevant doctor, but he had sent her away, telling her only that she should come back tomorrow for more information. Her actual interaction with the doctor was not recorded, but the extract below quotes the conclusion of her narrative, with its vivid recollection of her strong feelings of anger, and how these feelings frustrated her second language-medium attempts to force the doctor to give her proper attention.

B: il me dit que je sorte tout de suite de/*del hospital* pasque bon je crois que c'est l'heure pasque + c'est la/la neuf + vingt ↑/vingt et un ↑ vingt et un heure je crois que c'est possible *por* ça
he told me that i leave at once from/from the hospital because well i think it is the time because + it is nine + twenty ↑/ twenty-one ↑ twenty-one i think it is possible that's why

N: Oui mais c'est quand même pas normal
Yes but it is not really normally like that

B: oui c'est ça *lo que* jé dis pasque je suis très fâchée avec lui je le dis bon je n'/*yo/yo* voudrais que vous m'expliquiez qu'est-ce qui passe non non non il me dit
yes it is what i said because i was very angry with him i told him well i don't /i i wish you would explain to me what happens no no no he told me

N: qu'est'ce que tu as fait alors ↑
what did you do then ↑

B: bon je suis fâchée avel/avec lui *y* je le dis beaucoup de choses avec m/ + :et + je m'énervé beaucoup
well i got angry with h/ with him and i told him a lot of things with m/ + and + i got very worked up

N: ah oui + je comprends ça oui + et tu es partie ↑
Yes + i understand it yes + and did you go ↑

B: alors oui il est parti pasque je n'avais le/ avais le + que je suis fâchée je ou/
je oubliais les mots en français *por por* dire + je ne/je ne trouvais + rien
de mots *por* dire les choses que/ que je le dis à lui *por* pasque n'est
pas bon la manière qu'il me dit au revoir
then yes he went because i did not have the/ have the + that i was angry for/ i
forget the words in french to say + i did not/ did not find + nothing of words to
say the things which/ which i tell him because it is not good the manner he said
goodbye to me

(Bremer *et al.*, 1996, p. 94)

In a classroom study, Rampton (2002) observed the foreign language German lessons on offer to a group of adolescents at a multi-ethnic London secondary school. The audiolingual-style lessons were strongly structured and controlled, and students' own agendas and experience were 'kept at arms length', much more so than in other curriculum subjects. Active public commitment to German was expected, through involvement in the collective practices of oral drills, etc., and the students showed their ambivalent response in class by 'ragged and reluctant participation' (Rampton, 2002, p. 502). However, in other lessons, unexpectedly, Rampton documented these same students as using bits and pieces of 'management German', at moments of potential conflict with other teachers. The following example comes from an English lesson:

1	Mr N:	As I've said before
2		I get a bit fed up with saying (.)
3		shshsh
4	John:	*(addressed to Mr N?)* LOU/DER
5	Mr N:	You're doing your SATs *(tests)* now
6	Hanif:	VIEL LAUTER SPRECHEN
		speak much louder
7		VIEL LAUTER SPRECHEN
		speak much louder
8	John:	*(smile-voice)* lauter spricken
9		Whatever that is

(Rampton, 2002, p. 506)

Rampton suggests that as far as the students were concerned, 'language lessons turned German into a ritual language, and that this ritual dimension was both acknowledged and taken in vain in the subversive orientation to order and propriety displayed in impromptu *Deutsch* [German]' (Rampton, 2002, p. 511). This downgrading of German to a ritual language from which their personal experience was excluded, made German only useful immediately for procedural management, and led in the longer term to language learning failure.

Norton (2000) further shows that learners' motivation to succeed in SLL, and the amount of effort that Eva, Mai and the other women in her study were willing to 'invest' in practising English, is closely related to the social identities they were aiming to construct over time. This variable investment is also seen among the Chinese teenagers studied by McKay and Wong (1996), some of whom concentrated on developing the English literacy skills needed for a 'good student' identity, while others concentrated on developing speaking skills, so as to be accepted among the students' informal networks. (Interestingly, these students seemed to invest in those aspects of English needed for acceptance in their immediate surroundings, rather than those which would eventually be needed to meet their parents' aspirations for them, or those of the wider society.) In an extensive ethnographic study of a French-medium high school in the English-dominant city of Toronto, Heller (1999) compared the social motivations for learning French of local white students, with those of students of migrant background (e.g. from Francophone Africa). The African students held ambivalent views towards both French and English, as languages of colonialism, and rejected them as languages of personal cultural significance. Nonetheless, they saw excellent mastery of the standard varieties of both languages as central to their individual economic success, as skilled multilingual individuals. In contrast, Heller cites a white female student, whose dominant language is English, who is pleased to have studied through French, as part of her family identity, but whose ambitions, for example, for French literacy are self-limiting, as she does not see herself needing or using French in her future career:

> So I mean like people on my Mom's side and my Dad's side, like they know French sort of thing. So it's kind of like that's kind of not the background, but a lot of . . . they always knew French, so I also want my kids to speak French as well. It's like it's my background you know. They spoke French, so I think I should keep it up as well.
> (. . .)
> I know I'm going to an English university because, first of all, they offer more programmes, like the programmes that I want, and it will be easier for me to like explain myself in English, you know, especially when I'm going to have to do like a lot of essays and stuff. English is my first language and I can write better and stuff.
>
> (Student Sandra, in Heller, 1999, pp. 144–5)

8.7   Evaluation: the scope and achievements of sociolinguistic enquiry

In this chapter we have introduced several different strands of socio-linguistic theorizing about second language use and second language development. One of these strands, the quantitative study of second language variation, is very different from the others, focusing on interlanguage variability at the lexical and morphological level. Here, we have seen that sociolinguistic factors play a role of increasing importance as learners become more advanced, but it is clear that much variability must be attributed primarily to psycholinguistic influences.

The remaining strands deal with SLL in a broad way, embedded in its social context. This work is typically qualitative and interpretive in nature, using the techniques of ethnography or of conversational analysis, and providing longitudinal accounts of the social processes of second language interaction and development. It frequently involves case studies of individuals or groups of learners; great attention is paid to the personal qualities and ambitions of the learner, and their own social contribution to the learning context. Valuable concepts such as the 'community of practice' have been introduced to this field in recent work, which have been helpful for theorizing SLL as a social practice, in an integrative way. On the other hand, it is still rare to find in sociolinguistic work of this kind, any close attention being paid to the linguistic detail of the learning path being followed (i.e. to the precise learning *route*), or the cognitive processes involved (*see* comments of Watson-Gegeo and Nielsen, 2003).

8.7.1   Sociolinguistic perspectives on interlanguage and interlanguage communication

One of the obvious strengths of the sociolinguistic tradition in second language acquisition is the rich accounts offered of cross-cultural second language communication. In Chapter 5, we noted that the functionalist tradition in second language acquisition had paid relatively little attention to second language interaction, despite being very interested in learners' naturalistic second language output. The interactionist tradition reviewed in Chapter 6 does of course systematically analyse second language interaction, but adopts a mainly quantitative approach, tallying the occurrence or non-occurrence of significant functions such as the negotiation of meaning, recasts, etc. The ethnographers of second language communication whose work we sampled in this chapter explore complete speech events in a much more holistic way. They take a multi-level view of conversational interaction; they are concerned with the relationships between linguistic and non-linguistic aspects of communication, and with the development of pragmatic and discourse competence appropriate to particular identities and communities of practice, rather than centring on the linguistic aspect *per se*, which is not seen as autonomous or pre-eminent.

In contrast, the variationists discussed in Section 8.3 look at a range of relatively 'micro' linguistic features in learner language. They have demonstrated that such variability is patterned rather than random, and that it is linked to some extent to social factors, though much less so than first language varieties. The emergence of socially patterned variation among more advanced or more integrated learners can be linked to learners' aspirations to develop appropriate second language identities, and thus to the themes discussed in later sections of the chapter. However, it has not been shown that interlanguage contains 'variable rules' of a formal kind.

8.7.2   Sociolinguistic perspectives on language learning and development

As far as language learning itself is concerned, sociolinguistically oriented research has provided rich descriptions of the context for language learning, and the speech events (from gatekeeping encounters to classroom lessons) through which it is presumed to take place. Like the Vygotskyan socio-cultural theorists discussed in Chapter 7, the second language ethnographers studied here believe that learning is a collaborative affair, and that language knowledge is socially constructed through interaction. They have paid less attention than the socio-cultural theorists to the linguistic detail of expert or novice interaction, or to the 'microgenesis' of new language forms in the learner's second language repertoire. There is no real parallel as yet in second language 'language socialization' studies to the detailed work of Ochs (1988) on linguistic development in first language socialization. Thus, while Ochs offers evidence to support her claim that the actual *route* of first language development can be influenced by the nature and quality of interactions in which the child becomes engaged, this idea has not yet seriously been investigated for second language development, from a 'socialization' perspective. (For a small-scale exception, *see* Tarone and Liu, 1995.)

On the other hand, current ethnographies of second language communication and of second language socialization offer a great deal of evidence about how the learning context, and the learner's evolving style of engagement with it, may affect the *rate* of SLL. The patterning of learning opportunities, through communities of practice with structured and sometimes very unequal power relationships, has been invoked to explain learners' differential success even where motivation is high.

8.7.3   Sociolinguistic accounts of the second language learner

Second language ethnographies take an interest in a wide variety of second language learners, from the youngest classroom learners to adult migrants. The second language ethnographers that we have encountered take a more rounded view of the learner as a social being, than is true for other perspectives we have surveyed. Thus, for example, dimensions such as gender and ethnicity are seen as significant for language learning success (Sunderland, 2000).

Most striking, though, is the emphasis placed by contemporary ethnographic researchers such as Norton on the dynamic and alterable nature of learners' identity and engagement with the task of SLL. Self-esteem, motivation, etc., are believed to be both constructed and reconstructed in the course of second language interaction, with significant consequences for the rate of learning and ultimate level of success. Alongside rich characterizations of the learning context, the importance attributed to agency and investment is one of the most distinctive current themes offered by this particular perspective on SLL.

9
Conclusion

9.1   One theory or many?

Having come to the end of our survey of current trends in second language learning (SLL) research, we are left with a reinforced impression of great diversity. Different research groups are pursuing theoretical agendas that centre on very different parts of the total language learning process; while many place the modelling of learner grammars at the heart of the enterprise, others focus on language processing, or on second language interaction. Each research tradition has developed its cluster of specialized research procedures, ranging from the grammaticality judgement tests associated with Universal Grammar-inspired research, to the naturalistic observation and recording practised by ethnographers and language socialization theorists. On the whole, grand synthesizing theories, which try to encompass all aspects of SLL in a single model, have not received general support. Rather than a process of theory reduction and consolidation, of the kind proposed by Beretta and others (1993), we find that new theoretical perspectives (such as connectionism or socio-cultural theory) have entered the field, without displacing established ones (such as Universal Grammar).

On the other hand, some attempts have been made at the principled linking of specific theories on a more modest scale, to account for different aspects of the SLL process; a clear example is that made by Towell and Hawkins (1994) to link Universal Grammar theory with a theory of information processing.

9.2   Main achievements of recent second language learning research

Drawing on the wealth of studies that have been carried out in the last 15 years or so, what are the most significant changes that can be noted in SLL theorizing in its many forms?

From a linguistic perspective, the continuing application of Universal Grammar to the modelling of second language competence has led to an increasingly sophisticated and complex range of proposals about the possible contents of that mysterious black box originally imported by Krashen into second language research, the 'Language Acquisition Device'. One complication is the growing view among some Universal Grammar specialists that the innate language module may itself be modular, with different aspects of language knowledge being learnt and stored relatively autonomously. The Universal Grammar approach has also been instrumental in providing sharper linguistic descriptions of learner language, and has helped to better document the linguistic route followed by second language learners and to explain cross-linguistic influences.

From a cognitive perspective, the main evolutionary developments have been the application of information processing models to domains complementary to the learning of grammar, for example the application of Anderson's ACT* model to the acquisition of learning strategies, or the development of fluency. As far as grammar learning itself is concerned, connectionist models offer a much more radical challenge to traditional linguistic thinking, given that they make do without the accepted paraphernalia of abstract rules and symbolic representations, and suggest that a network of much more primitive associationist links can underlie language learning and performance. However, the empirical evidence supporting these claims remains limited, and contentious in its interpretation.

Descriptively, recent work in the functionalist tradition has added substantially to our understanding of the course of second language development, and especially the key role played by pragmatics and lexis in interlanguage communication, in particular in the early stages. Variationist studies also suggest that much second language variability can be accounted for by evolving links between form and function.

In terms of descriptive accounts, we have also learnt much from recent research about the contexts within which SLL takes place, and the kinds of interactions in which learners become engaged, and have also started seriously to investigate the links between interactional engagement and SLL itself. In their different ways, the interactionist, socio-cultural and sociolinguistic perspectives all address this issue. The sociolinguistic perspective has shown us how learners' engagement in second language interaction is influenced by power relations and other cultural factors. On the other hand, we have seen that these factors are not inalterably fixed, but can be renegotiated as learners build new identities. Both interactionist and socio-cultural research, in their different ways, show how the ongoing character of second language interaction can systematically affect the learning opportunities it makes available, and have started to demonstrate how learners actually use these opportunities.

However, a major limitation shared by these particular strands remains that identified by Braidi (1995) in her commentary on the interactionist tradition in particular: the continuing scarcity of studies which track and document learners' linguistic development in detail over time, and link their evolving control of linguistic structure, to a narrative account of their interactional experiences. As researchers in the socio-cultural tradition have explicitly recognized, even in longitudinal studies, such as that of Ohta (2001), links have so far been made on a limited scale, in respect of small 'patches' of language knowledge only. We have not yet seen the systematic linking over time of longitudinal accounts of interlanguage development like those provided by the functionalist strand, with evolving accounts of second language negotiation, scaffolding, etc.

9.3   Future directions for second language learning research

For the foreseeable future, it seems that SLL will be treated as a modular phenomenon, with different research programmes addressing different aspects. The influence of linguistics on the modelling of second language competence is unlikely to diminish, so that we can expect to see continuing reflexes of evolving linguistic thinking in second language research, as we have already seen in the application of successive versions of Universal Grammar theory to the second language problem. On the other hand, the application of general learning theories derived from cognitive psychology, neural science, etc., can also be expected to continue, as can be seen clearly, for example, in Doughty and Long (2003); the attempts to bring to bear on SLL such diverse general learning theories as connectionism, on the one hand, and Vygotskyan socio-cultural theory, on the other, are current examples, but others may follow.

Although we believe these different research strands within second language acquisition will retain their autonomy and individual impetus, however, it is clear that attempts to cross-refer between them and examine relations between different learning 'modules' in a systematic way, a process already exemplified in, for example, Towell and Hawkins (1994) and Carroll (2000), will continue to prove a productive way of developing our understanding of the specific modular domains. Much recent work has examined various interfaces in detail, for example between syntax and morphology, between the lexicon and syntax, or between semantics and syntax (Juffs, 1998, 2000; Lardière 1998; Parodi, 2000; Prévost and White, 2000;

Franceschina, 2001; Hawkins, 2001, 2003; Herschensohn, 2001; Van Hout *et al.*, 2003; Myles, in press a).

From a methodological point of view, one productive development within certain strands of second language research is the greater use of computer-aided techniques for the analysis of second language data. In the past, corpus-based studies of second language development or second language interaction have usually involved manual analysis of a very labour-intensive kind. Child language research has shown the potential of computer-aided analysis for the handling of corpus data, using software such as the CHILDES package (MacWhinney 2000a, 2000b). The development of electronic second language corpora, plus work to devise appropriate tools for analysis, is making possible the more systematic linking of second language grammar development with second language interaction (Granger, 1998; Granger *et al.*, 2002; Marsden *et al.*, 2003; Rule *et al.*, 2003). They also facilitate much closer attention to second language lexis and lexico-grammar, and to the role of prefabricated chunks and routines in second language use and SLL. Recent advances in computer technology have also enabled the development of computer modelling of SLL (e.g. the recent application of connectionism to SLL).

Such technical developments do not challenge the fundamental assumptions of SLL research, which by and large have remained those of rationalist 'modern' science. In recent years, however, a number of critiques have developed of 'autonomous' applied linguistics and second language acquisition, from more socially engaged perspectives (Phillipson, 1992; Pennycook, 1994); Rampton (1995b) charts what he sees as the rise of more 'ideological' forms of applied linguistics. We can find in contemporary theoretical discussions, proposals for more socially engaged forms of second language acquisition research, on the one hand (Block, 1996), and for post-modern interpretations of second language use and learning, on the other (reviewed by Brumfit, 1997). Post-modernism offers a relativist critique of 'attempts to see human activity as part of a grand scheme, driven by notions of progressive improvement of any kind' (Brumfit, 1997, p. 23). As far as language is concerned, it highlights problems of textuality, and the complex relationship between language and any sort of external reality; 'we are positioned by the requirements of the discourse we think we adopt, and our metaphors of adoption hide the fact that *it* adopts *us*' (Brumfit, 1997, p. 25). The post-modern concept of intertextuality – the idea that all language use is a patchwork of borrowings from previous users – has been claimed to be of central importance for SLL (Hall, 1995).

So far, however, the critical and post-modern commentary on second language acquisition has not dislodged its central modernist assumptions.

It will be for the future to tell how much impact it eventually makes on pro-grammes of second language empirical enquiry; this evolution will evi-dently be linked to wider ongoing debates in the social sciences.

9.4   Second language learning research and language education

We noted in Chapter 2 that theorizing about SLL has its historic roots in reform movements connected to the practical business of language teach-ing. Howatt (1984, pp. 12–72) shows that this has been true since Renaissance times at least. In the last quarter-century, however, as we have clearly seen, it has become a much more autonomous field of enquiry, with an independent, 'scientific' rationale.

But what kind of connections should this now relatively independent research field maintain, with its language teaching origins? From time to time, it has been argued that the 'scientific' findings of second language acquisition should guide the practices of classroom teachers; the recom-mendations that flowed from Krashen's Input hypothesis, in the form of the 'Natural Approach' to language pedagogy, are an obvious example (Krashen and Terrell, 1983). Another example that we encountered briefly earlier is the Teachability hypothesis, advanced by Pienemann, who suggests that new second language items might most effectively be taught in sequences that imitate empirically documented developmental sequences.

R. Ellis (1997) reviews a number of well-known difficulties with such a top-down, rationalist approach to linking research-derived theory and classroom practice. The findings of second language acquisition research are not sufficiently secure, clear and uncontested, across broad enough domains, to provide straightforward prescriptive guidance for the teacher (nor, perhaps, will they ever be so). They are not generally presented and disseminated in ways accessible and meaningful to teachers; the agenda of second language acquisition research does not necessarily centre on the issues which teachers are most conscious of as problematic. But most importantly, teaching is an art as well as a science, and irreducibly so, because of the constantly varying nature of the classroom as a learning community. There can be no 'one best method', however much research evidence supports it, which applies at all times and in all situations, with every type of learner. Instead, teachers 'read' and interpret the changing dynamics of the learning context from moment to moment, and take what seem to them to be appropriate contingent actions, in the light of largely implicit, proceduralized pedagogic knowledge. This has been built up over time very largely from their own previous experience, and usually derives only to a much more limited extent from study or from organized training.

However, present second language acquisition research offers a rich variety of concepts and descriptive accounts, which can help teachers to interpret and make better sense of their own classroom experiences, and significantly broaden the range of pedagogic choices open to them. For example, SLL research has produced descriptive accounts of the course of interlanguage development, which show that learners follow relatively invariant routes of learning, but that such routes are not linear, including phases of restructuring and apparent regression. Such accounts have helped teachers to understand patterns of learner error and its inevitability, and more generally, to accept the indirect nature of the relationship between what is taught and what is learnt. Similarly, in the recent literature, discussions about the role of recasts and negative evidence in learning (reviewed in Chapter 6), about scaffolding and microgenesis (Chapter 7), or about language socialization (Chapter 8) have great potential to stimulate teacher reflections on the discourse choices available to them, when enacting their own role as second language guide and interlocutor.

Of course, the sub-field of research on 'instructed second language acquisition' (R. Ellis, 1990; Spada, 1997; Norris and Ortega, 2000; Cook, 2001; Lyster, 2001; Robinson, 2001; Doughty, 2003) plays a special role in addressing concerns somewhat closer to those of the classroom teacher, and may offer opportunities for more direct involvement of teachers as research partners. But even 'instructed second language acquisition' research is not identical with problem solving and development in language pedagogy, and does not ensure a shared agenda between teachers and researchers. There is a continuing need for dialogue between the 'practical theories' of classroom educators, and the more decontextualized and abstract ideas deriving from programmes of research. Researchers thus have a continuing responsibility to make their findings and their interpretations of them as intelligible as possible to a wider professional audience, with other preoccupations. We hope that this book continues to contribute usefully to this dialogue.

References

Aarts, J. 1991: Intuition-based and observation-based grammars. In Aijmer, K. and Altenberg, B. (eds), *English corpus linguistics*. Harlow: Longman, 44–62.

Adams, M. 1978: Methodology for examining second language acquisition. In Hatch (ed.), *Second language acquisition*. Rowley, MA: Newbury House, 278–96.

Aitchison, J. 1989: *The articulate mammal*. London: Unwin Hyman.

Aljaafreh, A. and Lantolf, J.P. 1994: Negative feedback as regulation and second language learning in the Zone of Proximal Development. *Modern Language Journal* **78**, 465–83.

Allen, J. and Seidenberg, M.S. 1999: The emergence of grammaticality in connectionist networks. In MacWhinney, B. (ed.), *The emergence of language*. Mahhwah, NJ: Lawrence Erlbaum, 115–52.

Andersen, R. (ed.) 1983: *Pidginisation and creolisation as language acquisition*. Rowley, MA: Newbury House.

Andersen, R. 1984: *Second languages: A cross-linguistic perspective*. Rowley, MA: Newbury House.

Andersen, R. 1990: Models, processes, principles and strategies: second language acquisition inside and outside of the classroom. In Van Patten, B. and Lee, J. (eds), *Second language acquisition – foreign language learning*. Clevedon: Multilingual Matters, 45–68.

Andersen, R.W. 1991: Developmental sequences: the emergence of aspect marking in second language acquisition. In Huebner, T. and Ferguson, C.A. (eds), *Crosscurrents in second language acquisition and linguistic theories*. Amsterdam: John Benjamins, 305–24.

Andersen, R. and Shirai, Y. 1994: Discourse motivations for some cognitive acquisition principles. *Studies in Second Language Acquisition* **16**, 133–56.

Anderson, J. 1980: *Cognitive psychology and its implications*. New York, NY: Freeman.

Anderson, J. 1983: *The architecture of cognition*. Cambridge, MA: Harvard University.

Anderson, J. 1985: *Cognitive psychology and its implications* (2nd edn). New York, NY: Freeman.

Anderson, J. 1993: *Rules of the mind*. Hillsdale, NJ: Erlbaum.

Anderson, J. and Fincham, J. 1994: Acquisition of procedural skill from examples. *Journal of Experimental Psychology: Learning, Memory and Cognition* **20**, 1322–40.

Anton, M. and DiCamilla, F.J. 1999: Socio-cognitive functions of L1 collaborative interaction in the L2 classroom. *Modern Language Journal* 83, 233–47.

Atkinson, M. 1996: Now, hang on a minute: some reflections on emerging ortho-doxies. In Clahsen, H. (ed.), *Generative perspectives on language acquisition.* Amsterdam: John Benjamins, 451–85.

Ayoun, D. 2001: The role of negative and positive feedback in the second language acqusition of the *passé composé* and *imparfait. Modern Language Journal* **85**, 226–43.

Bailey, N., Madden, C. and Krashen, S. 1974: Is there a 'natural sequence' in adult second language learning? *Language Learning* 24, 235–43.

Bardovi-Harlig, K. 2000: Tense and aspect in second language acquisition: Form, meaning and use. *Language Learning* **50**, Supplement 1.

Bayley, R.J. 1994: Interlanguage variation and the quantitative paradigm: past tense marking in Chinese–English. In Gass, S., Cohen, A. and Tarone, E. (eds), *Research methodology in second language acquisition.* Hillsdale, NJ: Erlbaum, 157–81.

Bayley, R. 1996: Competing constraints on variation in the speech of adult Chinese learners of English. In Bayley, R. and Preston, D.R. (eds), *Second language acquisition and linguistic variation.* Amsterdam: John Benjamins, 97–120.

Bayley, R. and Preston, D.R. (eds) 1996: *Second language acquisition and linguistic variation.* Amsterdam: John Benjamins.

Becker, A. and Carroll, M. 1997: *The acquisition of spatial relations in a second language.* John Benjamins.

Bellugi *et al.* 1993: Bellugi, U., Van Hoek, K., Lillo-Martin, D., and O'Grady, L. 1993: The acquisition of syntax in young deaf singers. In Bishop, D. and Mogford, K. (eds) *Language development in exceptional circumstances.* Hove: Lawrence Erlbaum Associates, 132–50.

Beretta, A. (ed.) 1993: Theory construction in SLA. *Applied Linguistics,* **14** special issue.

Berko, J. 1958: The child's learning of English morphology. *Word* 14, 150–77.

Bialystok, E. 1991: Metalinguistic dimensions of bilingual language proficiency. In Bialystok, E. (ed.), *Language processing in bilingual children.* Cambridge: Cambridge University Press, 113–40.

Bickerton, D. 1971: Inherent variability and variable rules. *Foundations of Language* 7, 457–92.

Bickerton, D. 1977: Pidginisation and creolisation: language acquisition and lan-guage unversals. In Valdman, A. (ed.), *Pidgin and creole linguistics.* Bloomington: Indiana University Press, 49–69.

Birdsong, D. (ed.) 1999: *Second language acquisition and the Critical Period Hypothesis.* Mahwah, NJ: Lawrence Erlbaum.

Bishop, D. (ed.) 2001: *Language and cognitive processes in developmental disorders.* Hove: Psychology Press.

Bishop, D. and Mogford, K. (eds) 1993: *Language development in exceptional circum-stances.* Hove: Erlbaum.

Bley-Vroman, R. 1989: What is the logical problem of foreign language learning? In Gass, S. and Schachter, J. (eds), *Linguistic perspectives on second language acquisi-tion.* Cambridge: Cambridge University Press, 41–68.

Block, D. 1996: Not so fast: some thoughts on theory culling, relativism, accepted findings and the heart and soul of SLA. *Applied Linguistics* **17**, 63–83.

Bloomfield, L. 1933: *Language.* New York, NY: Holt, Rinehart & Winston.

Bohannon, J.N., MacWhinney, B. and Snow, C. 1990: No negative evidence revisited: beyond learnability or who has to prove what to whom. *Developmental Psychology* **26**, 221–6.

Bohannon, J.N., Padgett, R.J., Nelson, K.E. and Mark, M. 1996: Useful evidence on negative evidence. *Developmental Psychology* **32**, 551–5.

Bourdieu, P. 1977: The economics of linguistic exchanges. *Social Science Information* **16**, 645–68.

Braidi, S.M. 1995: Reconsidering the role of interaction and input in second language acquisition. *Language Learning* **45**, 141–75.

Bremer, K., Broeder, P., Roberts, C., Simonot, M. and Vasseur, M-T. 1993: Ways of achieving understanding. In Perdue, C. (ed.), *Adult language acquisition: Cross-linguistic perspectives*. Volume 2: The Results. Cambridge: Cambridge University Press, 153–95.

Bremer, K., Roberts, C., Vasseur, M.-T., Simonot, M. and Broeder, P. 1996: *Achieving understanding: Discourse in intercultural encounters*. Harlow: Longman.

Broeder, P. 1995: Adult language acquisition: the establishment, shift and maintenance of reference in narratives. In Geiger, R.A. (ed.) *Reference in multidisciplinary perspective*. Hildesheim: Olms.

Brown, R. 1973: *A first language: The early stages*. Cambridge, MA: Harvard University Press.

Brumfit, C.J. 1997: Theoretical practice: applied linguistics as pure and practical science. *AILA Review* **12**, 18–30.

Brumfit, C.J. and Johnson, K. (eds) 1979: *The communicative approach to language teaching*. Oxford: Oxford University Press.

Brumfit, C.J. and Mitchell, R. 1990: The language classroom as a focus for research. In Brumfit, C.J. and Mitchell, R. (eds) *Research in the language classroom*. ELT Documents 133. Modern English Publications/ The British Council, 3–15.

Bruner, J. 1985: Vygotsky: a historical and conceptual perspective. In Wertsch, J. (ed.), *Culture, communication and cognition: Vygotskian perspectives*. Cambridge: Cambridge University Press, 21–34.

Budwig, N. 1995: *A developmental-functionalist approach to child language*. Mahwah, NJ: Lawrence Erlbaum Associates.

Butterworth, B. and Harris, M. 1994: *Principles of developmental psychology*. Hove: Lawrence Erlbaum.

Butterworth, G. and Hatch, E. 1978: A Spanish-speaking adolescent's acquisition of English syntax. In Hatch, E. (ed.), *Second language acquisition*. Rowley, MA: Newbury House, 231–45.

Caplan, D. 1987: *Neurolinguistics and linguistic aphasiology: An introduction*. Cambridge: Cambridge University Press.

Caplan, D. 1992: *Language: Structure, processing, and disorders*. Cambridge, MA: MIT Press.

Carroll, S. 1995: The hidden danger of computer modelling: remarks on Sokolik and Smith's connectionist learning model of French gender. *Second Language Research* **11**, 193–205.

Carroll, S. 2000: *Input and evidence: The raw material of second language acquisition*. Amsterdam: John Benjamins.

Carter, R. 1998: *Mapping the mind*. London: Weidenfeld & Nicolson.

Cazden, C. 1972: *Child language and education*. New York: Holt, Rinehart & Winston.

Cazden, C.B., Cancino, H., Rosansky, E. and Schumann, J. 1975: *Second language acquisition sequences in children, adolescents and adults: Final report*. Washington, DC: National Institute of Education.

Chaudron, C. 1988: *Second language classrooms: Research on teaching and learning*. Cambridge: Cambridge University Press.

Chaudron, C. 2003: Data collection in SLA research. In Doughty, C. and Long, M. (eds), *The handbook of second language acquisition*. Malden, MA: Blackwell, 762–828.

Chomsky, N. 1957: *Syntactic structures*. The Hague: Mouton.

Chomsky, N. 1959: Review of B.F. Skinner, *Verbal behavior. Language* 35, 26–58.

Chomsky, N. 1965: *Aspects of the theory of syntax*. Cambridge, MA: MIT Press.

Chomsky, N. 1981: *Lectures on government and binding*. Dordrecht: Foris.

Chomsky, N. 1986a: *Knowledge of language, its nature, origin, and use*. New York, NY: Praeger.

Chomsky, N. 1986b: *Barriers*, Cambridge, MA: MIT Press.

Chomsky, N. 1987: Transformational grammar: past, present and future. In *Studies in English language and literature*. Kyoto: Kyoto University, 33–80.

Chomsky, N. 1995: *The minimalist program*. Cambridge, MA: MIT Press.

Chomsky, N. 2000: *New horizons in the study of language and mind*. Cambridge: Cambridge University Press.

Chomsky, N. 2002: *On nature and language*. Cambridge: Cambridge University Press.

Christiansen, M. and Chater, N. 2001: Connectionist psycholinguistics: capturing the empirical data. *Trends in Cognitive Sciences* 5, 82–8.

Clahsen, H. 1982: *Spracherwerb in der Kindheit: eine Untersuchung zur Entwicklung der Syntax bei Kleinkindern*. Tübingen: Gunter Narr.

Clahsen, H. 1984: The acquisition of German word order: a test case for cognitive approaches to L2 development. In Andersen, R. (ed.), *Second languages: A crosslinguistic perspective*. Rowley, MA: Newbury House, 219–42.

Clahsen, H. (ed.) 1996: *Generative perspectives on language acquisition: Empirical findings, theoretical considerations and crosslinguistic comparisons*. Amsterdam: John Benjamins.

Clahsen, H. and Muysken, P. 1986: The availability of universal grammar to adult and child learners – a study of the acquisition of German word order. *Second Language Research* 2, 93–119.

Clark, E. 1985: The acquisition of Romance, with special reference to French. In Slobin, D. (ed.), *The crosslinguistic study of language acquisition*. Hillsdale, NJ: Lawrence Erlbaum, 687–782.

Cook, V. 1997: *Inside language*. London: Arnold.

Cook, V. 2001: *Second language learning and language teaching*. London: Arnold.

Cook, V. and Newson, M. 1996: *Chomsky's Universal Grammar. An introduction*. Oxford: Blackwell.

Corder, S.P. 1967: The significance of learners' errors. *International Review of Applied Linguistics* 5, 161–9.

Coughlan, P. and Duff, P.A. 1994: Same task, different activities: analysis of an SLA task from an activity theory perspective. In Lantolf, J.P. and Appel, G. (eds), *Vygotskian approaches to second language research*. Norwood, NJ: Ablex Publishing Corporation, 173–94.

Coupland, N. and Jaworski, A. 1997: *Sociolinguistics: A reader and coursebook*. Basingstoke: Macmillan.

Crystal, D. 1991: *A dictionary of linguistics and phonetics*. Oxford: Blackwell.

Curtiss, S. 1977: *Genie: A psycholinguistic study of a modern-day 'wild child'*. New York, NY: Academic Press.

Curtiss, S. 1988: Abnormal language acquisition and the modularity of language. In Newmeyer, F.J. (ed.), *Linguistics: The Cambridge survey* Vol. 2. Cambridge: Cambridge University Press, 96–116.

De Graaff, R. 1997: The eXperanto experiment: effects of explicit instruction on second language acquisition. *Studies in Second Language Acquisition* 19, 249–76.

DeGraff, M. 1999: Creolisation, language change and language acquisition: an epilogue. In DeGraff, M. (ed.), *Language creation and language change*. Cambridge, MA: MIT Press, 473–528.

De Guerrero, M.C.M. 1999: Inner speech as mental rehearsal: the case of advanced L2 learners. *Issues in Applied Linguistics* 10, 27–55.

DeKeyser, R. 1993: The effect of error correction on L2 grammar knowledge and oral proficiency. *Modern Language Journal* 77, 501–14.

DeKeyser, R. 1997: Beyond explicit rule learning: automatizing second language morphosyntax. *Studies in Second Language Acquisition* 19, 195–222.

DeKeyser, R. 2001: Automaticity and automatization. In Robinson, P. (ed.), *Cognition and second language instruction*. Cambridge: Cambridge University Press, 125–51.

DeKeyser, R. 2003: Implicit and explicit learning. In Doughty, C. and Long, M. (eds), *The handbook of second language acquisition*. Oxford: Blackwell Publishing, 313–48.

de la Fuente, M.J. 2002: Negotiation and oral acquisition of L2 vocabulary. *Studies in Second Language Acquisition* 24, 81–112.

Deutsch, W. and Budwig, N. 1983: Form and function in the development of possessives. *Papers and Reports on Child Language Development* 22, 36–42.

De Villiers, P.A. and De Villiers, J.G. 1973: A cross-sectional study of the development of grammatical morphemes in child speech. *Journal of Psycholinguistic Research* 1, 299–310.

Dewaele, J.-M. and Regan, V. 2002: Maitriser la norme socioliguistique en interlangue française: le cas de l'omission variable de 'ne'. *Journal of French Language Studies* 12, 123–48.

Dietrich, R., Klein, W. and Noyau, C. 1995: *The acquisition of temporality in a second language*. Amsterdam: John Benjamins.

Dittmar, N. 1984: Semantic features of pidginised learners of German. In Andersen, R. (ed.), *Second languages: A cross-linguistic perspective*. Rowley, MA: Newbury House, 243–70.

Dittmar, N. 1993: Proto-semantics and emergent grammars. In Dittmar, N. and Reich, A. (eds) 1993, *Modality in language acquisition*. Berlin: Walter de Gruyter, 213–33.

Dittmar, N. and Reich, A. 1993: *Modality in language acquisition*. Berlin: Walter de Gruyter.

Donato, R. 1994: Collective scaffolding in second language learning. In Lantolf, J.P. and Appel, G. (eds), *Vygotskian approaches to second language research*. Norwood, NJ: Ablex Publishing Corporation, 33–56.

Donato, R. and McCormick, D. 1994: A sociocultural perspective on language learning strategies: the role of mediation. *Modern Language Journal* 78, 453–64.

Dopke, S. (ed.) 2000: *Cross-linguistic structures in simultaneous bilingualism.* Amsterdam: John Benjamins.

Dörnyei, Z. 2001a: New themes and approaches in second language motivation research. *Annual Review of Applied Linguistics* 21, 43–59.

Dörnyei, Z. 2001b: *Teaching and researching motivation.* Harlow: Longman.

Dörnyei, Z. 2002: Attitudes, orientations, and motivations in language learning: advances in theory, research, and applications. *Language Learning* 53, 3–32.

Dörnyei, Z. and Skehan, P. (eds) 2002: *Individual differences in second language acquisition.* Amsterdam: John Benjamins.

Dörnyei, Z. and Skehan, P. 2003: Individual differences in second language learning. In Doughty, C. and Long, M. (eds), *The handbook of second language acquisition.* Oxford: Blackwell Publishing, 589–630.

Doughty, C.J. 1999: The cognitive underpinnings of focus on form. *University of Hawaii Working Papers in ESL* 18, 1–69.

Doughty, C.J. 2003: Instructed SLA: constraints, compensation, and enhancement. In Doughty, C.J. and Long, M.H. (eds), *The handbook of second language acquisition.* Oxford: Blackwell Publishing, 256–310.

Doughty, C.J. and Long, M.H. (eds) 2003: *The handbook of second language acquisition.* Oxford: Blackwell Publishing.

Dulay, H. and Burt, M. 1973: Should we teach children syntax? *Language Learning* 24, 245–58.

Dulay, H. and Burt, M. 1974: Natural sequences in child second language acquisition. *Language Learning* 24, 37–53.

Dulay, H. and Burt, M. 1975: Creative construction in second language learning and teaching. In Burt, M. and Dulay, H. (eds), *New directions in second language learning, teaching, and bilingual education.* Washington, DC: TESOL, 21–32.

Dulay, H., Burt, M. and Krashen, S. 1982: *Language two.* New York, NY: Oxford University Press.

Dunn, W. and Lantolf, J.P. 1998: Vygotsky's zone of proximal development and Krashen's I + 1: incommensurable constructs; incommensurable theories. *Language Learning* 48, 411–42.

Eckert, P. and McConnell-Ginet, S. 1992: Think practically and look locally: language and gender as community-based practice. *Annual Review of Anthropology* 21, 461–90.

Ellis, N.C. 1996a: Sequencing in SLA: phonological memory, chunking and points of order. *Studies in Second Language Acquisition* 18, 91–126.

Ellis, N.C. 1996b: Analyzing language sequence in the sequence of language acquisition: some comments on Major and Ioup. *Studies in Second Language Acquisition* 18, 361–8.

Ellis, N.C. 1998: Emergentism, connectionism and language learning. *Language Learning* 48, 631–64.

Ellis, N.C. 2001: Memory for language. In Robinson, P. (ed.), *Cognition and second language instruction.* Cambridge: Cambridge University Press, 33–68.

Ellis, N.C. 2003: Constructions, chunking, and connectionism: the emergence of second language structure. In Doughty, C. and Long, M. (eds), *The handbook of second language acquisition.* Oxford: Blackwell Publishing, 63–103.

Ellis, N.C. and Schmidt, R. 1997: Morphology and longer distance dependencies: laboratory research illuminating the A in SLA. *Studies in Second Language Acquisition* **19**, 145–71.

Ellis, N.C., and Schmidt, R. 1998: Rules or associations in the acquisition of morphology? The frequency by regularity interaction in human and PDP learning of morphosyntax. *Language and Cognitive Processes* **13**, 307–36.

Ellis, R. 1985a: Sources of variability in interlanguage. *Applied Linguistics* **6**, 118–31.

Ellis, R. 1985b: *Understanding second language acquisition.* Oxford: Oxford University Press.

Ellis, R. 1990: *Instructed second language acquisition.* Oxford: Blackwell.

Ellis, R. 1991: *Second language acquisition and language pedagogy.* Clevedon: Multilingual Matters.

Ellis, R. 1994: *The study of second language acquisition.* Oxford: Oxford University Press.

Ellis, R. 1997: *SLA research and language teaching.* Oxford: Oxford University Press.

Ellis, R. 1999a: Item versus system learning: explaining free variation. *Applied Linguistics* **20**, 460–80.

Ellis, R. 1999b: Theoretical perspectives on interaction and language learning. In Ellis, R. (ed.), *Learning a second language through interaction.* Amsterdam: John Benjamins, 3–32.

Ellis, R. and He, X 1999: The roles of modified input and output in the incidental acquisition of word meanings. *Studies in Second Language Acquisition* **21**, 285–301.

Elman, J., Bates, E., Johnson, M., Karmiloff-Smith, A., Parisi, D. and Plunkett, K. 1996: *Rethinking innateness: A connectionist perspective on development.* Cambridge, MA: MIT Press.

Eubank, L. 1996: Negation in early German–English interlanguage: more valueless features in the L2 initial state. *Second Language Research* **12**, 73–106.

Eubank, L. and Gregg, K. 1999: Critical periods and (second) language acquisition: divide and impera. In Birdsong, D. (ed.), *Second language acquisition and the Critical Period Hypothesis.* Hillsdale, NJ: Lawrence Erlbaum, 65–99.

Farrar, M.J. 1992: Negative evidence and grammatical morpheme acquisition. *Developmental Psychology* **28**, 90–8.

Felix, S. 1978: Some differences between first and second language acquisition. In Waterson, N. and Snow, C. (eds), *The development of communication.* New York, NY: Wiley and Sons, 469–79.

Flynn, S. 1983: *A study of the effects of principal branching direction in second language acquisition: The generalization of a parameter of Universal Grammar from first to second language acquisition.* Cornell University, Ithaca, New York: doctoral dissertation.

Flynn, S. 1984: A universal in L2 acquisition based on a PBD typology. In Eckman, F., Bell, L. and Nelson, D. (eds), *Universals of second language acquisition.* Rowley, MA: Newbury House, 75–87.

Flynn, S. 1987: *A parameter-setting model of L2 acquisition: Experimental studies in anaphora.* Dordrecht: Reidel.

Flynn, S. 1996: A parameter-setting approach to second language acquisition. In Ritchie, W. and Bhatia, T. (eds), *Handbook of second language acquisition.* San Diego, CA: Academic Press, 121–58.

Foley, W.A. 1997: *Anthropological linguistics: an introduction.* Oxford: Blackwell.

Fodor, J.A. 1983: *The modularity of mind.* Cambridge, MA: MIT Press.

Foster, P. and Skehan, P. 1996: The influence of planning and task type on second language performance. *Studies in Second Language Acquisition* **18**, 299–323.

Foster-Cohen, S.H. 1999: *An introduction to child language development.* London: Longman.

Franceschina, F. 2001: Morphological or syntactic deficits in near-native speakers? An assessment of some current proposals. *Second Language Research* **17**, 213–47.

Frawley, W. and Lantolf, J. 1985: Second language discourse: a Vygotskian perspective. *Applied Linguistics* **6**, 19–44.

Fromkin, V. and Rodman, R. 1997: *An introduction to language.* Stamford, CT: Thomson Learning.

Gair, J. 1998: Functional categories in L2 acquisition: homegrown or imported? Commentary on Part 1. In Flynn, S., Martohardjono, G. and O'Neil, W. (eds), *The generative study of second language acquisition.* Hillsdale, NJ: Erlbaum, 79–86.

Gallaway, C. and Richards, B.J. (eds) 1994: *Input and interaction in language acquisition.* Cambridge: Cambridge University Press.

Gardner, R.C. and MacIntyre, P.D. 1992: A student's contributions to second language learning. Part I: cognitive variables. *Language Teaching* **25**, 211–20.

Gardner, R.C. and MacIntyre, P.D. 1993: A student's contributions to second language learning. Part II: affective variables. *Language Teaching* **26**, 1–11.

Gass, S.M. 1996: Second language acquisition and linguistic theory: the role of language transfer. In Ritchie, W.C. and Bhatia, T.K. (eds), *Handbook of second language acquisition.* San Diego, CA: Academic Press, 317–45.

Gass, S.M. 2003: Input and interaction. In Doughty, C.J. and Long, M.H. (eds), *The handbook of second language acquisition.* Oxford: Blackwell Publishing, 224–55.

Gass, S. and Selinker, L. 1994: *Second language acquisition: An introductory course.* Hillsdale, NJ: Lawrence Erlbaum.

Gass, S.M. and Varonis, E.M. 1994: Input, interaction and second language production. *Studies in Second Language Acquisition* **16**, 283–302.

Gee, J. and Savasir, I. 1985: On the use of 'will' and 'gonna': towards a description of activity-types for child language. *Discourse Processes* **8**, 143–75.

Gerhardt, J. 1990: The relation of language to context in children's speech: the role of HAFTA statements in structuring 3-year-olds' discourse. *Papers in Pragmatics* **4**, 1–57.

Giacalone Ramat, A. 1997: Progressive periphrases, markedness and second-language data. In Eliasson, S. and Jahr, E.H. (eds), *Language and its ecology.* Berlin: Mouton, 261–85.

Givón, T. 1979: From discourse to syntax: grammar as a processing strategy. In Givón, T. (ed.), *Syntax and semantics.* New York, NY: Academic Press, 81–112.

Givón, T. 1985: Function, structure and language acquisition. In Slobin, D. (ed.), *The cross-linguistic study of language acquisition.* Hillsdale, NJ: Lawrence Erlbaum, 1005–27.

Goldberg, A.E. 1999: The emergence of argument structure semantics. In MacWhinney, B. (ed.) *The emergence of language.* London: Lawrence Erlbaum Publications.

Goldberg, A. and Sethuraman, N. 1999: Learning argument structure generalisations. University of Illinois at Urbana-Champaign, unpublished paper.

Gopnik, M. and Crago, M.B. 1991: Familial aggregation of a developmental language disorder. *Cognition* **39**, 1–50.

Graddol, D. 1997: *The future of English?* London: The British Council.

Graddol, D., Cheshire, J. and Swann, J. 1994: *Describing language* (2nd edn). Buckingham: Open University Press.

Granger, S. 1998: *Learner English on computer*. London and New York: Addison Wesley Longman.

Granger, S., Hung, J. and Petch-Tyson, S. 2002: *Computer learner corpora, second language acquisition and foreign language teaching*. Amsterdam: John Benjamins.

Gregg, K. 1984: Krashen's monitor and Occam's razor. *Applied Linguistics* **5**, 79–100.

Gregg, K. 2003: SLA theory: construction and assessment. In Doughty, C.J. and Long, M.H. (eds), *The handbook of second language acquisition*. Oxford: Blackwell Publishing, 831–65.

Grondin, N. and White, L. 1996: Functional categories in child L2 acquisition of French. *Language Acquisition* **5**, 1–34.

Haegeman, L. 1996: Root infinitives, clitics and truncated structures. In Clahsen, H. (ed.), *Generative perspectives on language acquisition*. Amsterdam: John Benjamins, 271–307.

Hahn, U. and Nakisa, R.C. 2000: German inflection: single or dual route? *Cognitive Psychology* **41**, 313–60.

Hall, J.K. 1995: (Re)creating our worlds with words: a sociohistorical perspective of face-to-face interaction. *Applied Linguistics* **16**, 206–32.

Halliday, M.A.K. 1985: *An introduction to functional grammar*. London: Arnold.

Hamann, C., Rizzi, L. and Frauenfelder, U. 1996: On the acquisition of subject and object clitics in French. In Clahsen, H. (ed.), *Generative perspectives on language acquisition*. Amsterdam: John Benjamins, 309–34.

Hamers, J. and Blanc, M. 1989: *Bilinguality and bilingualism*. Cambridge: Cambridge University Press.

Han, Z. 2002: A study of the impact of recasts on tense consistency in L2 output. *TESOL Quarterly* **36**, 543–72.

Hansen, J.G. and Liu, J. 1997: Social identity and language: theoretical and methodological issues. *TESOL Quarterly* **31**, 567–76.

Harley, B. and Hart, D. 1997: Language aptitude and second language proficiency in classroom learners of different starting ages. *Studies in Second Language Acquisition* **19**, 379–400.

Harley, T.A. 1995: *The psychology of language: from data to theory*. Hove: Erlbaum (UK) Taylor & Francis.

Harris, M. and Coltheart, M. 1986: *Language processing in children and adults: An introduction*. London: Routledge.

Harris, T. and Wexler, K. 1996: The optional-infinitive stage in child English: evidence from negation. In Clahsen, H. (ed.), *Generative perspectives on language acquisition*. Amsterdam: John Benjamins, 1–42.

Hatch, E.M. 1978: Discourse analysis and second language acquisition. In Hatch, E.M. (ed.), *Second language acquisition: A book of readings*. Rowley, MA: Newbury House, 401–35.

Hawkins, R. 2001: *Second language syntax: A generative introduction*. Oxford: Blackwell.

Hawkins, R. 2003: Locating the source of defective past tense marking in advanced L2 English speakers. In Van Hout, R., Hulk, A., Kuiken, F. and Towell, R. (eds), *The lexicon–syntax interface in second language acquisition*. Amsterdam: John Benjamins, 21–44.

Hawkins, R. and Chan, C.Y-H. 1997: The partial availability of Universal Grammar in second language acquisition: the 'failed functional features hypothesis'. *Second Language Research* **13**, 187–226.

Haznedar, B. 2001: The acquisition of the IP system in child L2 English. *Studies in Second Language Acquisition* **23**, 1–39.

Heath, S.B. 1983: *Ways with words*. Cambridge: Cambridge University Press.

Heath, S.B. 1986: What no bedtime story means: narrative skills at home and school. In Schieffelin, B.B. and Ochs, E. (eds), *Language socialisation across cultures*. Cambridge: Cambridge University Press, 97–124.

Heller, M. 1999: *Linguistic minorities and modernity*. Harlow: Longman.

Herschensohn, J. 2000: *The second time around: Minimalism and second language acquisition*. Amsterdam: John Benjamins.

Herschensohn, J. 2001: Missing inflection in L2 French: accidental infinitives and other verbal deficits. *Second Language Research* **17**, 273–305.

Hernandez-Chavez, E. 1972: Early code separation in the second language speech of Spanish-speaking children. Paper presented at the Stanford Child Language Research Forum, Stanford: Stanford University.

Hickey, T. 1993: Identifying formulas in first language acquisition. *Journal of Child Language* **20**, 27–41.

Holmes, J. 2001: *An introduction to sociolinguistics* (2nd edn). Harlow: Longman.

Houck, N., Robertson, J. and Krashen, S. 1978: On the domain of the conscious grammar: morpheme orders for corrected and uncorrected ESL student transcripts. *TESOL Quarterly* **12**, 335–9.

Howatt, A.P.R. 1984: *A history of English language teaching*. Oxford: Oxford University Press.

Howatt, A.P.R. 1988: From structural to communicative. *Annual Review of Applied Linguistics* **8**, 14–29.

Huebner, T. 1983: *The acquisition of English*. Ann Arbor, MI: Karoma.

Hulstijn, J. 1997: Second language acquisition research in the laboratory: possibilities and limitations. *Studies in Second Language Acquisition* **19**, 131–43.

Hulstijn, J. 2001: Intentional and incidental second language vocabulary learning: a reappraisal of elaboration, rehearsal and automaticity. In Robinson, P. (ed.), *Cognition and second language instruction*. Cambridge: Cambridge University Press, 258–86.

Hulstijn, J. 2003: Incidental and intentional learning. In Doughty, C. and Long, M. (eds), *The handbook of second language acquisition*. Oxford: Blackwell Publishing, 349–81.

Hulstijn, J. and Hulstijn, W. 1984: Grammatical errors as a function of processing constraints and explicit knowledge. *Language Learning* **34**, 23–43.

Hyams, N. 1996: The underspecification of functional categories in early grammar. In Clahsen, H. (ed.), *Generative perspectives on language acquisition*. Amsterdam: John Benjamins, 91–128.

Hymes, D. 1972: Models of the interaction of language and social life. In Gumperz, J. and Hymes, D. (eds), *Directions in sociolinguistics: The ethnography of communication.* New York, NY: Holt, Rinehart & Winston, 35–71.

Ionin, T. and Wexler, K. 2000: Evidence for defaults in child L2 acquisition of finiteness. Cambridge, MA: MIT, unpublished manuscript.

Izumi, S. and Bigelow, M. 2000: Does output promote noticing and second language acquisition? *TESOL Quarterly* **34**, 239–78.

Izumi, S., Bigelow, M., Fujiwara, M. and Fearnow, S. 1999: Testing the output hypothesis: effects of output on noticing and second language acquisition. *Studies in Second Language Acquisition* **21**, 421–52.

Jenkins, L. 2000: *Biolinguistics.* Cambridge: Cambridge University Press.

Johnson, J. and Newport, E. 1989: Critical period effects in second language learning: the influence of maturational state on the acquisition of ESL. *Cognitive Psychology* **21**, 60–99.

Johnson, K. 1996: *Language teaching and skill learning.* Oxford: Blackwell.

Juffs, A. 1998: Some effects of first language argument structure and morphosyntax on second language sentence processing. *Second Language Research* **14**, 406–24.

Juffs, A. 2000: An overview of the second language acquisition of links between verb semantics and morpho-syntax. In Archibald, J. (ed.) *Second language acquisition and linguistic theory.* Oxford: Blackwell, pp. 187–227.

Kanagy, R. 1999: Interactional routines as a mechanism for L2 acquisition and socialisation in an immersion context. *Journal of Pragmatics* **31**, 1467–92.

Kaplan, R. and Bresnan, J. 1982: Lexical-functional grammar: a formal system for grammatical representation. In Bresnan, J. (ed.) *The mental representation of grammatical relations.* Cambridge, MA: MIT Press, 173–281.

Karmiloff-Smith, A 1979: *A functional approach to child language.* Cambridge: Cambridge University Press.

Karmiloff-Smith, A. 1987: Function and process in comparing language and cognition. In Hickmann, M. (ed.), *Social and functional approaches to language and thought.* London: Academic Press, 185–202.

Kasper, G. and Rose, K.R. 2003: Pragmatic development in a second language. *Language Learning* **52**, Supplement 1. Oxford: Blackwell Publishing.

Kempe, V. and Macwhinney, B. 1998: The acquisition of case-marking by adult learners of Russian and German. *Studies in Second Language Acquisition* **20**, 543–87.

Kinginger, C. 2001: I + 1 ≠ ZPD. *Foreign Language Annals* **34**, 417–25.

Klein, W. 1995: The acquisition of English. In Dietrich, R., Klein, W. and Noyau, C. (eds), *The acquisition of temporality in a second language.* Amsterdam: John Benjamins, 31–70.

Klein, W., Dietrich, R. and Noyau, C. 1993: The acquisition of temporality. In Perdue, C. (ed.), *Adult language acquisition: Cross-linguistic perspectives.* Volume 2: The Results. Cambridge: Cambridge University Press, 73–118.

Klein, W. and Perdue, C. 1992: *Utterance structure: Developing grammars again.* Amsterdam: John Benjamins.

Klima, E. and Bellugi, V. 1966: Syntactic regularities in the speech of children. In Lyons, J. and Wales, R. (eds), *Psycholinguistic papers.* Edinburgh: Edinburgh University Press, 183–219.

Klingner, J.K. and Vaughn, S. 2000: The helping behaviors of fifth graders while using collaborative strategic reading during ESL content classes. *TESOL Quarterly* **34**, 69–98.

Krashen, S. 1977a: The monitor model of adult second language performance. In Burt, M., Dulay, H. and Finocchiaro, M. (eds), *Viewpoints on English as a second language*. New York, NY: Regents, 152–61.

Krashen, S. 1977b: Some issues relating to the monitor model. In Brown, H., Yorio, C. and Crymes (eds), *Teaching and learning English as a second language: Some trends in research and practice*. Washington, DC: TESOL, 144–8.

Krashen, S. 1978: Individual variation in the use of the monitor. In Ritchie, W. (ed.), *Second language acquisition research: issues and implications*. New York, NY: Academic Press, 175–83.

Krashen, S. 1981: *Second language acquisition and second language learning*. Oxford: Pergamon.

Krashen, S. 1982: *Principles and practice in second language acquisition*. Oxford: Pergamon.

Krashen, S. 1983: Newmark's ignorance hypothesis and current second language acquisition theory. In Gass, S. and Selinker, L. (eds), *Language transfer in language learning*, Rowley, MA: Newbury House, 135–53.

Krashen, S. 1985: *The input hypothesis: issues and implications*. Harlow: Longman.

Krashen, S.D. 1998: Comprehensible output? *System* **26**, 175–82.

Krashen, S. and Scarcella, R. 1978: On routines and patterns in second language acquisition and performance. *Language Learning* **28**, 283–300.

Krashen, S. and Terrell, T. 1983: *The natural approach: Language acquisition in the classroom*. Hayward, CA: Alemany Press.

Labov, W. 1972: *Sociolinguistic patterns*. Philadelphia, PA: University of Pennsylvania Press.

Lado, R. 1964: *Language teaching: a scientific approach*. New York, NY: McGraw Hill.

Lai, C., Fisher, S., Hurst, J., Vargha-Khadem, F. and Faraneh, M. 2001: A forkhead-domain gene is mutated in a severe speech and language disorder. *Nature* **413**, 519–23.

Lakshmanan, U. 1993: The boy for the cookie – some evidence for the non-violation of the case filter in child second language acquisition. *Language Acquisition* **3**, 55–91.

Lakshmanan, U. and Selinker, L. 1994: The status of CP and the tensed complementizer *that* in the developing L2 grammars of English. *Second Language Research* **10**, 25–48.

Lam, W.S.E. 2000: L2 literacy and the design of the self: a case study of a teenager writing on the internet. *TESOL Quarterly* **34**, 457–82.

Lange, D. 1979: Negation in natürlichen Englisch–Deutschen Zweitsprachenerwerb: eine Fallstudie. *International Review of Applied Linguistics* **17**, 331–48.

Lantolf, J.P. (ed.) 1994: Sociocultural theory and second language learning: Special issue, *Modern Language Journal* **78**, 4.

Lantolf, J. P. and Appel, G. 1994 (eds): *Vygotskian approaches to second language research*. Norwood, NJ: Ablex Publishing Corporation.

Lantolf, J.P. 1996: Second language acquisition theory building? In Blue, G. and Mitchell, R. (eds), *Language and education*. Clevedon: BAAL/Multilingual Matters, 16–27.

Lantolf, J.P. 2000: Second language learning as a mediated process. *Language Teaching* **33**, 79–96.

Lantolf, J.P. (ed.) 2000b: *Sociocultural theory and second language learning*. Oxford: Oxford University Press.

Lardière, D. 1998: Dissociating syntax from morphology in a divergent L2 end-state grammar. *Second Language Research* **14**, 359–75.

Larsen-Freeman, D. and Long, M.H. 1991: *An introduction to second language acquisition research*. Harlow: Longman.

Lave, J. and Wenger, E. 1991: *Situated learning: Legitimate peripheral participation*. Cambridge: Cambridge University Press.

Leeman, J. 2003: Recasts and second language development: beyond negative evidence. *Studies in Second Language Acquisition* **25**, 37–64.

Lenneberg, E. 1967: *Biological foundations of language*. New York, NY: Wiley.

Leontiev, A.N. 1981: *Problems of the development of mind*. Moscow: Progress Publishers.

Levelt, W. 1989: *Speaking: From intention to articulation*. Cambridge, MA: MIT Press.

Lieven, E.V.M. 1994: Crosslinguistic and crosscultural aspects of language addressed to children. Chapter 3 in Gallaway, C. and Richards, B. (eds), *Input and interaction in language acquisition*. Cambridge: Cambridge University Press, 56–73.

Lightbown, P. and Spada, N. 1993: *How languages are learned*. Oxford: Oxford University Press.

Long, M.H. 1980: *Input, interaction and second language acquisition*. University of California, Los Angeles, PhD dissertation.

Long, M.H. 1981: Input, interaction and second language acquisition. In Winitz, H. (ed.), Native language and foreign language acquisition. *Annals of the New York Academy of Sciences* **379**, 259–78.

Long, M.H. 1983a: Native speaker/non-native speaker conversation and the negotiation of comprehensible input. *Applied Linguistics* **4**, 126–41.

Long, M.H. 1983b: Linguistic and conversational adjustments to non-native speakers. *Studies in Second Language Acquisition* **5**, 177–93.

Long, M.H. 1985: Input and second language acquisition theory. In Gass, S.M. and Madden, C.G. (eds), *Input in second language acquisition*. Rowley, MA: Newbury House, 377–93.

Long, M.H. 1990a: The least a second language acquisition theory needs to explain. *TESOL Quarterly* **24**, 649–66.

Long, M.H. 1990b: Maturational constraints on language development. *Studies in Second Language Acquisition* **12**, 251–85.

Long, M.H. 1993: Assessment strategies for SLA theories. *Applied Linguistics* **14**, 225–49.

Long, M.H. 1996: The role of the linguistic environment in second language acquisition. In Ritchie, W.C. and Bhatia, T.K. (eds), *Handbook of second language acquisition*. San Diego, CA: Academic Press, 413–68.

Long, M.H. and Doughty, C.J. 2003: SLA and cognitive science. In Doughty, C.J. and Long, M.H. (eds), *The handbook of second language acquisition*. Oxford: Blackwell, 866–70.

Long, M.H., Inagaki, S. and Ortega, L. 1998: The role of implicit negative feedback in SLA: models and recasts in Japanese and Spanish. *Modern Language Journal* **82**, 357–71.

Lorenzo, G. and Longa, V. 2003: Minimizing the genes for grammar. The minimalist program as a biological framework for the study of language. *Lingua* **113**, 643–57.

Loschky, L. 1994: Comprehensible input and second language acquisition: What is the relationship? *Studies in Second Language Acquisition* **16**, 303–23.

Losey, K.M. 1995: Gender and ethnicity as factors in the development of verbal skills in bilingual Mexican American women. *TESOL Quarterly* **29**, 635–61.

Lyster, R 1998: Negotiation of form, recasts, and explicit correction in relation to error types and learner repair in immersion classrooms. *Language Learning* **48**, 183–218.

Lyster, R. 2001: Form-focused instruction and second language learning. In Ellis, R. (ed.), *Form-focused instruction and second language learning*. Oxford: Blackwell, 265–301.

Lyster, R. and Ranta, E. 1997: Corrective feedback and learner uptake: negotiation of form in communicative classrooms. *Studies in Second Language Acquisition* **19**, 37–61.

MacIntyre, P.D., Baker, S.C., Clement, R. and Donovan, L.A. 2002: Sex and age effects on willingness to communicate, anxiety, perceived competence, and L2 motivation among junior high school French immersion students. *Language Learning* **52**, 537–64.

Mackey, A. 1999: Input, interaction and second language development: an empirical study of question formation in ESL. *Studies in Second Language Acquisition* **21**, 557–88.

Mackey, A., Gass, S. and McDonough, K. 2000: How do learners perceive implicit negative feedback? *Studies in Second Language Acquisition* **19**, 37–66.

Mackey, A., Oliver, R. and Leeman, J. 2003: Interactional input and the incorporation of feedback: an exploration of NS–NNS and NNS–NNS adult and child dyads. *Language Learning* **53**, 35–56.

Mackey, A. and Philp, J. 1998: Conversational interaction and second language development: recasts, responses and red herrings? *Modern Language Journal* **82**, 338–56.

MacWhinney, B. (ed.) 1999: *The emergence of language*. Mahwah, NJ: Lawrence Erlbaum.

MacWhinney, B. 2000a: *The CHILDES project: Tools for analyzing talk. Volume 1: Transciption format and programs* (3rd edn). Mahwah, NJ: Lawrence Erlbaum.

MacWhinney, B. 2000b: *The CHILDES project: Tools for analyzing talk. Volume 2: The database.* (3rd edn). Mahwah, NJ: Lawrence Erlbaum.

MacWhinney, B. 2001: The competition model: the input, the context, and the brain. In Robinson, P. (ed.), *Cognition and second language instruction*. Cambridge: Cambridge University Press, 60–90.

MacWhinney, B. and Anderson, J. 1986: The acquisition of grammar. In Gopnik, I. and Gopnik, M. (eds), *From models to modules*. Norwood, NJ: Ablex, 3–23.

MacWhinney, B. and Leinbach, J. 1991: Implementations are not conceptualizations: revising the verb learning model. *Cognition* **29**, 198–256.

Marsden, E., Myles, F., Rule, S. and Mitchell, R. 2002: Oral French interlanguage corpora: tools for data management and analysis. *Centre for Language in Education Occasional Papers* **58**. Southampton: University of Southampton.

Marsden, E., Myles, F., Rule, S. and Mitchell, R. 2003: Using CHILDES tools for researching second language acquisition. In Sarangi, S. and Van Leeuwen, T. (eds), *Applied linguistics and communities of practice*. London: Continuum.

Masgoret, A.-M. and Gardner, R.C. 2003: Attitudes, motivation, and second language learning: a meta-analysis of studies conducted by Gardner and associates. *Language Learning* 53, 123–63.

McCafferty, S. 1992: The use of private speech by adult second language learners: a cross-cultural study. *Modern Language Journal* 76, 179–89.

McCafferty, S. 1994: Adult second language learners' use of private speech: a review of studies. *Modern Language Journal* 78, 421–36.

McCafferty, S.G., Roebuck, R.F. and Wayland, R.P. 2001: Activity theory and the incidental learning of second-language vocabulary. *Language Teaching Research* 10, 289–94.

McKay, S.L. and Wong, S-L.C. 1996: Multiple discourses, multiple identities: investment and agency in second-language learning among Chinese adolescent immigrant students. *Harvard Educational Review* 66, 577–608.

McLaughlin, B. 1987: *Theories of second language learning*. London: Edward Arnold.

McLaughlin, B. 1990: Restructuring. *Applied Linguistics* 11, 113–28.

McLaughlin, B. and Heredia, R. 1996: Information-processing approaches to research on second language acquisition and use. In Ritchie, W. and Bhatia, T. (eds), *Handbook of second language acquisition*. San Diego, CA: Academic Press, 213–28.

McNamara, T. 1997: What do we mean by social identity? Competing frameworks, competing discourses. *TESOL Quarterly* 31, 561–7.

Meisel, J. 1997: The acquisition of the syntax of negation in French and German: contrasting first and second language development. *Second Language Research* 13, 227–63.

Meisel, J., Clahsen, H. and Pienemann, M. 1981: On determining developmental stages in natural second language acquisition. *Studies in Second Language Acquisition* 3, 109–35.

Mellow, J.D., Reeder, K. and Forster, E. 1996: Using time-series research designs to investigate the effects on instruction on SLA. *Studies in Second Language Acquisition* 18, 325–50.

Mercer, N. 1995: The guided construction of knowledge. Clevedon: Multilingual Matters.

Mercer, N. 1996: Language and the guided construction of knowledge. In Blue, G. and Mitchell, R. (eds), *Language in education*. Clevedon: BAAL/Multilingual Matters, 28–40.

Mercer, N. 2000: *Words and minds*. London: Routledge.

Mesthrie, R., Swann, J., Deumert, A. and Leap, W.L. 2000: *Introducing sociolinguistics*. Edinburgh: Edinburgh University Press.

Milon, J.P. 1974: The development of negation in English by a second language learner. *TESOL Quarterly* 8, 137–43.

Mitchell, R. and Martin, C. 1997: Rote learning, creativity and 'understanding' in classroom foreign language teaching. *Language Teaching Research* 1, 1–27.

Morgan, J.L., Bonamo, K.M. and Travis, L.L. 1995: Negative evidence on negative evidence. *Developmental Psychology* 31, 180–97.

Myles, F. in press a: The emergence of morpho-syntactic structure in French L2. In Dewaele, J-M. (ed.), *Focus on French as a foreign language: Multidisciplinary approaches*. Clevedon: Multilingual Matters.

Myles, F. in press b: From data to theory: the over-representation of linguistic knowledge in SLA. In Hawkins, R. (ed.), *Empirical evidence and theories of representation in current research in Second Language Acquisition*: Transactions of the Philological Society.

Myles, F., Hooper, J. and Mitchell, R. 1998: Rote or rule? Exploring the role of formulaic language in classroom foreign language learning. *Language Learning* 48, 323–63.

Myles, F., and Mitchell, R. 2003: *Rote-learnt chunks and interlanguage development: a corpus-based study*. Paper presented at the American Association of Applied Linguistics Conference, Washington, DC, March 2003.

Myles, F., Mitchell, R. and Hooper, J. 1999: Interrogative chunks in French L2: a basis for creative construction? *Studies in Second Language Acquisition* 21, 49–80.

Nassaji, H. and Swain, M. 2000: A Vygotskian perspective on corrective feedback in L2: the effect of random versus negotiated help in the learning of English articles. *Language Awareness* 8, 34–51.

Nation, I.S.P. 2001: *Learning vocabulary in another language*. Cambridge: Cambridge University Press.

Nicholas, H., Lightbown, P.M. and Spada, N. 2001: Recasts as feedback to language learners. *Language Learning* 51, 719–58.

Ninio, A. and Snow, C.E. 1999: The development of pragmatics: learning to use language appropriately. In Ritchie, W.C. and Bhatia, T.K. (eds), *Handbook of child language acquisition*. London: Academic Press, 347–83.

Nobuyoshi, J. and Ellis, R. 1993: Focused communication tasks and second language acquisition. *ELT Journal* 47, 203–10.

Norris, J. and Ortega, L. 2000: Effectiveness of L2 instruction: a research synthesis and quantitative meta-analysis. *Language Learning* 50, 417–528.

Norton, B. 2000: *Identity and language learning*. Harlow: Pearson Education.

Ochs, E. 1988: *Culture and language development: Language acquisition and language socialisation in a Samoan village*. Cambridge: Cambridge University Press.

Ochs, E. and Schieffelin, B.B. 1984: Language acquisition and socialisation: three developmental stories and their implications. In Shweder, R. and LeVine, R. (eds), *Culture theory: Essays on mind, self and emotion*. Cambridge: Cambridge University Press, 276–320.

Ochs, E. and Schieffelin, B. 1995: The impact of language socialisation on grammatical development. In Fletcher, P. and MacWhinney, B. (eds), *The handbook of child language*. Oxford: Blackwell, 73–94.

Ohara, Y. 2001: Finding one's voice in Japanese: a study of the pitch levels of L2 users. In Pavlenko, A., Blackledge, A., Piller, I. and Teutsch-Dwyer, M. (eds), *Multilingualism, second language learning and gender*. Berlin: Mouton de Gruyter, 231–54.

Ohta, A.S. 1999: Interactional routines and the socialisation of interactional style in adult learners of Japanese. *Journal of Pragmatics* 31, 1493–512.

Ohta, A.S. 2000: Rethinking interaction in SLA: developmentally appropriate assistance in the zone of proximal development and the acquisition of L2 grammar. In Lantolf J. P. (ed.), *Sociocultural theory and second language learning*. Oxford: Oxford University Press, 51–78.

Ohta, A.S. 2001: *Second language acquisition processes in the classroom: Learning Japanese.* Mahwah, NJ: Lawrence Erlbaum.

Olson, D.R. 1995: Writing and the mind. In Wertsch, J.V., Del Rio, P. and Alvarez, A. (eds), *Sociocultural studies of mind.* Cambridge: Cambridge University Press, 95–123.

Oliver, R. 1995: Negative feedback in child NS–NNS conversation. *Studies in Second Language Acquisition* 17, 459–81.

Oliver, R. 2000: Age differences in negotiation and feedback in classroom and pair-work. *Language Learning* 50, 119–51.

O'Malley, J. and Chamot, A. 1990: *Learning strategies in second language acquisition.* Cambridge: Cambridge University Press.

Pallotti, G. 2001: External appropriations as a strategy for participating in intercultural multi-party conversations. In Di Luzio, A., Gunthner, S. and Orletti, F. (eds), *Culture in communication.* Amsterdam: John Benjamins, 295–334.

Panova, I. and Lyster, R. 2002: Patterns of corrective feedback and uptake in an adult ESL classroom. *TESOL Quarterly* 36, 573–95.

Parodi, T. 2000: Finiteness and verb placement in second language acquisition. *Second Language Research* 16, 355–81.

Pavlenko, A. 1998: Second language learning by adults: testimonies of bilingual writers. *Issues in Applied Linguistics* 9, 3–19.

Pavlenko, A. 2001: 'How am I to become a woman in an American vein?' Transformations of gender performance in second language learning. In Pavlenko, A., Blackledge, A., Piller, I. and Teutsch-Dwyer, M. (eds), *Multilingualism, second language learning and gender.* Berlin: Mouton de Gruyter, 133–74.

Penner, Z. and Weissenborn, J. 1996: Strong continuity, parameter setting and the trigger hierarchy: on the acquisition of the DP in Bernese Swiss German and High German. In Clahsen, H. (ed.), *Generative perspectives on language acquisition.* Amsterdam: John Benjamins, 161–200.

Pennycook, A. 1994: *The cultural politics of English as an international language.* Harlow: Longman.

Perdue, C. (ed.) 1993a: *Adult language acquisition: Cross-linguistic perspectives.* Volume 1, Field Methods. Cambridge: Cambridge University Press.

Perdue, C. (ed.) 1993b: *Adult language acquisition: Cross-linguistic perspectives.* Volume 2, The Results. Cambridge: Cambridge University Press.

Perdue, C. (ed). 2000: The structure of learner varieties. *Studies in Second Language Acquisition* 22 (4) [special issue].

Perdue, C. and Klein, W. 1993: Concluding remarks. In Perdue, C. (ed.), *Adult language acquisition: Cross-linguistic perspectives.* Volume 2 The Results. Cambridge: Cambridge University Press, 253–72.

Phillipson, R. 1992: *Linguistic imperialism.* Oxford: Oxford University Press.

Philp, J. 2003: Constraints on 'noticing the gap': nonnative speakers' noticing of recasts in NS–NNS interaction. *Studies in Second Language Acquisition* 25, 99–126.

Piaget, J. 1970: *Genetic epistemology.* Columbia, OH: Columbia University Press.

Piaget, J. and Inhelder, B. 1966: *The psychology of the child* (trans. H. Weaver). New York, NY: Basic Books, 1969.

Piatelli-Palmarini, M. (ed.) 1980: *Language and learning: The debate between Jean Piaget and Noam Chomsky.* London: Routledge and Kegan Paul.

Pica, T. 1994: Research on negotiation: what does it reveal about second-language learning conditions, processes and outcomes? *Language Learning* **44**, 493–527.

Pica, T., Young, R. and Doughty, C. 1987: The impact of interaction on comprehension. *TESOL Quarterly* **21**, 737–58.

Pienemann, M. 1981: *Der Zweitsprachenerwerb ausländischer Arbeitskinder.* Bonn: Bouvier.

Pienemann, M. 1987: Determining the influence of instruction on L2 speech processing. *Australian Review of Applied Linguistics* **10**, 83–113.

Pienemann, M. 1989: Is language teachable? Psycholinguistic experiments and hypotheses. *Applied Linguistics* **10**, 52–79.

Pienemann, M. 1998: *Language processing and second language acquisition: Processability theory.* Amsterdam: John Benjamins.

Pienemann, M. 2003: Language processing capacity. In Doughty, C. J. and Long, M. H. (eds), *The handbook of second language acquisition.* Oxford: Blackwell Publishing, 679–714.

Pienemann, M. and Johnston, M. 1987. Factors influencing the development of language proficiency. In Nunan, D. (ed.), *Applying second language acquisition research.* Adelaide, Australia: National Curriculum Resource Centre, 45–141.

Pierce, A. 1992: *Language acquisition and syntactic theory: A comparative analysis of French and English child grammars.* London: Kluwer.

Pierce, B.N. 1995: Social identity, investment, and language learning. *TESOL Quarterly* **29**, 9–31.

Pine, J.M. 1994: The language of primary caregivers. In Gallaway, C. and Richards, B.R. (eds), *Input and interaction in language acquisition.* Cambridge: Cambridge University Press, 15–37.

Pine, J. and Lieven, E. 1993: Reanalysing rote-learned phrases: individual differences in the transition to multi-word speech. *Journal of Child Language* **20**, 551–71.

Pine, J. and Lieven, E. 1997: Slot and frame patterns in the development of the determiner category. *Applied Psycholinguistics* **18**, 123–38.

Pine, J., Lieven, E. and Rowland, C. 1998: Comparing different models of the development of the English verb category. *Linguistics* **36**, 807–30.

Pinker, S. 1989: *Learnability and cognition.* Cambridge, MA: MIT Press.

Pinker, S. 1991: Rules of language. *Science* **253**, 530–5.

Pinker, S. 1994: *The language instinct.* London: Penguin Books.

Pinker, S. and Prince, A. 1988: On language and connectionism: analysis of a parallel distributed processing model of language acquisition. *Cognition* **28**, 73–193.

Platt, E. and Brooks, F.B. 1994: The 'acquisition-rich environment' revisited. *Modern Language Journal* **78**, 497–511.

Platt, E. and Brooks, F.B. 2002: Task engagement: a turning point in foreign language development. *Language Learning* **52**, 365–400.

Plunkett, K. (ed.). 1998: *Special issue on connectionist models of language* (Vol. 13).

Plunkett, K. and Marchman, V. 1991: U-shaped learning and frequency effects in a multi-layered perception: implications for child language acquisition. *Cognition* **38**, 43–102.

Poole, D. 1992: Language socialisation in the second language classroom. *Language Learning* **42**, 593–616.

Preston, D. 1989 *Sociolinguistics and second language acquisition.* Oxford: Blackwell.

Preston, D. 1996a: Variationist linguistics and second language acquisition. In Ritchie, W.C. and Bhatia, T.K. (eds), *Handbook of second language acquisition.* San Diego, CA: Academic Press.

Preston, D. 1996b: Variationist perspectives on second language acquisition. In Bayley, R. and Preston, D.R. (eds) *Second language acquisition and linguistic variation.* Amsterdam: John Benjamins, 1–45.

Prévost, P. and White, L. 2000: Missing surface inflection or impairment in second language acquisition? Evidence from tense and agreement. *Second Language Research* **16**, 103–33.

Radford, A. 1990: *Syntactic theory and the acquisition of English syntax.* Oxford: Basil Blackwell.

Radford, A. 1996: Towards a structure-building model of acquisition. In Clahsen, H. (ed.), *Generative perspectives on language acquisition.* Amsterdam: John Benjamins, 43–90.

Radford, A. 1997: *Syntax: A minimalist introduction.* Cambridge: Cambridge University Press.

Rampton, B. 1995a: *Crossing: Language and ethnicity among adolescents.* Harlow: Longman.

Rampton, B. 1995b: Politics and change in research in applied linguistics. *Applied Linguistics* **16**, 233–56.

Rampton, B. 2002: Ritual and foreign language practices at school. *Language in Society* **31**, 491–525.

Raupach, M. 1984: Formulae in second language speech production. In Dechert, D., Möhle, D. and Raupach, M. (eds), *Second language production.* Tübingen: Gunter Narr, 114–37.

Raupach, M. 1987: Procedural learning in advanced learners of a foreign language. In Coleman, J. and Towell, R. (eds), *The advanced language learner.* London: AFLS/SUFLRA/CILT, 123–55.

Ravem, R. 1968: Language acquisition in a second language environment. *International Review of Applied Linguistics* **6**, 175–85.

Regan, V. 1996: Variation in French interlanguage: a longitudinal study of sociolinguistic competence. In Bayley, R. and Preston, D.R. (eds), *Second language acquisition and linguistic variation.* Amsterdam: John Benjamins, 177–201.

Rehner, K., Mougeon, R. and Nadasdi, T. 2003: The learning of sociolinguistic variation by advanced FSL learners: the case of nous versus on in immersion French. *Studies in Second Language Acquisition* **25**, 127–56.

Richards, B.J. 1994: Child-directed speech and influences on language acquisition: methodology and interpretation. Chapter 4 in Gallaway, C. and Richards, B.J. (eds), *Input and interaction in language acquisition.* Cambridge: Cambridge University Press, 74–106.

Richards, B.J. and Gallaway, C. 1994: Conclusions and directions. Chapter 11 in Gallaway, C. and Richards, B.J. (eds), *Input and interaction in language acquisition.* Cambridge: Cambridge University Press, 253–69.

Richards, J. (ed.) 1974: *Error Analysis: Perspectives on second language learning.* London: Longman.

Rispoli, M. 1999: Functionalist accounts of first language acquisition. In Ritchie, W.C. and Bhatia, T.K. (eds), *Handbook of child language acquisition.* London: Academic Press, 221–46.

Ritchie, W.C. and Bhatia, T.K. (eds), 1996: *Handbook of second language acquisition.* San Diego: Academic Press.

Rivers, W.M. 1964: *The psychologist and the foreign-language teacher.* Chicago, IL: University of Chicago Press.

Rivers, W.M. 1968: *Teaching foreign-language skills.* Chicago, IL: University of Chicago Press.

Robinson, P. 1986: Constituency or dependency in the units of language acquisition? An approach to describing the learner's analysis of formulae. *Linguisticae Investigationes* **10**, 417–37.

Robinson, P. 1997: Individual differences and the fundamental similarity of implicit and explicit adult second language learning. *Language Learning* **47**, 45–99.

Robinson, P. 2001. *Cognition and second language instruction.* Cambridge: Cambridge University Press.

Robinson, P. (ed.) 2002: *Individual differences and instructed language learning.* Amsterdam: John Benjamins.

Robinson, P. 2003: Attention and memory during SLA. In Doughty, C. and Long, M. (eds), *The handbook of second language acquisition.* Oxford: Blackwell Publishing, 631–78.

Roebuck, R. 2000: Subjects speak out: how learners position themselves in a psycholinguistic task. In Lantolf, J.P. (ed.), *Sociocultural theory and second language learning.* Oxford: Oxford University Press, 81–98.

Rogoff, B. 1990: *Apprenticeship in thinking.* Cambridge: Cambridge University Press.

Rogoff, B. 1995: Observing sociocultural activity on three planes: participatory appropriation, guided participation and apprenticeship. In Wertsch, J.V., Del Rio, P. and Alvarez, A. (eds), *Sociocultural studies of mind.* Cambridge: Cambridge University Press, 139–64.

Romaine, S. 1988: *Pidgin and creole languages.* Harlow: Longman.

Romaine, S. 1995: *Bilingualism* (2nd edn). Oxford: Blackwell.

Romaine, S. 2003: Variation. In Doughty, C.J. and Long, M.H. (eds), *The handbook of second language acquisition.* Oxford: Blackwell Publishing, 409–35.

Rule, S., Marsden, E., Myles, F. and Mitchell, R. 2003: Constructing a database of French interlanguage oral corpora. In: Archer, D. Rayson, P. Wilson, A. and McEnery, A. (eds) *Proceedings of the Corpus Linguistics 2003 Conference.* Lancaster University: UCREL Technical Papers 16, 669–77.

Rumelhart, D. and McClelland, J. 1986: On learning the past tense of English verbs. In McClelland, J. and Rumelhart, D. (eds), *Parallel distributed processing: Explorations in the microstructure of cognition. Vol. 2: Psychological and biological models.* Cambridge, MA: MIT Press, 216–71.

Rutherford, W. and Thomas, M. 2001: The *Child Language Data Exchange System* in research on second language acquisition. *Second Language Research* **17**, 195–212.

Sabouraud, O. 1995: *Le langage et ses maux.* Paris: Editions Odile Jacob.

Salaberry, M.R. 1999: The development of past tense verbal morphology in classroom L2 Spanish. *Applied Linguistics* **20**, 151–78.

Salkie, R. 1990: *The Chomsky update: linguistics and politics.* London: Routledge.

Salsbury, T. and Bardovi-Harlig, K. 2000: Oppositional talk and the acquisition of modality in L2 English. In Swierzbin, B., Morris, F., Anderson, M., Klee, C.A. and Tarone, E. (eds), *Social and cognitive factors in second language acquisition.* Somerville, MA: Cascadilla Press.

Sato, C. 1990: *The syntax of conversation in interlanguage development.* Tübingen: Gunter Narr Verlag.

Saville-Troike, M. 1989: *The ethnography of communication: An introduction* (2nd edn). Oxford: Basil Blackwell.

Schachter, J. 1986: In search of systematicity in interlanguage production. *Studies in Second Language Acquisition* **8**, 119–34.

Schachter, J. 1996: Maturation and the issue of Universal Grammar in second language acquisition. In Ritchie, W. and Bhatia, T. (eds), *Handbook of second language acquisition.* San Diego, CA: Academic Press, 159–93.

Schieffelin, B.B. 1985: The acquisition of Kaluli. In Slobin, D.I. (ed.), *The cross-linguistic study of language acquisition,* Volume 1. Hillsdale, NJ: Lawrence Erlbaum, 525–95.

Schieffelin, B.B. 1990: *The give and take of everyday life: Language socialisation of Kaluli children.* Cambridge: Cambridge University Press.

Schmidt, R. 1990: The role of consciousness in second language learning. *Applied Linguistics* **11**, 129–58.

Schmidt, R. 1992: Psychological mechanisms underlying second language fluency. *Studies in Second Language Acquisition* **14**, 357–85.

Schmidt, R. 1994: Deconstructing consciousness in search of useful definitions for applied linguistics. *AILA Review* **11**, 11–26.

Schmidt, R. 2001: Attention. In Robinson, P. (ed.), *Cognition and second language instruction.* Cambridge: Cambridge University Press, 3–32.

Schmidt, R. and Frota, S. 1986: Developing basic conversational ability in a second language: a case study of an adult learner of Portuguese. In Day, R.R. (ed.), *Talking to learn: Conversation in second language acquisition.* Rowley, MA: Newbury House, 237–322.

Schumann, J. 1978a: *The pidginisation process: A model for second language acquisition.* Rowley, MA: Newbury House.

Schumann, J. 1978b: The acculturation model for second language acquisition. In Gingras, R. (ed.), *Second language acquisition and foreign language teaching.* Arlington, VA: Center for Applied Linguistics, 27–50.

Schumann, J. 1978c: Social and psychological factors in second language acquisition. In Richards, J. (ed.), *Error Analysis: Perspectives on second language learning.* London: Longman.

Schwartz, B. 1993: On explicit and negative evidence affecting and affecting competence and 'linguistic behavior'. *Studies in Second Language Acquisition* **15**, 147–63.

Schwartz, B. 1998: On two hypotheses of 'transfer' in L2A: minimal trees and absolute L1 influence. In Flynn, S., Martohardjono, G. and O'Neil, W. (eds), *The generative study of second language acquisition.* Hillsdale, NJ: Erlbaum, 35–60.

Schwartz, B., and Eubank, L. 1996: What is the 'L2 initial state'? *Second Language Research* **12**, 1–6.

Schwartz, B. and Sprouse, R. 1994: Word order and nominative case in nonnative language acquisition: a longitudinal study of (L1 Turkish) German interlanguage. In Hoekstra, T. and Schwartz, B. (eds), *Language acquisition studies in generative grammar: Papers in honor of Kenneth Wexler from the GLOW 1991 Workshops.* Amsterdam: John Benjamins, 317–68.

Schwartz, B. and Sprouse, R. 1996: L2 cognitive states and the Full Transfer/Full Access model. *Second Language Research* **12**, 40–72.

Sebba, M. 1997: *Contact languages: Pidgins and creoles.* Basingstoke: Macmillan Press.

Segalowitz, N. 2003: Automaticity and second languages. In Doughty, C. and Long, M. (eds), *The handbook of second language acquisition.* Oxford: Blackwell Publishing, 382–408.

Selinker, L. 1972: Interlanguage. *International Review of Applied Linguistics* **10**, 209–31.

Selinker, L. 1992: *Rediscovering interlanguage.* London: Longman.

Sharwood Smith, M. 1994: *Second language learning: theoretical foundations.* Harlow: Longman.

Shehadeh, A. 2002: Comprehensible output, from occurrence to acquisition: an agenda for acquisitional research. *Language Learning* **52**, 597–647.

Shiffrin, R.M. and Schneider, W. 1977: Controlled and automatic human information processing. II: perceptual learning, automatic, attending, and a general theory. *Psychological Review* **84**, 127–90.

Sinclair, J. 1991: *Corpus, concordance, collocation.* Oxford: Oxford University Press.

Singleton, D. 1995: A critical look at the critical period hypothesis in second language acquisition research. In Singleton, D. and Lengyel, Z. (eds), *The age factor in second language acquisition.* Clevedon: Multilingual Matters, 1–29.

Singleton, D. 1999: *Exploring the second language mental lexicon.* Cambridge: Cambridge University Press.

Skehan, P. 1998: *A cognitive approach to language learning.* Oxford: Oxford University Press.

Skinner, B.F. 1957: *Verbal Behavior.* New York: Appleton-Century-Crofts.

Slabakova, R. 2000: L1 transfer revisited: the L2 acquisition of telicity marking in English by Spanish and Bulgarian native speakers. *Linguistics* **38**, 739–70.

Slobin, D. 1970: Universals of grammatical development in children. In Flores d'Arcais, G. and Levelt, W. (eds), *Advances in psycholinguistics.* Amsterdam: North-Holland Publishing.

Slobin, D. 1973: Cognitive prerequisites for the development of grammar. In Ferguson, C. and Slobin, D. (eds), *Studies of child language development.* New York, NY: Holt, Rinehart & Winston, 175–208.

Slobin, D. 1979: *Psycholinguistics* (2nd edn). Glenview, IL: Scott, Foresman and Company.

Slobin, D. 1985: Crosslinguistic evidence for the language-making capacity. In Slobin, D. (ed.), *The crosslinguistic study of language acquisition*, Volume 2. Hillsdale, NJ: Lawrence Erlbaum Associates, 1159–249.

Smith, N. 1999: *Chomsky: Ideas and ideals.* Cambridge: Cambridge University Press.

Smith, N.V. and Tsimpli, I-M. 1995: *The mind of a savant: Language learning and modularity.* Oxford: Blackwell.

Snow, C.E. 1994: Beginning from baby talk: twenty years of research on input and interaction. In Gallaway, C. and Richards, B.R. (eds), *Input and interaction in language acquisition.* Cambridge: Cambridge University Press, 3–12.

Sokolik, M.E. 1990: Learning without rules: PDP and a resolution of the adult language learning paradox. *TESOL Quarterly* **24**, 685–96.

Sokolik, M. and Smith, M. 1992: Assignment of gender to French nouns in primary and secondary language: a connectionist model. *Second Language Research* **8**, 39–58.

Sokolov, J.L. and Snow, C.E. 1994: The changing role of negative evidence in theories of language development. In Gallaway, C. and Richards, B.R., (eds) *Input and interaction in language acquisition.* Cambridge: Cambridge University Press, 38–55.

Sorace, A. 1996: The use of acceptability judgements in second language acquisition research. In Ritchie, W. and Bhatia, T. (eds), *Handbook of second language acquisition.* San Diego, CA: Academic Press, 375–409.

Sorace, A. 2000: Syntactic optionality in non-native grammars. *Second Language Research* **16**, 93–102.

Spada, N. 1997: Form-focussed instruction and second language acquisition: a review of classroom and laboratory research. *Language Teaching* **30**, 73–87.

Spolsky, B. 1989: *Conditions for second language learning.* Oxford: Oxford University Press.

Steinberg, D. 1993: *An Introduction to psycholinguistics,* London: Longman.

Storch, N. 2002: Patterns of interaction in ESL pair work. *Language Learning* **52**, 119–58.

Stubbs, M. 1996: *Text and corpus analysis.* Oxford: Blackwell.

Sunderland, J. 2000: Issues of language and gender in second and foreign language education. *Language Teaching* **33**, 203–23.

Swain, M.1985: Communicative competence: some roles of comprehensible input and comprehensible output in its development. In Gass, S.M. and Madden, C.G. (eds), *Input in second language acquisition.* Rowley, MA: Newbury House, 235–53.

Swain, M 1995: Three functions of output in second language learning. In Cook, G. and Seidlhofer, B. (eds), *Principle and practice in applied linguistics: Studies in honour of H. G. Widdowson.* Oxford: Oxford University Press, 125–44.

Swain, M. 2000: The output hypothesis and beyond: mediating acquisition through collaborative dialogue. In Lantolf, J. (ed.) *Sociocultural theory and second language learning.* Oxford: Oxford University Press, 97–114.

Swain, M., Brooks, L. and Tocalli-Beller, A. 2002: Peer–peer dialogue as a means of second language learning. *Annual Review of Applied Linguistics* **22**, 171–85.

Swain, M. and Lapkin, S. 1995: Problems in output and the cognitive processes they generate: a step towards second language learning. *Applied Linguistics* **16**, 371–91.

Swain, M. and Lapkin, S. 1998: Interaction and second language learning: two adolescent French immersion students working together. *Modern Language Journal* **82**, 320–37.

Taraban, R. and Kempe, V. 1999: Gender processing in native (L1) and non-native (L2) Russian speakers. *Applied Psycholinguistics* **20**, 119–48.

Tarone, E. 1988: *Variation in interlanguage.* London: Edward Arnold.

Tarone, E. and Liu, G.-Q. 1995: Situational context, variation, and second language acquisition theory. In Cook, G. and Seidlhofer, B. (eds), *Principle and practice in applied linguistics.* Oxford: Oxford University Press, 107–24.

Thomas, M. 1991: *Universal Grammar and knowledge of reflexives in a second language.* Harvard University, Cambridge, MA, doctoral dissertation.

Thorndike, E. 1932: *The fundamentals of learning.* New York, NY: Columbia Teachers College.

Tokuhama-Espinosa, T. 2000. *Raising multilingual children: Foreign language acquisition and children.* Westport, CT: Greenwood Press.

Tomasello, M. 1992: *First verbs: A case study of early grammatical development.* Cambridge: Cambridge University Press.

Tomasello, M. 2003: *Constructing a language: a usage-based theory of language acquisition.* Cambridge, MA: Harvard University Press.

Tomasello, M. and Brooks, P. 1999: Early syntactic development: a construction grammar approach. In Barrett, M. (ed.), *The development of language.* Hove: Psychology Press, 161–90.

Toohey, K. 2000: *Learning English at school: Identity, social relations and classroom practice.* Clevedon: Multilingual Matters.

Toohey, K. 2001: Disputes in child L2 learning. *TESOL Quarterly* **35**, 257–78.

Toohey, K. and Norton, B. 2001: Changing perspectives on good language learners. *TESOL Quarterly* **35**, 307–22.

Towell, R. and Hawkins, R. 1994: *Approaches to second language acquisition.* Clevedon: Multilingual Matters.

Towell, R. and Hawkins, R. in press: *Empirical evidence and theories of representation in current research in Second Language Acquisition:* Transactions of the Philological Society.

Towell, R., Hawkins, R. and Bazergui, N. 1996: The development of fluency in advanced learners of French. *Applied Linguistics* **17**, 84–115.

Tran-Chi-Chau. 1975: Error analysis, contrastive analysis and students' perception: a study of difficulty in second language learning. *International Review of Applied Linguistics* **13**, 119–43.

Vainikka, A. and Young-Scholten, M. 1996a: The early stages in adult L2 syntax: additional evidence from Romance speakers. *Second Language Research* **12**, 140–76.

Vainikka, A. and Young-Scholten, M. 1996b: Gradual development of L2 phrase structure. *Second Language Research* **12**, 7–39.

Vainikka, A. and Young-Scholten, M. 1998: The initial state in the L2 acquisition of phrase structure. In Flynn, S., Martohardjono, G. and O'Neil, W. (eds), *The generative study of second language acquisition.* Hillsdale, NJ: Erlbaum, 17–34.

Valian, V. 1990: Null subjects: a problem for parameter-setting models of language acquisition. *Cognition* **35**, 105–22.

Van der Lely, H. 1996: Empirical evidence for the modularity of language from grammatical SLI children. In Stringfellow, A., Cahana-Amitay, D., Hughes, E. and Zukowsky, A. (eds), *Proceedings of the 20th Annual Boston University Conference on Language Development.* Somerville, MA: Cascadilla Press, 792–803.

Van der Lely, H. 1998: Guest Editor: Special Issue on Specific Language Impairment. *Language Acquisition* **72** (4).

Van der Lely, H. and Battell, J. 2003: Wh-movement in children with grammatical SLI: a test of the RDDR hypothesis. *Language* **79**, 153–81.

Van der Lely, H. and Ullman, M. 1996: The computation and representation of past-tense morphology in normally developing and specifically language impaired children. In Stringfellow, A., Cahana-Amitay, D., Hughes, E. and Zukowsky, A. (eds), *Proceedings of the 20th annual Boston University Conference on Language Development.* Somerville, MA: Cascadilla Press, 804–15.

Van der Lely, H. and Ullman, M. 2001: Past tense morphology in specifically language impaired and normally developing children. *Language and Cognitive Processes* **16**, 177–217.

Van Hout, R., Hulk, A., Kuiken, F., and Towell, R. (eds) 2003: *The lexicon–syntax interface in second language acquisition*. Amsterdam: John Benjamins.

Van Lier, L. 1994: Forks and hope: pursuing understanding in different ways. *Applied Linguistics* 15, 328–46.

VanPatten, B. 1996: *Input processing and grammar instruction: Theory and research*. Norwood, NJ: Ablex.

VanPatten, B. 2002: Processing instruction: an update. *Language Learning* 52, 755–803.

VanPatten, B. and Cadierno, T. 1993: Explicit instruction and input processing. *Studies in Second Language Acquisition* 18, 495–510.

Van Valin, R.D. 1992: An overview of ergative phenomena and their implications for language acquisition. In Slobin, D.I. (ed.), *The crosslinguistic study of language acquisition*, Volume 3. Hillsdale, NJ: Lawrence Erlbaum.

Vendler, Z. 1967: Verbs and times. In Vendler, Z. (ed.), *Linguistics and philosophy*. Ithaca, NY: Cornell University Press, 97–121.

Vihman, M. 1982: Formulas in first and second language acquisition. In Obler, L. and Menn, L. (eds), *Exceptional language and linguistics*. New York, NY: Academic Press, 261–84.

Vygotsky, L.S. 1978: *Mind in society: The development of higher psychological processes*. Cambridge, MA: Harvard University Press.

Vygotsky, L.S. 1987: *The collected works of L. S. Vygotsky: Volume 1. Thinking and speaking*. New York, NY: Plenum Press.

Wardhaugh, R. 2002: *An introduction to sociolinguistics* (4th edn). Oxford: Blackwell.

Watson, J. 1924: *Behaviorism*. New York, NY: Norton.

Watson-Gegeo, K.A. and Nielsen, S. 2003: Language socialisation in SLA. In Doughty, C. and Long, M.H. (eds), *Handbook of second language acquisition*. Oxford: Blackwell, 155–77.

Weinert, R. 1995: The role of formulaic language in second language acquisition: a review. *Applied Linguistics* 16, 180–205.

Weissenborn, J. 1992: Null subjects in early grammars: implications for parameter-setting theories. In Weissenborn, J. and Goodluck, H. (eds), *Theoretical issues in language acquisition: Continuity and change in development*. Hillsdale, NJ: Lawrence Erlbaum.

Wells, G. 1999: *Dialogic inquiry: toward a sociocultural practice and theory of education*. Cambridge: Cambridge University Press.

Wenger, E. 1998: *Communities of practice: Learning, meaning, and identity*. Cambridge: Cambridge University Press.

Wertsch, J.V. 1995: The need for action in sociocultural research. In Wertsch, J.V., Del Rio, P. and Alvarez, A. (eds), *Sociocultural studies of mind*. Cambridge: Cambridge University Press, 56–74.

Wertsch, J.V. 1998: *Mind as action*. Oxford: Oxford University Press.

Wertsch, J.V., Del Rio, P. and Alvarez, A. (eds) 1995: *Sociocultural studies of mind*. Cambridge: Cambridge University Press.

Wexler, K. and Culicover, P.W. 1980: *Formal principles of language acquisition*. Cambridge, MA: MIT Press.

Wexler, K. and Harris, T. 1996: The optional infinitives, head movement and the economy of derivations. In Clahsen, H. (ed.), *Generative perspectives on language acquisition*. Amsterdam: John Benjamins, 1–42.

White, L. 1992: Long and short verb movement in second language acquisition. *Canadian Journal of Linguistics* **37**, 273–86.

White, L. 1996: Universal Grammar and second language acquisition: Current trends and new directions. In Ritchie, W. and Bhatia, T. (eds.), *Handbook of second language acquisition*. San Diego, CA: Academic Press, 85–120.

White, L. 2003: *Second language acquisition and Universal Grammar*. Cambridge: Cambridge University Press.

White, L., Travis, L. and MacLachlan, A. 1992: The acquisition of wh-question formation by Malagasy learners of English: evidence for Universal Grammar. *Canadian Journal of Linguistics* **37**, 341–68.

Willett, J. 1995: Becoming first graders in an L2: an ethnographic study of L2 socialisation. *TESOL Quarterly* **29** (3), 473–503.

Wode, H. 1978: Developmental sequences in naturalistic L2 acquisition. In Hatch, E. (ed.), *Second language acquisition*. Rowley, MA: Newbury House, 101–17.

Wode, H. 1981: *Learning a second language*. Tübingen: Gunter Narr Verlag.

Wong-Fillmore, L. 1976: The second time around: cognitive and social strategies in second language acquisition. Stanford University, Stanford, CA, unpublished doctoral dissertation.

Wood, D., Bruner, J. and Ross, G. 1976: The role of tutoring in problem solving. *Journal of Child Psychology and Psychiatry* **17**, 89–100.

Wray, A. 2002: *Formulaic language and the lexicon*. Cambridge: Cambridge University Press.

Wray, A. and Perkins, M. 2000: The functions of formulaic language: an integrated model. *Language and Communication* **20**, 1–28.

Young, R. 1991: *Variation in interlanguage morphology*. New York, NY: Peter Lang.

Young, R. and Bayley, R. 1996: VARBRUL analysis for second language acquisition research. In Bayley, R. and Preston, D.R. (eds), *Second language acquisition and linguistic variation*. Amsterdam: John Benjamins, 253–306.

Yuan, B. 1998: Interpretation of binding and orientation of the Chinese reflexive *ziji* by English and Japanese speakers. *Second Language Research* **14**, 324–40.

Yuan, B. 2001: The status of thematic verbs in the second language acquisition of Chinese. *Second Language Research* **14**, 248–72.

Zinchenko, V.P. 1995: Cultural-historical psychology and the psychological theory of activity: retrospect and prospect. In Wertsch, J.V., Del Rio, P. and Alvarez, A. (eds), *Sociocultural studies of mind*. Cambridge: Cambridge University Press, 37–55.

Zobl, H. 1980: The formal and developmental selectivity of L1 influence on L2 acquisition. *Language Learning* **30**, 43–57.

Zobl, H. 1995: Converging evidence for the 'acquisition-learning' distinction. *Applied Linguistics* **16**, 35–56.

Subject Index

Author Index